Experience and the Absolute

John D. Caputo, *series editor*

JEAN-YVES LACOSTE

Experience and the Absolute
Disputed Questions on the Humanity of Man

TRANSLATED BY MARK RAFTERY-SKEHAN

FORDHAM UNIVERSITY PRESS
New York ■ 2004

Experience and the Absolute: Disputed Questions on the Humanity of Man was originally published in French under the title *Expérience et absolu,* © 1994, Presses Universitaires de France.

Perspectives in Continental Philosophy Series, No. 40
ISSN 1089-3938

Library of Congress Cataloging-in-Publication Data

Lacoste, Jean-Yves.
    [Expérience et absolu. English]
    Experience and the absolute: disputed questions on the humanity of man / Jean-Yves Lacoste; translated by Mark Raftery-Skehan. — 1st ed.
        p. cm. — (Perspectives in continental philosophy; no. 40)
    Includes bibliographical references and index.
    ISBN 0-8232-2375-2 (hardcover) — ISBN 0-8232-2376-0 (pbk.)
 1. Philosophical anthropology. 2. Philosophical theology. 3. Experience (Religion) 4. Liturgics. I. Title. II. Series.
    BD450.L19513   2004
    128 — dc22

                                                                    2004018984

Printed in the United States of America
08 07 06 05 04   5 4 3 2 1
First edition

Contents

Translator's Note and Acknowledgments

Wherever possible, I have referred to English translations of French and German works and articles cited by Lacoste, modifying certain translations to conform with Lacoste's own renderings. My translation of the last sections (§§ 63–73) of this work, though enlightened by David Thompson's translation in *Postmodern God: A Theological Reader* (ed. Graham Ward, Oxford: Blackwell, 1997), 249–94, differs considerably from Thompson's in some respects.

I would like to express my deep gratitude to Louis-Philippe Zebst for his tireless and generous assistance and to Mark Dooley for his long-abiding expertise, support, and encouragement. I am also indebted to John D. Caputo for initiating this project and for much advice given on many issues: he has dedicated himself to this work of translation at all levels and every stage. Finally, I would like to thank the author for exchanges that have been richly rewarding and of great assistance in producing an English translation as faithful as possible to the letter and spirit of the French.

Mark Raftery-Skehan

In Memory of Henri de Lubac

Experience and the Absolute

Introduction

The work I publish here is without doubt nothing more than an attempt to introduce a concept, and to do so at the cost of a displacement in meaning. It is a question of speaking of man, of the Absolute, and of putting their potential encounter into the terms of the language of experience—the superficially banal intention of "religious anthropology." This adjective and this noun are nonetheless absent from this text, and this absence is entirely deliberate. (a) To name from the very outset the contemporary philosopher who has given me a little more to think than others, I subscribe entirely to the words of Heidegger (in appendix 10 to "The Age of the World Picture"), according to whom: "Anthropology is an interpretation of man that already knows at bottom what man is, and cannot therefore ask what he is."[1] Thus this work is not an anthropology (be it philosophical or theological matters little, for, as we will see, the supposed border between these two kinds of knowledge tends to disappear in the present work, which is dedicated to drawing up, perhaps on too great a scale, a map of the outer limits of this field). It is certainly not for reasons of style that I deemed it necessary to speak of the "*disputatio de homine*," but in order not to use a lexicon linked to a conceptuality I would prefer to avoid as much as possible. To speak of the "humanity of man" as a reality and a problem, even if the word *humanity* does appear here and there, is not to practice anthropology. (b) This is not, symmetrically, an inquiry into "religion," and still less a study of "religious experience." The reasons for this will become clear enough; I will content myself by indicating the principal one here: the destiny of "religion," since Schleiermacher, has been to find itself annexed to the sphere of *feeling*, an ill-fated destiny it would seem to me. Here again it was necessary to avoid a word, and so I chose instead to speak of "liturgy." According to Littré, *liturgy* is defined as "order and ceremonies of divine worship." The reader who has seen the term arise in the table of contents of this work must therefore be advised: what "liturgy" designates in these pages is, in fact, as convention would have it, the logic that presides over the encounter between man and God writ large. I am not denying that this encounter is also attested to in worship, or that worship has an order and that this order is rule governed. But the limits of what I understand here by "liturgy" exceed the limits of worship—though I concede unreservedly that anything to do with worship is not foreign to the domain of the "liturgical."

The limited ambition of the present book is, in other respects, to pose some questions I believe to be important, which I might perhaps have posed better, and which we may already be in a position to discuss here briefly. If phenomenology, and phenomenology alone, furnishes us the coordinates with which to coherently question who we are, and with which to rigorously debate what we are, will it not also provide us with the means to understand how *Dasein*, how *mortals*, who concern themselves solely with an atheistic world and a familiar earth, with the sky and the deities, can also be concerned with a God with whom they maintain a relation steeped in ambiguity? If a phenomenology of what I am here calling "liturgy" is possible, will we not come to a better understanding of the meaning of the liturgical encounter between man and God, and redefine what we commonly understand by the term "experience"? If liturgy cannot be deduced from the a priori laws that bear always and everywhere on everyone and his presence in the world, is not the transcendental akin to a divertissement? If liturgy is proposed as the possible center around which to organize an inquiry into the humanity of man, do not the models and conceptualities classically employed in this inquiry then prove themselves incapable of letting what is essential be thought? The responses largely follow on from the formulation of these questions. In a certain way, therefore, they matter less to me than do the questions: the responses imposed themselves upon me.

Two names do not appear in this text, those of Dietrich Bonhoeffer and John of the Cross. To the former, I am indebted not only for the term "next to last" but also for an entire part of its treatment. To the latter, I obviously owe the thematic of the night. My silence, however, in no way bespeaks a refusal to acknowledge my indebtedness; it simply indicates that to acknowledge this debt to its full extent (and not to attribute to others more intelligent than I whatever errors of interpretation I may have made) would have required analyses that seemed to me beyond the scope of the present inquiry. What I do not in fact owe to Bonhoeffer and John of the Cross is, to tell the truth, obvious enough. I chose to use their notions freely rather than to grant myself peremptorily the authority belonging to those who have forged them or to those who gave them their entire conceptual depth (the night).

A very rough draft of this book has already appeared in the form of articles: *RT* 87 (1987): 357–90, 547–78, and 89 (1989): 5–39, 569–98.

I gladly take this opportunity to thank the Alexander von Humboldt Foundation, which epitomizes what university hospitality means; Clare Hall, Cambridge, for the intellectual stimulation offered by an interdisciplinary and intercontinental scientific community; Jérôme de Gramont for criticisms I have taken into account; Roger de Bazelaire; Rémi Brague, unerring corrector of my orthographic mistakes; Marie-Béatrice Mesnet, who spent a great deal of her time rereading proofs greatly in need of correction; E. F. Benson and P. G. Wodehouse for evenings spent in their company; Jean-Luc Marion, who welcomed this work into the series he edits; and all those who help me to live and who know who they are.

Finally, this book is dedicated to a recently departed friend, whose exquisite courteousness never impaired his critical faculty, and who I am sure would not have done me the disservice of sparing me his objections. My simple hope is that he would have rediscovered here and there what he taught me.

PART I

Man and His Place

Topology and Liturgy

§ 1 Place

To the question "Who am I?" it is highly unlikely we could provide a response without prior meditation on another question: "Where am I?" It is doubtless of no importance to the comprehension of my humanity (even if it is of importance to the comprehension of my preferences or the practical necessities bearing on my work) that I am here or there, in Cambridge or in Paris. It is, on the other hand, of preeminent importance that I transcendentally be either here or there, that I have an essential relation with the here or there—or, to put it more succinctly, that I be in a *place* [*avoir un* lieu]. Although this may appear to be stating the obvious, it is in fact anything but a truism and, as such, demands to be thought. Is it not proper to the body, and to the body alone, to be here or there? What sense would it make to speak of a "consciousness" (or of a "spirit" or a "soul") that is here or there? Every philosophy capable of distancing itself from the overly convenient way out commonly known as "Cartesian dualism" can respond to these questions. Since Maine de Biran's rewriting of the *cogito*, we have known that the self—ipseity—does not come under the exclusive jurisdiction of the incorporeal. The problem of the body is that it is an I [*un je*]: not some "thing" that we may or may not possess, but something we are: and, more rigorously, something that defines us as man: as someone. (Could one say of a soul separated from a body that it is a man?) Ordinary language, then, does not deceive us when we state that we—ourselves—are here or there. The here and the there are not proper to flesh independent of spirit, or to flesh in its pure difference from spirit. Just as the body has to be in a place, so, too, does the spirit.

One learns thus that *place* is not another word for space. Space is a geometric concept: speaking of it enables us only to determine the coordinates of extended things, and to do so abstractly. We cannot take account of the things themselves such as they present themselves to everyone using this concept alone: the "space" they occupy is a concrete space that needs more than to be measured—which is why, a fortiori, we would say nothing worthy of being thought were we to restrict ourselves to stating that man is inscribed in space. Place is something other than space because it furnishes us the coordinates of life and of existence: the logic of the latter, in its most elementary phenomenality, allows itself to be comprehended as a logic of place— as a topology.

This applies not only to exteriority but also to interiority, and this point is crucial. If ipseity and corporeality are indissociable, can we in fact think of an interiority that does not imply a relation to place? The thinking substance does not think by abstracting itself from the world of extended things, and we know of no pathology of experience that would permit such an abstraction. We can thematize no pure relation of the I [*du moi*] to itself in which it does not know itself as a carnal being. We do not retreat within ourselves without ceasing to remain in the midst of things, where we are in a place [*nous avons lieu*].[1] The angels can think or praise God (this perhaps being one and the same activity for them) without being in a place. But we are not angels, and it is over the I in its entirety, "body and soul," that place exercises its authority. No experience of the self can bracket the body, and thus bracket the relations of proximity to which the body binds us; the experience of the self is the experience of place as much as of time. Interiority can certainly be transformed by an anchoretic desire; it can wish to erase from itself all that is not conscious. But this desire is irrational. My body is thus inescapable for me: both as a condition of consciousness and as perpetually present to consciousness. My place is thus inescapable for me as well. To "mental life" ["*vie intérieure*"] therefore belongs neither incorporeality nor atopism.

§ 2 World

The most obvious realities are often the last to be brought to conceptualization. Thus it happens that location, as a transcendental feature of the humanity of man, had not really been thought before 1927, when, before proceeding to an imposing reorganization of the *quaestio de homine*, Heidegger proposed to understand what we are through the primordial figure of being-in-the-world. We have spoken of place before speaking of world so as to avail ourselves of it in introducing this all-encompassing concept. From the concept of the world, then, what do we learn that the description of our location in broad outline does not teach us? If the world is not a synonym for place, what is it?

It is first as the horizon of place—of all places—that we can form the concept of world. This horizon amounts by definition to being the insuperability that recedes into the distance as quickly as one imagines oneself to be approaching it. The logic of place establishes itself as a logic of corporeal existence. As such, it goes hand in hand with proximity, and thus (when it is a question of the proximity of things) with manipulability. It is organized as a logic of the here, of being-here; and every here is near to us or capable of becoming so; nothing in principle defies "approximation." Indeed, we can lay our hands on every form of manipulation, whether it be the actual manipulation of an object or simply the gaze that sizes up an object—and even on the "thinking substance." And yet, in unfolding as world, in having the structure of a horizon, place escapes manipulability just as it escapes measurement. This does not mean—unimaginably—that things cease to be (possibly or actually) ready to hand, or that they lose all proximity and cease to be accessible to us when we think our existence in terms of "world," and no longer in terms of "place." But it does mean, however, that the world, as the horizon unfolding around every place we might occupy, is in perpetual retreat in relation to place and to what our presence makes possible there. I can be in possession of a place because it always defines itself as my place. And yet the world constantly indicates the limit of every "here" by indicating the "there" beyond it. Its horizontal structure challenges the controllable finitude of our place. We do, of course, go from place to place; and we meet with the same degree of accessibility in things—nothing is inaccessible within the horizon of the world—just as we meet with the same amenability to appropriation. But from place to place, in contrast to what it shelters, the world always manifests itself as a figure of inaccessibility and reintroduces distance into every proximity—it manifests itself as the intranscendable par excellence.

This tells us then that being-there is a being-in: that our relation with the world demands to be thought as *inherence*. The world is phenomenologically insuperable, the logic of being-in-the-world being thus a logic of immanence. But we must come to understand what we mean by the modes of this immanence. I am not in the world as water is in a glass or a fish is in water. Just as place is an egological reality, so, too, is the world. Man "has" a world; the animal does not: the latter "is bereft of a world" and possesses only an environment.[2] And insofar as we use the term "inherence," it is to think the precise form of immanence proper to a being (to the I present as flesh) that is capable of confronting the limit represented by a horizon. Inherence is proper only to the I: it thus implies a point of view on the world. Place is therefore perceived as world, and location is lived as being-in-the-world because what is accessible (the beings and things present, nearby, comprehensible, etc.) stands out for us from the inaccessibility of a horizon. And inherence can be defined as the mode of immanence that amounts to perpetually coming up against the limit that encloses it, while recognizing this limit to be inaccessible. Hence the fact that there exists no analogous relation between the world and the aquarium, in which the fish constantly comes up against its inner walls.

§ 3 "Disclosure"

The world presents itself both as near, under the category of accessibility, and as distant, by being what no experience can circumscribe. It is, on the other hand, something we cannot abstract ourselves from without losing all conceptual grasp of what we are. This requires that we specify the power it exercises over us. In Heidegger's lexicon, this power is grounded in a fundamental characteristic of our being to which is given the name of "opening" or "disclosure [aperité]" — Erschlossenheit. What does this mean? It would be easy for us to think the relation of the I to the world as a relation between the subjective and the objective. Accordingly, the world would represent the other to consciousness — the capacity to relate itself to this other or to take cognizance of every contact between the I and the not-I. This theory could be clarified, in terms of Husserlian phenomenology, by discerning in consciousness a radical sphere of activity where intentionality governs the relation of self to self as the relation of self to world. On the one hand, the world is not a being [un étant] but the condition under which being [l'étant] is given: I am not present to it as a "subject" is to an "object." And yet, on the other hand, does our inherence in the world fundamentally have to do with consciousness? To this question, which is not formulated in *Sein und Zeit*, the book responds unambiguously.

The world has already taken possession of Dasein prior to any conscious action or awareness. "Open" to the world, Dasein cannot, in this respect, avail itself of any form of protection from it. Not only does it shelter the world within itself, where it exists in the flesh, but with regard to the world it also contradicts the Leibnizian definition of the monad. In a certain sense, Dasein is nothing but doors and windows. There is, of course, no being-in-the-world that is not reflected in a consciousness. But because consciousness does reflect, it thereby finds itself deprived of every constitutive function; and the world is no longer a spectacle for it. It is more fundamentally "preoccupied" with the world than it is with its relation to itself so that it can accept its presence and annex it, in the form of intentional contents, to its sphere of immanence. As paradoxical as it may be, it is nonetheless accurate to say that a standpoint on the *quaestio de homine* governed by the question of place avoids uttering both the name of man to designate the privileged being existing there and the notion of consciousness [*la conscience*] (*Bewusstsein*, although we know that conscience [*la conscience morale*], *Gewissen*, is not absent from the text). Consciousness does not create the opening of Dasein—on the contrary, this opening is first the condition for the exercise of consciousness. The logic of inherence is of a sovereignty that place, in the form of the world, exercises over the I. (This makes all the more remarkable and surprising the conduct of someone who refuses to exist under the sole and necessary form of Dasein by subverting his relation to place in the name of a relation he maintains with the Absolute.) The life of consciousness is therefore uninterpretable insofar as being-in-the-world is not thematized and inherence not perceived as an opening.

§ 4 "Foreignness"

Inherence is native to us. It is essential to what we are. But it does not follow that the logic of being-in-the-world compels the world to be a residence in which we would feel at home—or, if you prefer, that the topology of existence is an "oikology." On the contrary, being-in-the-world, Heidegger says, amounts to being fundamentally determined as *Unzuhause*, as a not-being-at-home, a *non-domiciliation*.[3] Without a doubt, nothing is more familiar to us than the immemorial presence of the world. The world is always already there, at the horizon of every manifestation, at the bottom of every conscious life, as the condition of our carnal being. We do not have to grant ourselves access to it—it has already taken possession of us. The unexpected does, of course, come to pass. But it is always within the horizon of the world that it does so.[4] How is it, then, that we can feel ourselves not at home in the only place given to us, it being understood (for Heidegger) that we do not come from elsewhere (that being-in-the-world is originary), and that no other place that would be a homeland will be given to us? The response is easily provided: if we belong to the world (in the mode of inherence or in the mode of opening), then the world is not something that fundamentally belongs to us or that we have established. It precedes us as something for which we have not wished, as that which preexists and outlives us, and where the mode of our presence in it must be understood as that of house arrest. We know how to make the world ours. Daily experience recognizes in it familiarity and not uncanniness [*étrangeté*]. We cannot be there without dwelling in it and without it also becoming, in a sense, a dwelling place of which we are the architects—in the simplest acts of consciousness that appropriate place as in the richest cultural works. But this appropriation does not accurately describe the originary manifestation of our relation to the world. When the analysis retraces the dawn of experience up to the simple discovery that I am, and that I am in the world, then it encounters nothing of import if not the realization of a pure limitation: the world is not ours [*n'est pas à nous*]; on the contrary, its reality takes possession of us and determines us, and it is we who in the first place must submit to its authority. One thus understands that the instinctive strategies by which we make the world ours and give to *In-sein* the appearance of a dwelling place [*habitat*], of a *Wohnen*, are not inscribed in the logic of primitive experience. On the contrary, this logic confronts us with the not-ours. The condition of Dasein is that of the not-at-home: *Unheimlichkeit*, "foreignness" ["*étrangéité*"].[5]

The status of the foreigner [*étranger*] defines man essentially rather than accidentally, even though he neither comes from elsewhere nor is going anywhere else. This means that the *Unheimlichkeit* of the Heideggerian Dasein is not a contemporary variation on a classical philosophico-religious theme but a novel concept in the strict sense. Whoever recognizes himself to be a foreigner in one place, according to the ordinary usage of the concept, possesses a homeland in another. The metic of "here" is autochthonous to some other "there." A foreigner in the world, the Gnostic argues from the premise of an allogeneity. And yet no homeland, whether lost or to come, can be attributed to those who exist in the mode of inherence in the world and in this mode alone. Not-being-at-home, *Unzuhause*, is not a metaphysical "accident"; it cannot give rise to the nostalgia of a *protologia*, and is most certainly not the index of a relation with the world gone awry: it is the originary (this concept will have to be made more precise, but we will use it without troubling ourselves unduly here), the truth of being-in-the-world, and being-in-the-world is to all appearances the truth of our being. As we have already remarked, this originary truth is one that daily experience vehemently challenges: the latter is thus constituted by man's appropriation of his place, and it therefore denies in practice this figure of place that the "world" represents. One might, of course, put forward that this appropriation nevertheless has its roots in the very structure of our facticity. The world is present to us in the availability of things to hand or ready to hand that solicit their usage; ultimately, it is present in the humanization of the world. There also exists in *Sein und Zeit* a dynamic according to which Dasein does nothing but "be" in the world, and has available to it certain ways of dwelling [*habiter*] in it.[6] But the appropriation of the world meets with a powerful reminder of the originary: anxiety. Anxiety is thus the "fundamental mood" of experience in which Dasein finds itself redirected to the originary fact of its "dereliction," of the abandonment that hands it over to the world in a groundless trial, without it being anyone or anything that has abandoned it. With anxiety, the familiar face of the world disappears; from the world of common "lived" ["*habité*"] experience, we are redirected to the innermost depths of our worldliness; the I accustomed [*habitué*] to the world that it has brought under control finds itself returned to the primordial fact of its uncanniness [*étrangeté*] in the world, and to its foreignness [*étrangéité*] in the world. Anxiety succeeds therefore in undermining everydayness and its superficiality—moreover, this undermining is ever present in a "latent" way.[7] This is well known and is said here simply for the record.

§ 5 World and Earth

We know the considerable fluctuations the theses of *Sein und Zeit* were to undergo in Heidegger's subsequent works, from his very first commentaries on Hölderlin, when, along with the concept of the world, there came the concept of "earth." Though less spectacular (or rather less commented on by interpreters), this shift is perhaps as important as the *Kehre*, the "turn" intending to think Being [*l'être*] from itself and no longer from being [*l'étant*]. The issues at stake here are numerous. But only one aspect of this shift is of importance for our purposes: the restitution or concession of a homeland, of a basic right to redress the misfortune of *Unzuhause*. The world gave rise to anxiety (or boredom); and the unpleasantness of the "there" was all the more intense because no beyond was thinkable. However, from the lectures of 1934–35 and the treatise *The Origin of the Work of Art* (1935–36) on, Heidegger's world will have no fundamental determination other than that of the "opening" of the field in which the real manifests itself. And the "earth" is contradistinguished from this opening, to which is opposed an originary "difference," by revealing itself as that which shelters and protects. What this amounts to, the treatise on the work of art says, is that the world provides the light in which being appears to us; and it is for the earth to provide the shelter from out of which being can reach the light—the world cannot thus be thought without the earth (nor the earth of course without the world). What is valid for every being [*tout étant*] is more valid still for being [*l'étant*], for which the truth, as the play of concealing and revealing, manifests itself in the "the difference" of world and earth. The "all-sustaining" ["*omniportante*"] earth, *das alles Tragende*, corresponds to the opening of the world as the "ground which closes up upon itself," *der sich verschliessende Grund*, corresponds to the "unconcealedness of Being," *Unverborgenheit des Seins*.[8] This does not tell us— since it is not the intention of the treatise to do so—that the play of world and earth opens up an originary space of bliss to man. But the text does harbor an important avowal: "Upon the earth and in it, historical man grounds his dwelling in the world."[9] The conceptual system in which earth plays its part enables us to think a world that is a dwelling place where we can feel at home.

The right to be in the world for those dwelling there contradicts therefore, in a fruitful way, the position adopted in *Sein und Zeit*. This Heidegger will never recant. World and earth no longer strike as foreign those for whom their play is that of opening and shelter. It is easy to understand how the idea of a homeland can then become central. A commentary on Hölderlin in 1943 brings to light the reasons for this centrality perfectly. The homeland is "the very place of nearness to the origin"; "the homecoming (*Heimkunft*) is the return to the nearness to the origin."[10] In Hölderlin's text and the commentary on it, it is a question of a specific homeland: the German homeland or, more precisely, the Swabian land. But the "belonging of man to the earth"[11] does not apply to the contingent borders of a single homeland; on the contrary, it means that on his earth (and in the world understood less and less as a "place" and more and more as a historical milieu), every man is perfectly at home, or at least can be so. (One might also suggest—but this would go beyond our purposes here—that his participation in the play of earth and world offers to every man the symbolic possibility of being a "Greek" or a "German," a man of the origin or of the new beginning [*recommencement*].) The homeland is perhaps what we have lost. But the control the earth exercises over us renders it forever accessible; and *Heimlosigkeit*, as Heidegger would later say, perhaps consists in man's ignoring that the veritable crisis of dwelling, *die eigentliche Wohnungsnot*, is the ultimate crisis.[12]

The consequences of such a thematization are obvious. The daily deeds that manifest man's familiarity with places cease to be superficialities masking a restless relation with originary realities. Anxiety [*angoisse*] as a "fundamental mood" will be succeeded by joy and (in later texts) serenity. The philosopher will rediscover the atavistic trust which links man to the soil. In the play of earth and world, place holds the conditions for the joy of being, which does not however abolish the conditions under which we exist—the horizon of death and the right to contemplate our death as our ownmost possibility, actually more often present in Heidegger's "later" works than it is in *Sein und Zeit*—but which permits the "mortal" something not permitted Dasein, that is, dwelling in a present no longer preoccupied by cares but determined by a peacefulness. In the circle that unites earth and world, human finitude receives yet greater emphasis than when being-in-the-world came to be thematized. But this finitude ceases to be tragic. The very work of thought thus finds itself bearing the imprint of dwelling [*de l'habiter*], of *Wohnen*; it is by the same act—the title of the conference given in 1951 saying so expressly—that man *dwells* on the earth, that the act of dwelling is in fact an act of *building*, and that the work of thought finds itself convoked there. Such are the conditions of the *Ereignis*, of the "Event of Appropriation" in which Being properly falls to the lot of man, and man properly falls to Being.

§ 6 The Infinite Relation

All is not said and done in Heidegger's text when the unfolding of place as earth and as world brings to a close *Unzuhause* being proper to being-in-the-world. All is not said and done because world and earth, since Heidegger's first encounter with Hölderlin, no longer represent an ultimate horizon. A duality (man and world/earth) will be succeeded by a structure consisting of four terms of location. The "earth" will convoke the "sky," and "mortals" will convoke the "deities" or the "gods." These four, whose interaction will later receive the name of *Geviert*, the "Fourfold," mark out the space in which Being is meted out, and over which sovereignly reigns, even over the gods themselves, the sacred — *das Heilige*. In the his lecture "Hölderlin and the Essence of Poetry" in 1936, Heidegger puts forward his first commentary on two of the poet's verses, to which he would return on more than one occasion:

Voll Verdienst, doch dichterisch wohnet
Der Mensch auf dieser Erde.[13]

What does it mean to dwell poetically? It is "to stand in the presence of the gods and to be struck by the essential nearness of things."[14] Man no longer truly lives in the world or on the earth: he exists between the two, between the gods and earthly realities. In the commentary on the hymn "Griechenland" in 1959, Heidegger will tell us: "The earth is earth only as the earth of heaven; the heaven is heaven only insofar as it acts downward upon the earth."[15] The poet announces "the great beginning" or "that which is to come." To "that which is to come" the philosopher gives the name that he borrows from the poet: "the infinite relation." What is it, then, that is to "come"? "What comes is not the god by himself alone. What comes is the whole infinite relation, to which, along with the god and mankind, earth and heaven belong."[16]

It is possible that the language adopted by a philosopher who thinks by trying to come to grips with the poet in these and other texts is a mythological language — an issue we will not discuss here. Whatever may be said of it, this language does not fail to be clear. Dasein's location destines it to inherence in an essentially intranscendable world. And yet, in Heidegger's "later" texts, it is deemed appropriate to know where we are in order to know who we are; place finds itself totally redefined. The sovereignty that the sacred (or that Being) exercises over earth and sky, over mortals and deities, brings about a close correlation between them, and substantially enlarges the sphere of immanence. Inscription within the *Geviert* replaces being-in-the-world. Since the gods and their sky are inscribed there in the same way as man and earth, a location will accordingly be meted out to the gods. Transcendence refers to the sacred or to Being; inasmuch as the sacred or Being exercises the same control over them, or keeps them both under the same protection, mortals and deities are inextricably caught up in the same place: the "Fourfold" is the most vast place, the archi-place that alone enables us to provide the coordinates of what is, and thus the coordinates of the humanity of man. One could express this otherwise and say that with the "Fourfold," a fundamental order of relations replaces the logic of being-in, of *In-sein*. But it must be recognized that this order of relations does not in any way annul the topology that, as Heidegger was able to recognize, provided the basis for a logic of existence. The "infinite relation" constituted by the *Geviert* actually claims to tell us what the integral dimensions of place are. It is place, therefore, that receives all the benefits of the gift of Being (or of the sacred): the earth and sky, deities and mortals. Place thus exceeds the limits of the world, the phenomenological reality of which has ceased to be taken into account for itself. But this is not to say that it ceases to be.

The theoretical reorganization emanating from the reading of Hölderlin provided a homeland for man, and it leads to two major consequences:

a. The first is the paradoxical intervention of the numinous in the world. It was proper to Dasein to be in a godless world: it was his inherence in the world that was fundamental, and this left God, or the god, or the Absolute, and so on, nameless. The topological entailed no relation to God, no presence before God—or as we will say from now on: no "liturgy."[17] But from the moment that place saw itself unfold as world and as earth, and as soon as the earth was thought in relation to a "sky" that takes root in it, Dasein ceased to bear the destiny of man, and the latter—the "mortal"—exists in proximity to the gods just as surely as he exists in proximity to things. The gods and the deities, we know, are not God. And if the "one true God" can be an object of expectation, he is nevertheless absent today, and would himself come under the jurisdiction of the sacred. The gods, or the deities, are nevertheless sufficient [for expressing] what, without something seeming to resemble liturgy making its mark on experience, man cannot experience in the world (the term outlives Heidegger's conceptualization of the "Fourfold"). The mediation of the sacred then becomes indispensable to whoever wishes to know what the world is: Fink aptly develops the Heideggerian argument when he interprets the play of worship, when man encounters the divine, as a bringing to light of the ultimate stakes of being-there, as cosmophany.[18]

b. The paradoxical intervention of the numinous by which the difficult meditation on the "Fourfold" completely departs from what is commonly called the "profanity" of the "modern world" by no means permits us to utter the name of God. We need not enter into the problems raised by what Heidegger gives or does not give to think as regards God at this point. A brief aide-mémoire might be appropriate, however. The proximity of the gods within the *Geviert* at once both conceals and unveils the absence of God. But for whoever takes note of this absence, the rhythm that the experience assumes within the "Fourfold" can all too hastily take on the name of "liturgy." The sacred exercises its authority over the gods, and over God (over "the God") himself. But if it is necessary to speak of God in rigorous terms, then the current subordination of the gods to the sacred, and the potential subordination of God to the sacred, clearly shows that between the Heideggerian concept of the divine and the divinity of God, there is in fact an equivocal relation: if, for example, we should acknowledge with Schelling that the divinity of God makes of him the "Lord of Being,"[19] the gods (or even a God), over which the sacred, Being, or both reign, can only appear as radically other to God. We are justified, then, in departing from the terminology adopted by Heidegger; and we will say that in the field of experience the *Geviert* attempts to thematize, mortals become acquainted with an immanent sacred [*deviennent familiers d'un sacré immanent*], but not with a transcendent God. Just as Dasein was without God in the world, mortals live without God in the "Fourfold," and it is by no means certain that the God for which they wait is worthy of the name.

§ 7 The Dialectic of World and Earth

Must we choose between the phenomenological thematization of being-in-the-world and the conceptuality put in place some years after *Sein und Zeit*? No one would doubt that the conceptuality within which "earth" came to be marks a rupture with the conceptuality preceding it. However, it is not out of the question to suggest that with the names of "world" and "earth," we are not only faced with a theoretical alternative, but also with the dual unfolding of what, at the outset, we called "place." The concept of place is apparently more poorly determined than that of world or earth. But is not this poverty the pseudopoverty of the relation the possible maintains with the real? If we wish to respond to this question in the affirmative, we would not want for good reasons. Heidegger is not unaware in *Sein und Zeit*, as we have said, that the world offers itself to an appropriation that makes a dwelling place of its familiar reality—but it is a question here of an "everyday" rather than an originary mode of experience. In the subsequent texts of which we have already sketched an interpretation, the originary finds itself displaced: the "mortal" is basically a "dweller." Such is the letter of the texts and their conceptual coherence. We would not, however, proceed to a simplistic reconciliation were we to suppose that world and earth represent two antagonistic aspects of the same reality—place—and that the possibility of this antagonistic unfolding is perhaps, in fact, the originary, or to put it more prudently, the beginning, the initial. We will elucidate the distinction between the originary and the initial in due course (see §§ 12, 34). Before the world reveals to us that we are there without feeling at home, and before the earth offers itself as a shelter, dwelling place, and homeland, world and earth comprise the double secret of place. As Heidegger's interpretation develops, it becomes clear that the topologic of existence favors neither being-at-home nor not-being-at-home: it admits only that corporeality, which imprints itself on our being in its entirety, is in fact a being-here-or-there, a being natively defined by its place. We can no more doubt that being-there can be experienced as the discovery, behind the immemorial familiarity of things, of a restless or anxiety-inducing [*inquiétante ou angoissante*] dimension of the world (for this experience is common) than we can doubt that the joy of being and of being-there can derive from this same familiarity. The decision to assign to *Unzuhause* the rank of a phenomenon more originary than being-at-home, *Zuhause*, emphasized by the privilege accorded to anxiety, can then appear to us to be somewhat fragile. The exact status of the recourse to the originary must therefore be questioned and we will do so at a later stage. But prior to that, it would be prudent to recognize the dialectical power of place to present itself as world as much as earth, without either of its aspects putting itself forward as being more originary or more fundamental. We would say thus that the status of the not-at-home (*Unheimlichkeit*) is a given *possibility* at the origin— or more prudently, at the beginning—more than a given *reality* at the beginning, and that the same applies to the "homecoming" (*Heimkunft*). This, undoubtedly, is what Heidegger has failed to think. But if the transition that led him from an "existential-ontological" interpretation of being-in-the-world as foreignness [*étrangéité*] to a conceptual structure in which man is present on earth and has the status of a dweller must not be considered simply as a change in point of view, or as introducing into his work a hiatus pure and simple, we must return to the concept of place prior to the introduction of world and earth, and recognize that it holds within itself the possibility of their dual unfolding. If it is necessary then, by way of hypothesis, to say that place shelters the emergence of both world and earth within the order of its possibility, it would then be necessary to discern a dialectical link between the mutually contradictory world and earth. The native conditions of experience (the originary, or at least those at the beginning) will have gone hand-in-hand with a logic of ambiguity. The world contradicts the earth, although this does not consist in a lesser mode of experience contradicting an authentic mode, but rather, if we provisionally distinguish the native and the originary, of the contradiction of the originary by the co-originary. The world contradicts in advance the earth, from which it excludes the numinous — but here once again, the same field of possibility (location) presides over the actual emergence of the contradiction. World and earth are the two antagonistic aspects of place, but their antagonism has its roots in a common soil. In a sense, the experience of place and of our inherence can only tend one way or the other when organized exclusively as either experience of the world or as experience of the earth. The plenary sense of our location would, if place unfolded only as world or earth, therefore fail to come to light. The possible is not necessarily realized in reality, and with experience come inclinations [partialités]. But it is perhaps imperative that the dual unfolding of place be recognized (at the very least, because we will thereby avoid the incontestable, though not always commendable, tendency that leads to the distinction between the originary and the nonoriginary and, at best, because we will learn from it the topological limits of our ability-to-be). If we decide to exist in a way faithful to our essence, we are not doomed to the *Unzuhause* of Dasein. Nor is the mode of serene dwelling on the earth and familiarity with the sky and the sacred the only mode in which to sustain [*éprouver*] our relation to place in reality. One is as good as the other. And it is altogether possible that, if we cannot think the one truthfully, we will not be able to think the other either.

§ 8 Liturgy as Transgression

From being-in-the-world to dwelling on the earth serenely in the midst of the "Fourfold" where the deities and mortals exist side by side, the path is thus not that which would lead from an atheistic experience to a liturgical experience of place, but that which leads to the unveiling of a "pagan moment of facticity." It is of course in the "Open" that the mortals to whom a homeland has been granted conduct themselves. But such an opening constitutes the foundation of a liturgy only for those who confuse the deities (the "messengers" of the sacred) with the Absolute—and Heidegger's text permits no such confusion. Neither the world, such as *Sein und Zeit* thinks it, nor the play of earth and world, nor the "infinite relation" of earth and sky, offer to Dasein, and subsequently to mortals, the theoretical conditions which would enable them to come face-to-face to God—to the Lord of Being, to an Absolute who is someone, and who promises a relation with him. This is, with all due respect to him, reason enough to take leave of the philosopher. It is not, however, a reason to forget the paradoxical lesson of sobriety that even his most spellbinding texts do not fail to provide. It is justifiable—if we are right to place ourselves under the protection of an Absolute who is someone, and over whom there is no supreme and impersonal authority—to wish to observe the rights of liturgy in the interpretation of the relation we maintain with world and earth. But neither the world, nor the difference between earth and world, nor the wedding of earth and sky, possess for us its transcendental conditions.[20] We have to take place into consideration if we are to know [*pour savoir*] who we are, but we now know a little bit more than we did having learned to recognize from the outset that location has its roots in our flesh. Place, by way of hypothesis, unfolds for us as "world" and as "earth." The logic of inherence is sufficiently rich for it both to confer on us the status of the not-at-home as well as to provide us with a mother earth. But neither in the unfolding of place as world nor as earth can liturgy be included in the topological. One would see no problem here if we perceived in liturgy only an atopical work of the spirit. But one would thus regionalize the question of place and regress into the traditional standpoint of the *quaestio de homine*, which we have unreservedly admitted is no longer tenable for us. Paying close attention to the gestures of liturgy (here understood in its usual sense, as the practice of worship), however, is enough to understand that the encounter between man and the Absolute in no way overlooks location. The hands that raise themselves up for sacrifice do not reveal an inessential dimension of "Spirituality enriched by knowledge" (*wissende Geistigkeit*, as Hegel spoke of worship),[21] which in itself would be foreign to the order of the flesh and of place; they are not the exterior index of an interior reality: the exterior and the interior, the "body" and the "soul" correspond here to the face and obverse of a single reality. By building temples or churches, we would not be committing an error of misinterpretation either: we prove, on the contrary, that our relation to the Absolute has mobilized our aptitude to build and to dwell, and this is once again an essential characteristic of liturgy. It should be understood therefore that it is not by an arbitrary terminology that we have decided to give the general name of "liturgy" to everything that embodies the relation of man to God. By thus encompassing "spiritual life" or prayer, and their topological expression, "liturgy" is in fact the very concept that precludes the ruinous opposition of the interior and the exterior, of the "body" and the "soul": by thinking in terms of liturgy, we are constantly compelled to think in terms of place.

This is a point that needs to be emphasized. Liturgy is an act of freedom. As such, it does not share the native determinations of the topology of existence (it does not possess a clear and distinct existential signification), but accomplishes what we will call a "work of overdetermination." Place unfolds for us as a secular space but can just as easily unfold as a residence of the sacred, and this unfolding, far from requiring our consent, is imposed upon us. But only through deliberation can liturgical experience be established. Dwelling poetically on the earth permits Hölderlin, according to the Heideggerian interpretation, to know the unknown God [*connaître le Dieu inconnu*], who appears as Unknown across the manifestness (*Offenbarkeit*) of the sky:[22] far from being something we would choose, this is our destiny. To dwell liturgically in a place is, on the other hand, born of a decision we make. On our relation to place, this chosen path has perhaps one last word to offer. Liturgy may hold the secrets of the topological. But the God with which liturgy confronts us does not necessarily belong to the field of experience. Liturgy exceeds being-in-the-world and the relation to the earth. (Knowing whether it achieves a breakthrough toward an originary site that would erase the native experience of world or earth is a different issue.) Let us propose, in order to qualify this excess, a hypothesis we will have justify: it is perhaps by transgressing it that liturgy is integrated into topology.

Place and Nonplace

§ 9 The Vision of Saint Benedict: Exclusion

Does liturgy have the capacity to subvert topology from within? An initial sketch of our response to this question might well be furnished by an important text from the spiritual literature of the West: the story of the "vision of Saint Benedict" by Gregory the Great.[1] The text is well known. During a night of prayer, Saint Benedict is visited by a vision of the world, which appears to him as a little ball lost in the immensity of a sky. To the situation of man existing *within* the world, which at first glance seems the only one possible, Saint Benedict's experience provides an alternative: it is the situation of him who faces the world and finds himself momentarily *excluded* from it. How are we to understand this exclusion? Since the world is not a being, but is the condition under which beings [*les étants*] are made manifest to us, or the horizon from which they are offset, or even the horizon in which we exist; it is not something that we can apprehend from afar as one apprehends a thing. It is not objective for us; it is not ob-jected to us, but makes us participants in a game where it represents the intranscendable par excellence, and though itself inaccessible, it grants accessibility to all that it shelters. One can obviously cease to be in the world, understood according to its phenomenological concept, but this consists of exchanging a person's inherence for the mode of immanence proper to things (those which do not have a world)—in other words, death. And yet what is interesting about Saint Benedict's vision is precisely that it denies the dilemma according to which it is necessary to choose between inherence and death (or, if the question arises, between inherence and the possibility of a soul separated from the body, which, as we said in § 1, is not what we know by the name of man). The man to whom the world appears in its totality and from afar, within a new horizon, does not cease to be himself in the world. Benedict is graced with his vision, not in some seventh heaven, but somewhere in Italy: the exclusion has no ontic reality. But being in the world for whoever can create, or to whom can be granted enough distance from the world or himself to become a spectator is precisely what forces us to acknowledge that the topology of inherence can at least be exceeded symbolically and (since it is a question here of a new relation to the world) perhaps even ontologically.[2] How are we to understand this excess? Two sets of remarks can serve to delimit the field of our response.

a. It is, first of all, in the *meantime* that the topology of inherence finds itself subverted. Exclusion does not establish itself. It is not superimposed on being-in-the-world;[3] it does not substitute itself for it as a mode of being that could be inscribed within the duration and the order of the everyday. It presents itself rather as a violent phenomenological paradox. But this does not reduce it to the level of a pious absurdity. For if being-there finds itself bracketed [*nié*] during contemplation, this bracketing [*négation*] is itself the consequence of a particular standpoint. The relation of inclusion gives way to an other relation, that of confrontation: it is for the man who exists before [*devant*] God (the elucidation of the Latin preposition *coram*, "before," and of the spatial sense it normally possesses is one of the primordial tasks of all research devoted to the worldly relation between man and the Absolute), who thus exists liturgically, that the world ceases to be a horizon and appears as it is not, as a being that one can contemplate as a totality. Liturgy has of course had a right of citizenship [*a droit de cité*] in the world (this is a simple question of fact), and we do not have to choose—unimaginably—between being in the world and turning to face God. What, then, would an experience fully governed by the encounter with the Absolute be like? Benedict's vision puts forward a response: in such an experience, liturgy thwarts all the laws of topology; place would no longer be defined in terms of inherence, or more precisely, inherence would define man only secondarily. Man could "be in a place" [*"avoir lieu"*] without his being-in-the-world providing the coordinates of this place, which is thinkable evidently only on account of a grace that suspends the authority the world exercises over our being.

b. The liturgical subversion of the topological cannot thus be thought here (nor anywhere) except in terms of the *eschaton* or, in any case, in terms of eschatological anticipation. Historiality and being-in-the-world are inextricably linked. When man releases himself (whether symbolically, actually, or both) from his relation of inherence to the world, the horizon of history finds itself exceeded. What bearing does the historial have on the relation between man and the Absolute? We are not questioning the historical prevalence of religions; one does not doubt that they have indeed shaped history. We are asking, rather, whether he who encounters the Absolute exists within historical time, and is faithful to the logic of this time. But it seems difficult to respond to this question in the affirmative. When the world finds itself at a distance, so, too, does history. The reality of history has no more been annulled than has the reality of the world. But in the meantime [of liturgy], whoever no longer defines himself by his inherence in the world no longer dwells in history: he dwells in the accomplishment of the latter, the *eschaton*, and this accomplishment entails a transgression. In the act by which it subverts the topological, liturgy suggests a redefinition of place: no longer is it to be thought of as a being-there but as being-toward; inherence would be effaced to the benefit of the relation.

To the vision of Saint Benedict let us add a second reference, that of all the icons or statues in which the infant Christ is represented holding a globe in his hands, which is the universe—but which one might also say is the world. In the case of the infant of Nazareth, it is thus a question of the Absolute taking a place among men, of God assuming the form of being-in-the-world. And yet the theological paradox is redoubled when, beyond his being-in-the-world, a *man* who is also God has a hold over the world, when the man who is God present in the world simultaneously holds the world in his hands. I am, and we are in the world. But the world, which natively presents itself as intranscendable, can be symbolically objectivized (as Saint Benedict's vision teaches us), and this objectification reaches the point where the object it has become rests not only in the hands of God, but also in those of a man. We are obviously not suggesting that liturgy opens up the path to an inversion of the relation of inherence. One should nevertheless bear in mind the lesson to be learned here:

the man who finds complete repose in God escapes the world's rule over him, and participates in God's lordly reign over the universe.

The particular examples we have chosen are extreme. They enable us, however, to refine a question. The liturgical identity of man is at once a confirmation and a critique of his topological identity. It is a confirmation since its eschatological order is necessarily sheltered within the order of the world. But it is a critique of it since it removes from the world its status as a—by definition, insuperable—horizon. Liturgy—which each and every one of us can attempt to experience, provided we accept the existence of a God who does not belong to the transcendental field of experience, and with whom one is not insane enough to wish to maintain an experiential relationship, but with whom it is possible to exist "face-to-face"—most certainly promises us no ecstasy. Saint Benedict's vision and other analogous experiences represent nothing other than the accomplishment of the liturgical, toward which we have contributed nothing, and which by a special grace exceeds the common modes by which man is authorized to liturgically overdetermine his being-there. But, if the Absolute can assume the form of humanity, and thus that of being-there, as well as play with the a priori conditions of being-there, and if, on the other hand, it can authorize a singular experience that shows itself to be outside the play of being-there, do not these radical experiences indicate that liturgy necessarily leads to play with the topological? Or, to put it another way, do we not enter into liturgy only on condition that we bring into play the logic of its location? To respond to this question, it may be worthwhile to take into account two previously mentioned challenges to our relation to the world represented by monachism and Christian asceticism: *reclusion* and *dépaysement*.[4]

§ 10 Reclusion

Place unfolds for us as world and as earth: as the withholding and as the promise of a homeland. What is the recluse up to in the face of this unfolding? Before we attempt to determine whether his experience of place is of world or of earth, we must first, it would seem, recognize his perpetual being-in-a-place, which does not let itself be bracketed by his extreme behavior. It is of little import where we are—but that we are somewhere, the fact of our being somewhere, remains a basic given. The multiplicity of places is secondary to the universal and a priori laws of location; in this respect, the recluse is in his cell "as" I am in my office. But can we be certain of this? It goes without saying that reclusion is a way of being-in-a-place. But if the recluse confirms the facticity that governs every existence — and how could he do otherwise? — this confirmation serves to remind us that it is a question of the way of the ascetic, of a "practice" of existence, of the existentiell and not of the existential. "Remain in your cell, and it will teach you all," the *Apophthegmata Patrum* recites again and again.[5] Place is thus seen here to be determined less by what assimilates it to every other place than by what distinguishes it in principle from every other place. The recluse chooses to be *there* in the most rigorous way possible. But there is more to this than a rigorous exemplification of a common fate; this has nothing to do with a misinterpretation that would consist in believing that inherence is more radical for those who enclose themselves within four walls than for those who content themselves with being in the world. It could easily be proved that the recluse does not exclude the unfolding of place as world and as earth from his cell, or that his enclosure does not establish, in the first instance, a novel mode of existence within the topological. The world is not absent from the cell, for the desire for God never fails to unveil for the ascetic or remind him of his not-being-at-home and his foreignness. Nor is the earth absent from it, for even the most humble dwelling can embody a homeland for man.

The recluse submits himself to a law common to all. His reclusion can pass for a case of eccentric dwelling. Yet we would be deceived were we to fail to discern in these appearances a profound irony. By dint of consenting to be-there, the recluse actually disposes of place in order to be nowhere, or almost nowhere. His reclusion is a liturgical work whereby the gestures he makes before God subordinate all that falls within the category of the topological. It is within the conditions of the world that man concerns himself with the Absolute. Yet the remarkable case of reclusion nevertheless teaches us that the world can be reduced to its schematic reality, and be nothing more than the ineluctable point of contact between facticity (being-in) and the freedom that opts for liturgy. By equating the horizon of the world with that of his cell, the recluse thus divests himself of his concern with the logic of place. In his cell, even if world and earth can always besiege it [*l'investir*] (asceticism is a struggle from which one does not always emerge victorious), the recluse is neither a foreigner nor at home: he is there only to face up to the demands of the Absolute; and although the laws of facticity necessarily obtain, it must be admitted that the recluse wants at bottom to be nowhere — that, *symbolically*, his place is a *non*place. The recluse escapes neither the world, understood according to its phenomenological concept, nor the society of men: we have to work if we want to eat: thus we cannot but involve ourselves in relations of production. But understood as a society of men, the world is precisely what the ascetic seeks to marginalize completely. Understood as the transcendental horizon of existence, it is the law he attempts to thwart in the name of a more fundamental or more originary authority. Ostensibly settling in the outskirts of the city, having for his localized existence only the minimum demanded by his bodily condition, whoever chooses to be a recluse perhaps only runs the risk of exacerbating the worldliness he wishes to attenuate. Spiritual literature never fails to emphasize that asceticism is a risk one decides to take, rather than a decision whose outcome is a foregone conclusion. But whatever the risks of disqualifying topology in the name of "liturgy," the lessons furnished by reclusion must not be lost on us. To become a man as he conceives the task (and if the Absolute is the promise of a relation, such a project is certainly not for everyone, which is not to say that it ceases to have a sense and a validity), the recluse subversively distances himself from world and earth; enclosing himself, but seeming to manifest what being-in means to excess. And, though one needs no more than a cell to be in the world, he proves in the end that, by a complete reversal, by doing violence to the logic of place, one can unreservedly concern oneself with God. Our relation to the Absolute and our disposal of place thus appear to us not as independent phenomena—on the contrary, the relation to the Absolute implies a particular way of disposing of place. Where the solitary lives out the ironic subversion of his location matters little. But it is of great importance that his ascetic project deals with place and provides us with the lineaments of a novel conception of our location.

This novel conception can be expressed succinctly: the experiential practice of liturgy can open up a space where neither world nor earth is interposed between man and God. We have already said that liturgy is not a moment within but an overdetermination of topology; through the earth we may become familiar with the sacred [rend . . . les familiers du sacré], but not with God. But if such is the native condition of experience, the work of transgression accomplished by the recluse perhaps suggests that this is neither an originary condition nor one proper to the accomplishment of history. By throwing into turmoil the topology it subordinates, liturgy implies that the dialectic of world and earth is perhaps not the whole truth of place. It does not, of course, lead us to believe that we can conceive of man divested of place. But it does suggest the concept of a being-there or of a corporeal existence that simultaneously and essentially is tantamount to being a being-before-God. There is apparently nothing less eschatological than the experience of reclusion, nothing that would remind us more of the limitations imposed on us by history; the ascetic does not carve out a place in the *eschaton*. The way in which the recluse plays with his being-there, and thus finds himself grappling with his facticity is nonetheless born of a desire for the *eschaton*. In proving that history does not prevent man from structuring his experience around a relation that, though it cannot be deduced from the laws of being-in-the-world, confronts man with the Absolute, he is heralding the definitive realities (on condition that death is not the only figure of the definitive and that it does not govern the relationship between man and God as a desperate eschatology). In impoverishing his relation to place to the limit, and by subverting the meaning of his location, the ascetic does not deny the existence of place. On the contrary, he affirms the right and freedom to transfigure (albeit precariously) the logic of being-in-the-world in the name of a liturgical logic, and desires the eschatological establishment of this transfiguration.

§ 11 *Dépaysement*

From the perpetual pilgrimage that is the *xeniteia*, and thus from an apparently entirely opposed perspective, we receive a similar teaching. Not to dwell [*habiter*], whether here or there, not to reside [*demeurer*], not to distinguish between residence and exile in the world, or between homeland and foreign land [*terre étrangère*]: therein lies a clear-cut judgment on place and its dialectical unfolding. The pilgrim monk, who wishes to be neither here nor there, appears to realize the Stoic ideal of cosmopolitanism. For him, there no longer exists Greek or barbarian territory; no regional particularism, national or otherwise, can define or determine his humanity; and the quality of the metic, which for classical Greece represents a lesser form of belonging to the polis, a nonautochthony, seems to him a mode of citizenship on a world scale. One must not however be too hasty in arriving at such a conclusion. The *xeniteia*, which Peter Brown has rightly spoken of as a "bedouinization" of Christian asceticism,[6] is not a true cosmopolitanism inasmuch as the pilgrim monk does not furnish a model of boundless citizenship, but rather the exact paradigm of an experience conceived as a passage and as nonbelonging. A foreigner to national particularism, this Stoic sage knows that he embodies a universal rationality, and that the latter criticizes the former by teaching us that it is enough to exist in conformity with the nature of things. The distinction between the metic and the autochthon is no longer valid for him because there does not exist for him one, single earth [*terre*] to which we all have the same right politically and ontologically—politically because ontologically—to be at home. And yet the pilgrim monk provides no solution to the classical antagonism between the metic and the autochthon who respects the terms—both political and ontological—in which the problem is posed. In manifesting the extreme decision to dwell but in passing, peregrination invalidates every right that a belonging to place (this place here being the most vast place of all, namely, the earth on which we dwell, the *oikoumenē*] would have to determine the identity of man before some authority. This choice, as with that of the recluse, can always pass for a strange [*étrange*] manner of being in the world that can nevertheless be accounted for by the rationality governing the unfolding of place. The pilgrim flees perhaps because every place appears to him as world, and he is struck by the foreignness of his presence everywhere. Or, inversely, he refuses to be here rather than there, to come from one place rather than from another, because every land offers itself to him as a homeland. But the reasons behind his perpetual flight also enable us to perceive a symbolic subversion of place—the reasons behind which are also liturgical. Two points need to be emphasized here, and they apply equally and with as much precision to the interpretation of reclusion.

a. The freedom to determine existence as a transit actually denies that the experience of place is the experience of a land where one dwells at home [*chez soi*] in peace. The Heideggerian thematization of the "Fourfold," though still leaving room for expectation, can appear to be somewhat eschatological. The play of earth and sky, of mortals and the gods, does not bring history to a close—it grounds it. It does so by conferring on place a definitive order (while stipulating that the "salvation" that "only a God" could still provide us with has, in the age of nihilism, yet to come)[7] that enables us to maintain a relation of implicit trust with it. And yet the problem of Christian experience is the surprising nonrealization (surprising because all "is" completed between Good Friday and Easter Sunday) of the *eschaton*. The time of this experience can pass for being the "end." But it is not the time when the outpouring of the Spirit will have instituted the modes of a definitive presence of man before man and of man before God, and when man would have at his disposal on earth a definitive and given homeland. Rather, it is the time of an experience always lived in the shadow of death, when the rule of negation, or of sin, has been anything but abolished. This constitutes a major problem. A classical response is supplied by cenobitic monachism. The city of man, even in the history sealed by the event of Pentecost, cannot absolve itself of its complicity with the "world" (understood here in the Johannine or Pauline sense of the term—there is, after all, no equivocation between this sense and the phenomenological one; the horizon in which we exist is precisely what the Johannine and Pauline texts call, from a different though not contradictory perspective, the *kosmos*). Nevertheless, it may still be possible to build in its margins a city where man can, in anticipation, exist almost solely according to the eschatological dimension of his being: a city that would be nothing but the worldly icon of the City of God. And yet, if man shares with cenobitic monachism the same radical asceticism, the *xeniteia* gives us a little more to think by emphasizing that the liturgical experience, which must intensify the ethical experience of conversion (see §§ 27–29), also requires the subversion of that which possesses no ethical meaning, that is, our relationship to place. Since the *eschaton*, which can be anticipated, or to which one can allude in concrete terms, is the uninstitutable par excellence, place is unable to present itself to us in the form of the "earth." By refusing to enter into the logic of "building" and "dwelling," the pilgrim monk demonstrates more blatantly than the cenobite how he contradicts the historial determinations of his being. The recluse has taught us a similar lesson: his cell is for him but a place, not a residence he has built in which to live. There is perfect mutual confirmation here. Pursued to its ultimate consequences, the liturgical experience prevents man from dwelling peaceably on the earth—but *every* form of liturgy must learn this lesson.

b. It certainly does not follow that, by thinking of himself as a universal metic, the pilgrim monk confirms the unfolding of place simply as world and as the not-being-at-home that, according to Heidegger, "originarily" defines being-in-the-world. If we accept the hypothesis of the dialectical unfolding of place as world and as earth, it would already be surprising that one moment in this unfolding could be privileged over another. The not-being-at-home of Dasein can only superficially be linked to Christian experience: the philosopher is aware of this and expressly denies any connection.[8] But by defining himself as a perpetual passer-by, the pilgrim monk does not show favor to one aspect of place over another. Here again, it is prior to the dialectic of world and earth that the ascetic's reasons have their ground. It is not merely a possibility but an absolute certainty that the man who feels himself to have an eschatological vocation will find himself confined in the world, and refuse to dwell on his native earth without first acknowledging the transitory nature of every dwelling place. This, however, is neither the problem that the *xeniteia* manifests nor that to which he provides a solution. The relation to place he establishes is, in fact, a relation of indifference. It is of no import to the recluse whether he is here or there: world and earth can besiege [*investir*] his cell, but the earth formally represents the non-place in which liturgy symbolically brackets topology. The same applies to the pilgrim monk. His wanderings, as we have said, might pass for a way of dwelling on the earth in its totality without passing through the mediation of a dwelling place he would possess within it—but such an interpretation would be mistaken. It might also be said to pass for a refusal to dwell in the world, or for an expression of the uninhabitability of the world. But this again would be subject to the same error of interpretation. For the pilgrim monk really has but one thing to say to us: that no immanent logic of place is implied in liturgical experience. Just as it is not born of our "earthly" familiarity with the sacred, liturgy does not have a place prepared or carved out for it by the discontentment of being-in-the-world (even though, a posteriori, it enables a precise interpretation of this discontentment). It is a question of an overdetermination. Whether place unfolds as earth or as world, it is as a symbolic subversion of being-in-a-place that this overdetermination presents itself here.

§ 12 Liturgy Prior to World and Earth

It should therefore be clear to us that the liturgical dimension of experience does not leave intact the topology it overdetermines. On the contrary, in the extreme but exemplary cases of experience that we have briefly expounded, liturgy comes to break the circular return from world to earth and from earth to world, not by condemning us to think the "spiritual" atopically, but by requiring us to provide ourselves with the means to think place and body nearer to their origin or their accomplishment. The paradoxes of reclusion and of wandering are not nihilistic. On the contrary, the recluse and the wanderer are of importance by virtue of the affirmations that their attitudes reveal, and the first of these affirmations concerns the unquestionable relation between corporeal and liturgical experience. The recluse and the wanderer are not the artisans of an ulterior world: they subvert the world, or the earth—which is very different. The meaning of this subversion must not elude us. By involving the relation of man to his place, liturgy actually suspends, or treats with utter indifference, the dialectical unfolding by which the world can appear to whoever exists there as a homeland or a land of universal exile. This indifference merits our attention and needs to be interpreted. Place and carnality are a priori conditions from which there is no exemption for whoever takes the risk of liturgy, and which reveal in the first place the historial site of liturgy. But even though it implies a play between man and place, liturgy actually institutes what we have been calling "nonplaces": not the spaces from which the local and historial determinations of our humanity are absent, but rather the spaces where determinations enter into a new order of signification and a new order of finalities. It is precisely at this point that we can understand that the antagonism between earth and world has no bearing on the liturgical. The liturgical play between the ascetic and place (to which corresponds just as surely, even if in a more discreet mode, the play imposed on whoever wishes to exist before God) is the play of an overdetermination. In this regard, it no more grounds itself in the sacredness proper to places or to certain places (or to the "earth" in general) than it constitutes an objection against the profanity inherent in the world of Dasein. A certain existentiell relation to the world can give to the experience of such and such a thing its particular physiognomy. But it is a question here of the chance play of the existentiell that has no pretension to the universal—and we would be following a false trail were we to let the psychology of the mystics dictate to us the reasons underlying liturgy. We will readily concede that those who subvert their relation to place, through reclusion or through their wanderings, do not necessarily know what they are doing; or more precisely, they know what they are doing (they submit everything that can be opposed to their primary existence before God to the radical nature of their liturgical project) but are unaware of the philosophical implications. Though what is achieved may come about in a way unbeknownst to them, the ascetic's theoretical victory should not pass by unnoticed. Even if it should discover the ground to some essential property of place or of certain places, or to a certain a priori structure of our location, liturgy makes no judgment. It matters little to it whether place is governed a priori by the sacred or by the profane: "world" and "earth" are neither that which it approves of nor that which it contests, but that which it brackets. We are perhaps justified, then, in mentioning here for the first time the originary in its precise sense. Its order is not that of native experience: liturgy is absent from the dawn of experience, and man has not existed immemorially face-to-face with the Absolute.[9] It is possible, on the other hand, that the subversion of the native dialectics by which our topology is organized, when carried out in the name of an eschatology that does not have world and earth as its measure, speaks the language of the originary to us by including within it the language of the accomplishment. Liturgy is a historial work of man. But it is simultaneously this very work which separates itself most from the historial determinations of our being. By playing with place prior to world and earth, it is possible that it alludes to a mode of being faithful to the "origin," where the world does not interpose itself between God and man, and where the presence of the world and the presence of God would be jointly given.

§ 13 Building Dwelling Praying

The standpoint of recluse and wanderer alike reveals itself to us to be at once critique and affirmation; it affirms in such a way that negation is every bit as integral to it. Not least among these negations was the refusal to participate in the logic of dwelling [*habiter*], of *Wohnen*. Heidegger asserted that this logic is in solidarity with that of building, with *Bauen*. But it is certain that neither wandering nor reclusion participate in this logic: this is patently obvious of the *xeniteia*, but it requires little perspicacity to see that the recluse's cell is not a dwelling place he has built in which to dwell. Although "building" and "dwelling" are terms we use to speak about places we convert so as to be able to dwell there in the "Open" in such a way that the entire play of being in the world is reflected in them, reclusion is indifferent to this play. This should not, however, conceal from us that the nonplaces of liturgy do not contradict the topological structures that make us what we are from birth. On the contrary, the nonplace admits that our relation to the Absolute always possesses—at least in the time that leads us to death—a topological dimension. It is very much from within our location, and not by abstracting from it, that we must inscribe the modes of a relation to the Absolute—by knowing a priori that no place is holy, and that, as such, no place requires us to make of it our dwelling place, even though these places can shelter the sacred (we will allow ourselves to set aside the question of the Absolute itself occupying a place, such as in Christology and the theology of the sacraments, which furnish the best model). Those who reject that world and earth dictate what they are cannot make this refutation without transcribing it into a relation to place. A new example enables us to be more specific on this point: What is it that makes those builders of temples and churches set up places in the world where one can exist liturgically?

Here as before, the Heideggerian thematization of earth, and its insertion into the midst of the "Fourfold," enables us to bring to light what we would disallow ourselves to think—not arbitrarily but by being faithful to an elementary axiomatic—were we to understand by the name of God something sacred, proximity to which is guaranteed, rather than an Absolute that man faces only from an infinite distance. In *The Origin of the Work of Art*, Heidegger provides a well-known interpretation of religious architecture, the Greek temple being the particular case in point. Just as, in general, according to the philosopher, what is proper to the work of art consists in crystallizing or bringing together all that makes up the reality of earth and world, so the temple is not the index of any transcendence, and is not called upon to exceed the "difference" between world and earth. And just as the work of art is a place privileged by ontophany, so the temple is the privileged place for a demonstration of what is human (about which we have nothing to say here) and what is divine. But the divine that resides and manifests itself there has not descended into it; the logic of its manifestation is not that of a transcendent that has assumed the form of immanence: it simply resides in the temple more obviously than it resides in any other place; the building of the temple leads to the manifestation of the divine. The temple thus proves man and the gods' essential familiarity with each other. If the work of art must be thought as "a happening of truth," as *alēthophaneia*, the temple sets to work a truth that preexisted it: it does give shelter to the gods—but they were already there.

We rule out the possibility of such an interpretation, however, if we deny that the unfolding of place as earth would offer or provide us with an Eden where God would always have been familiar to us [*notre familier*], or promise a Kingdom where he would finally be. By the name of "world" or "earth," we are not thinking of a space we would share with the Absolute or which it would be up to the

Absolute to invest itself in—on the contrary, we are thinking of the space of historial experience, and the logic of this experience would have "earth" just as much as "world" interpose itself between God and us. We desire an eschatological proximity to God. But the liturgies that express this desire do not of course enjoy possession of [*jouit de*][10] the *eschaton*; the Absolute does not make itself present in the world without this presence conforming to the ambiguous modes by which the world manifests it (the world is not the field of theophany but that of the chiaroscuro, the field of a "kenotic" presence or of the sacraments). Moreover, if we acknowledge this fact, the truth at work in liturgical architecture is other than the truth at work in the temple where the sacredness of the earth is crystallized. The liturgical building brings together nothing that properly belongs to place. A cultural order was made possible—the vestiges of this order are still in our midst—where the *domus ecclesiae* reigned over a space that the men living there had organized. But this order did not reduplicate a cosmic order. Not only was it born of human freedom (which does not specifically differentiate it—the Greek temple did not come into being on the initiative of the gods), but it was also, and above all, superimposed on the native order by which man dwells on the earth. The temple, according to the Heideggerian interpretation, is unsurpassed as a harmonious expression of the rhythm native to things such are as they are, and the native rhythm at which the destiny of man and the gods is played out. And yet liturgical architecture is in tune with another destiny and another rhythm. This can be expressed in two ways in accordance with the dual unfolding of place. The church in fact obeys a logic we have already discussed, that of the nonplace. That it stands in the midst of the world, that its foundations rest on the earth, is no more a critique of the world than it is a crystallization of the signification of the earth. It has been built by us or our ancestors. But we do not live there. If the visibility of the church's presence recalls the claim that the Absolute holds over us, it nevertheless is our dwelling place only at intervals, when we accept that our time is the *kairos* of the encounter with God, and no longer the *chronos* that is the measure of our presence in the world. It can, in a trivial sense, be equated with every other place but is nevertheless at a distance from all of them. Liturgy alone must give form to what we are when in church; being-there is subordinate to it. The nonplaces of reclusion and of wandering have already taught us this by other means. And yet it must also be said that the church is not a shelter we would, on the authority of the Absolute, provide for ourselves against the uneasiness to which a world incapable of assuming the character of a homeland is prone. This place is, of course, a memorial or a lesson in theological thought. But we should come to know what this lesson is. The church does not thus put itself forward as a space established for definitive existence, and its narthex does not separate the unhappiness of history from the happiness of the *eschaton*. It puts itself forward as something else: the place of a fragile anticipation. The intervals during which it is our dwelling place, the time of worship or of silent contemplation, bracket the petitions of history and the laws that world and earth impose on us. The church does not, however, disentangle us from history, or from world or earth: the logic of place will always be able to make itself master of the liturgical nonplace. On the other hand, that architecture can be used to thwart, symbolically and in the mode of anticipation, both the historial reasons for "building" and for "dwelling" and the reasons for our "worldly" not-being-at-home is no small matter.

§ 14 Corporeality and Eschatology

We thus find ourselves redirected by our analyses to what constituted the point of departure for our interpretation of location: to the ineluctably carnal dimension of our being. Temporality, corporeality, and the passage toward death each refer to one another, and these reciprocal implications constitute the elementary structure of our presence in the world or on the earth.[11] But must we take the trouble to bring up the flesh once more when it is liturgy that is being thematized? If we are right to make the connection between topology and liturgy, this must be done: place cannot be thought independently of the body. Our inherence, we have said, is not a problem concerning the body but the ego, "body and soul." It is not the body but the I [*le moi*], the I that is a body and the body that is an I, that is at issue in the paradoxical behavioral forms that lead liturgy to put topology into question. It might also be surprising but not unreasonable to suppose that our relation to the divine Absolute also engages our bodies. The image of the *dance* can take our analysis forward here. The dance is not given a role in every liturgy—indeed, far from it. But when we speak of liturgy as a "gesture" we make, it is not simply a metaphor. We raise our hands toward God for the evening prayer. The figure of the man in prayer translates his veneration for the presence revealed to him into the language of the flesh. The body bows or prostrates itself to show one's adoration. It is this play of the body before God which justifies our speaking of the figure of the "dance"; and this play should appear to us as a challenge to every "worldly" or "earthly" relation we maintain with our body. There are other dances, which do nothing but celebrate the joy of being there, or the encounter with the sacred immanent in the earth. But this should not prevent us from recognizing the stakes proper to the "liturgical" dance. What, then, makes one dance before God? We can formulate a succinct response: the dance rejects every interpretation of corporeality that confines it to the limits of inherence, to the order of Being and that of manifestation. Just as liturgical architecture opens up a space in the world or on the earth in or on which one cannot dwell appropriately without carefully bracketing the historial rules of location, the liturgical "dance" transgresses these same rules. This transgression could, of course, be denied if the conditions we have assigned to liturgy were to be called into question, just as one could call into question every interpretation of liturgical architecture that refuses to perceive in it more than a shelter offered to a divinity with whom we are natively familiar [*soyons nativement les familiers*]. This negation—as with every negation that turns on the free act by which we overdetermine our facticity in the name of demands on us that the chiaroscuro of the world deprives of transparency—would nevertheless fail to see what liturgy means and does if it concerned itself with a God whose divinity takes world or earth, or the harmonic tension between earth and sky, as its measure. This is what is important here.

For what is in question in the liturgical "dance" is this: the body symbolically allows worldly or earthly logic to take leave of its inscription in place. We can leave aside the question of a possible eschatological destiny of the flesh, and refrain from asking whether the liturgical dance imitates in advance the definitive presence of man risen before God (which is not to dismiss or be indifferent to the question, but simply to say that the meaning of the liturgical dance is revealed with sufficient clarity in the time that leads man to his death). On the other hand, we should not fail to note how, during the privileged particular time it provides itself, the liturgical "dance" forces us to relate the question of God (when one poses it in experiential terms) and to the question of the body. As Claude Bruaire showed, there is a vital link between the modalities in which we think the Absolute and those in which we think the body.[12] This link is clearly apparent within the order of experience when the liturgical gestures no longer enable us to identify in ourselves a carnal dimension destined to confinement within this world and distinct from a "spiritual" dimension bearing the entirety of our relation to the Absolute. No one takes leave of the logic of place while still alive. But implicit in the liturgical "dance" is the possibility of being symbolically absent from world and earth, not so as to give the impression of death, but to make manifest a dimension of life that is neither worldly nor earthly. Even interiority, we have said (in § 1), is bound up with the logic of place. Reciprocally, even our exteriority is a question of liturgically revealing a meaning one cannot infer from a topology of inherence—a meaning that throws this logic into turmoil. We cannot say who we are without saying where we are. It falls to liturgy to do justice to the complexity of the question of place in a way that a phenomenology in which world and earth constitute the ultimate or the intranscendable par excellence cannot. What we are doing in the service of hermeneutics is thus of great importance.

§ 15 From Being-There to Being-Toward

Topology does not include liturgy within it, which it authorizes and which overdetermines it. Liturgy, on the other hand, cannot ground itself without maintaining an essential relation with topology. These two theorems should not be forgotten. Their exposition did not however claim, even in the form of a preliminary sketch, to respond to questions raised by the dual claim that world and the Absolute make over man, and by the tension that binds one to the other. It is always (the limits of this adverb are here those of the time that leads us to death since we are excluding from our inquiry the question of an eschatological destiny of the body) here or there that we exist before God. As regards our relation to this "here" or this "there," liturgy is capable of subverting it in a remarkable way. We are not, for all that, claiming that liturgy discloses all its secrets in the elucidation of its relation to topology. Though omnipresent, this relation does not sovereignly rule over liturgy. We have defined liturgy as the resolute deliberate gesture made by those who ordain their being-in-the-world a being-before-God, and who do violence to the former in the name of the latter. We know, because we have learned from a certain philosophical tradition, what presence in the world is. But what logic, over and above the symbolic subversion of the topological, structures man's presence in the shadow of death to God? We must reopen our questioning.

Nonexperience and Nonevent

§ 16 Opening and Exposition

In the conceptuality presiding over our interpretation of place, there figured the concept of *opening*. If, in Husserlian phenomenology, intentionality denotes the basic link between the I [*le moi*] (in the form of consciousness) and what one takes or receives as an object, in Heideggerian phenomenology, opening or disclosure, *Erschlossenheit*, designates a more basic link still. It is prior to every act of consciousness that Dasein is "open" to the world: the world takes possession of man and the function of his opening onto the world is to underpin his acts of consciousness, to provide them with a ground or a basis. Every closing over of man on himself is thus precluded. At the beginning, a relation is put in place, which takes the form of a making available: in the form of Dasein, the world has taken possession of man, and the world concerns him before he is concerned with the life of consciousness. Inherence is not, therefore, enclosure within a place: on the contrary, its opening gives to the there of being-there the dimensions of the world. It does, however, give only these dimensions. But when liturgy disturbs [*vient inquiéter*] the topological reality of our presence in the world or on the earth, the interpretation comes up against a receding horizon that the concept of opening would be unable to take into account. Liturgy plays with world and earth, and it therefore proves their existence and the essential commerce we maintain with them. But this very game is played out face-to-face with God and in his name. How are we to think this (noneschatological) face-to-face encounter which world and earth mediate but which exceeds our opening onto the world? Let us put forward a term and set ourselves the task of conceptualizing it: we are speaking here of "exposition."

It is a primary truth to state that, if the Absolute is a free subject, if man owes to it what he is, and if this debt should not pass by unacknowledged (or, at least, may not pass by unnoticed), then the elementary structures of experience do not destine us to atheism, paganism, or both. It would, however, be untrue to suppose that a relation to the Absolute natively structures experience. Dasein exists in the world without God—this does not presume the nonexistence of God but teaches only that the world, as world, draws a veil between Dasein and God. (And if the "deities" along with "mortals" enter into the composition of the "Fourfold," it is more certain still that this composition keeps God at a distance from man.) This provides us with a twofold teaching. On the one hand, no existential constitution of our being can necessitate an Absolute that comports itself toward us in the first place as that which lets us be to act in this or any other way. We will never necessarily exist before God, not even by virtue of a necessity unbeknownst to us. But, on the other hand, the existential reasons underlying what we are, are historial reasons: what is to be found at the beginning (the veiling over of God) is not perhaps to be found at the origin, and is not to be found at the end, if an end beyond our death is promised us. By the term "exposition," we do not thereby understand an existential right to exist within a horizon more vast than that of world or earth (this right could only be grounded in a hermeneutics of *restlessness*,[1] and restlessness does not bear clear and distinct witness to a desire for God, for it is a desire that does not know what it really desires). What we understand by it, in a more restrained fashion, is the possibility of such a horizon being given to us or that we ourselves would open up, the possibility of annulling our initial ignorance of God or of God himself annulling it, and the possibility of this donation and this opening relieving our restlessness of its uncertainties. Our exposition to God is thus radically distinct from our opening onto the world in that it speaks to us, not the language of facticity, but the language of an experience of surplus grounded in a divine donation or in an unveiling that we ourselves must undertake (see §§ 41–42). It is not the final secret of being-in-the-world because the world maintains God in the chiaroscuro, and since no native relation other than an ambiguous familiarity with the sacred patently links us to God (and thus because what is a priori to *religion,* if such apriorities exist, is not a priori to liturgy). It is what we cannot deduce either from ourselves, from our world, or from our earth; and it indicates a surplus from which, of course, no ontological foundation is lacking (restlessness is such a foundation), but which is only ever given distinctly in the element of the existentiell. Even if world and earth leave us dissatisfied, we cannot infer from this dissatisfaction with existence an Absolute with which we would maintain an immemorial relation. These remarks, however cursory, will suffice for us here.

They constitute only the first stage in the elucidation of the exposition to God, whose order totally exceeds that of our opening onto the world. If to infer a relation between the freedom of God and the possibility of his encountering us is a relatively basic point of philosophical grammar, this relation is itself qualified both by God's freedom (it would amount in this case to the type of relation that attempts to think the concept of providence, of the Absolute's interest in the relative that implies no interest on the part of the relative in the Absolute) and by those who choose not to let their opening onto the world and their dwelling on the earth exclusively define their humanity, who choose rather to let a liturgical system of presence — which does not leave the logic of place intact but establishes itself without such a logic being implicated once again — be superimposed onto the logic of place that structures experience. The logic of exposition is thus first that of approval given to a presence and to its many demands. Our inherence in the world, or the shelter given to us by the earth, can suffice to qualify what we are: we can choose to exist solely in the mode of Dasein or in that of the "mortal." But just as we are free to affirm the existence of an Absolute who is someone with whom a relation has been promised, so we can choose to exist in his presence: to expose ourselves to him. In so doing, we refuse to exist under any ultimate claim world and earth might make on us. Ex-position declares itself indifferent to our opening onto the world. This, of course, means that liturgy, if we take the risk (for risk there is since we thereby lose every verifiable measure of our being), may redistribute all the terms in which the question of our identity is posed.

§ 17 Dwelling at the Limit

Who, then, am I and where am I when I pray? To the second part of this question, a response has already been provided — we said that what was involved there was primary in all our investigations. This does not, however, exempt us from a more precise questioning of those who refuse to identify themselves other than by respectfully invoking the figures of the humanity of man that are Dasein and the "mortal." Liturgy is a worldly and historial work: it is also necessary to interpret the link that it maintains with the grounds of a worldly logic of existence furnished by the topological. It is, furthermore, a work that constantly reminds us of the distance that history establishes between man and the Absolute. We pray, of course, in order to praise—it is in praise that the prayer manifests its essence in its purity—and praise can pass for the historical image or inchoation of an eschatological practice. But we always pray in the knowledge of the inescapable reality of the world and in the knowledge that it interposes itself between us and a God (whose existence and presence it maintains in the realm of the chiaroscuro) who grants us both our existence and the chiaroscuro presence. It nevertheless remains, and this is the point we must bear in mind, that liturgy, though no experience can fail to recognize it, does not simply sanction this interposition. We pray here or there, but always while submitting our relation to place to a subversion. We must perhaps take another step forward in our inquiry. The liturgical subversion of the topological is still—paradoxically—a mode of inherence. It has neither the theoretical ambition nor the power to create a theophanic space out of world or earth. On the other hand, and as we have already seen in § 9, that it calls into question both our usage of place and, more radically, the reality of our inherence is an essential characteristic of liturgy: the world actually appears in the mode of closure, but of a closure that can be broken through.

To the world, or to the earth, which are not themselves beings but conditions presiding over the presencing of beings, we cannot attribute a closure, as we can, for example, to the cosmos; this would amount to a confusion of categories. But it is by no means absurd to affirm that, in liturgical experience, experience lived within the horizon of the world lets itself be interpreted as a figure enclosed by experience, and that liturgy enables us to break free from this closure. By giving itself, from within the world, a horizon not of the world, liturgy proves that the world is not intranscendable. Although it claims to represent a beyond only under the conditions obtaining on this side [*l'en deçà*], it very much proves that the world loses for it the structure of a horizon: inherence enables the passage to the limit that enables liturgy to have for its hermeneutic site the frontier between the world (between the stronghold of *In-sein*) and the *eschaton*, or their outer extremities. It is too early to assign to liturgy its precise experiential contents (see §§ 19–20, 54–55). But it is not too early to point out that it superimposes onto being-in a being-at-the-limit. By speaking in terms of the limit, we are obviously not implying that our relationship is analogous to the relationship maintained with an ontic totality, and we must not lose sight of the fact that the limit separates two orders of experience, not two regions of being (the "this side" is not a region from which the Absolute is absent). We are suggesting, however, that the world ceases, in a liturgical sense, to envelop us. It is not something we might leave behind us. On the contrary, it is a structure of presence from which we withdraw the right to be the ultimate determinant. It is a field of experience that holds no more promise for us, and we lose interest in its play in a more than symbolical way (in a restricted sense of the term) when we show ourselves to be capable of accepting another structure of presence.

This lack of interest, as we have said, certainly does not come without its dangers. Whoever prays does not cease to be in the grip [*être pris*] of the play of the world. In particular, the experience of closure, and the liturgical proof that we can break through it, gives us no hold [*nulle prise*] over the Absolute: the border between the world and definitive or eschatological realities lies between what is accessible and what is not. Liturgy acts as the negation and the adoption of a position: it denies that the logic of inherence unveils all that we are, and it affirms our desire to exist before God. But to affirm this is to accept that we have no right over God. When we pray, we contest that being-in-the-world accounts entirely for our being; and we are proposing that a relation to the Absolute can have the first and last word on the question of who we are. On the other hand, from the fact that we are exposed to the Absolute, and from the fact that we freely expose ourselves to God's condescension,[2] does it follow that, by breaking loose from the closed field of experience, we think in terms of the concept of "world," we accede to a novel mode of experience in which the Absolute comes to presence and to experience for us? To respond to this question, we are forced to examine a paradox: that which conjoins the expectation with the admission of a presence.

§ 18 Existing before He Who Is to Come

Liturgy manifests itself primordially as an act of presence. But if man is essentially exposed to an Absolute for which there is no a priori evidence, which he must unveil or have unveiled for him, and to which he must open himself up intentionally, we cannot understand the grammar of prayer without recognizing the perplexities introduced by the mention of God in any discourse that speaks of presence. What sense are we to attribute to the presence of God? Little acumen is needed to perceive that every concept of presence constructed by referring to a type of presence other than God's leads to ambiguities at best and to equivocations at worst. We cannot equate the presence of God with the presence of things or of people, or of the world that is the horizon in which all appearance unfolds. If the world is the measure of every presence, we would be obliged either to deny that God participated in any sensible way in an economy of presence or to propose that his participation is possible only if he puts himself in place in the world (which only the theology of the incarnation or the theology of the sacraments can think). If one denies the possibility of thinking his presence other than as the assumption of being-there or as a participation in the logic of being-there, must God therefore be thought of as absent? Would he come to be known as "the Absent" in the same way as he has come to be called "the Other"? Would we then have to understand liturgy as the hope that the present absence of God can "one day" be made whole? This last question makes a significant presupposition: it implies that, in contrast to the historial and worldly regimes of presence, the presence of God must first be understood as an eschatological reality or event. But, at the same time, it harbors a considerable conceptual weakness: it supposes in fact that the presence of God is only thinkable as Parousia, and that non-Parousia is identical to a nonpresence.

This is what we cannot concede, for, even if no eschatological proximity is granted to those who pray (except in the types of antic-ipation represented by certain forms of mystical experience), there nevertheless exists a historial mode through which God is present to us. The world that maintains God in the chiaroscuro, and which prohibits theophany (understood in the strict sense), does not doom liturgy to confronting nothing more than an absence. We will there-fore first qualify liturgy as the *expectation or desire for Parousia in the certitude of the nonparousiacal presence of God.* By this we will understand that one can unite the affirmation of a divine omnipresence (such that one necessarily avoids interpreting the nonparticipation of the Absolute in the play of presence proper to the world in the way the Gnostic interprets it, that is, on the grounds of a radical refusal to compromise himself by engaging in the world) and the request for

God to come. Liturgy strives for more than history and the veiled presence [*inévidence*] in which history maintains God. But the desire for the *eschaton* obviously does not bring about the Parousia (even though, as we will see in § 24, a moment in the liturgical logic compels whoever prays to imagine that the Absolute is present to him in the mode of Parousia). To pray in that way, even though it breaks through the closure of the world, is to dwell at the limit and not in the beyond. Though itself a paradigm of unveiling [*évidence*] and of every presence, the world keeps God and his nonparousiacal presence veiled over [*dans l'inévidence*]. This does not, however, constitute the aporia of liturgy: it constitutes the tension that is its lifeblood and that enables us to existence in the world turned toward God, while waiting for the definitive order of things in which the "world" would no longer present us with the veiled presence of God. The man who prays confesses his historiality and calls for the *eschaton* by asking that the already present God "come" into the chiaroscuro order of the world.

§ 19 The Nonevent

It is possible, then, to investigate with some precision the experiential contents of liturgy, not as an experience of the world, but as a hypothetical "experience" of the proximity or distance of God. The principal difficulty we encounter in liturgy is the following: author of his own presence before God [*présence à Dieu*] (even though theology might deem this act of presence itself to be the work of God in man), he who enters into prayer does not enter into a field of experience where the givens of consciousness would put the Absolute in question in any obvious way; rather, he does nothing but prepare the space of a possibility. For it may well be that nothing that could be described as the indisputable advent of God (subject to the theological condition already mentioned) occurs in liturgy, and that liturgy, in essence, reveals itself as a nonevent. The man who prays apparently "does" many things. These things—words uttered or phrases chanted, attention paid to what gets veiled over by the world at the expense of the attention we usually pay to what is unveiled in the world—have only the status of prolegomena (however much religious anthropology might think them to overflow with meaning). By demonstrating the ecstasy man feels toward God, they in no way prove God's condescension toward man (or, rather, they prove that this condescension is independent of every given of consciousness).

If liturgy rested on the single theoretical presupposition of the omnipresence of God, we could say that it is only man's gestures that need be considered real. And yet one prays only by presupposing more than the abstract omnipresence of God or his "general providence." Faced with an Absolute, whose freedom he recognizes, the man who prays first learns that, although he exposes himself to this Absolute or dwells at the limit between the historial and eschatological order, his expectation of God can never compel God's condescension. Insofar as the man who prays reveals his humanity, and reveals which conceptions of his humanity he exceeds, the proofs are not lacking—"religious anthropology" suffers, not from a dearth, but from too great an abundance of givens. But the man who prays does not do so in order to prove his existence or the possibility of a mode of existence: he prays, on the one hand, to subordinate what he and world and earth are unveiled as to God's veiled presence, while hoping, on the other hand, that the veiled and omnipresent God will provide proof of his presence. Despite the undeniable importance of a phenomenology of the expectation of God, liturgy must thus appear to us, first of all, as a human power to liberate a space where perhaps nothing can come to pass that, in the sphere of immanence of consciousness, would bear unequivocal witness to God's condescension. Insofar as the interpretation refers to words that commonly serve to speak to man, but which are also used by those who pray to speak to God, or to the silences we often keep in order to manifest the attention we are paying to things in the world, but which are also used by those who pray in order to direct their attention to God, liturgy assumes the character of an event. Moreover, it assumes it in a more radical fashion insofar as the interpretation makes itself the interpreter of the givens of a "consciousness." But it is also very much possible that the act of presence in which liturgy consists acknowledges in a more exacting fashion the intentions behind it, when man, having provided himself with a time and place to exist in the presence and in expectation of God, recognizes that God is in fact absent from his experience, or that the experience cannot ground itself in any content of consciousness to which the God's condescension would be unequivocally linked. (Or, to put it more directly, it is very much possible that we can interpret liturgy only by marginalizing the concept of consciousness and those bound up with it. We will return to this later—in §§ 25, 56.)

Our self-presencing before God [*présence à Dieu*] and the expectation of God—by definition—open up the field of liturgy. But this expectation can be frustrated, on the one hand (the Absolute may not come to conscious experiences, a fact we acknowledge to be the daily bread on which prayer lives), and accords me no right over whatever it is I am expecting, on the other. Not even the most beautiful architecture can summon up a presence. Our historiality, moreover, leads us to be defined in terms of expectation rather than of the joy of a plenary and unambiguous presence free of ambiguity. This implies that no one prays without acknowledging the conditions in which he prays, and which, even though they enable a sketch of gestures of praise laden with an eschatological meaning, first qualify his relation to the Absolute as inexperience. He who prays does, of course, know in principle to whom he addresses his praise or his requests: liturgy is established in the element of knowledge. But knowledge and inexperience *do not contradict each other.* It is not, therefore, senseless to say that man's transcendence toward God can have no other experiential content than that which man himself makes manifest in it, and that the proximity of the God we know [*Dieu connu*] does not itself come to experience—or, if you prefer, that the knowledge [le *savoir*] is ordinarily the only experience to which liturgy can commend itself and the only one to which it absolutely must commend itself.

§ 20 Nonevent and the Critique of Experience

In positing liturgy as being fundamentally determined by a nonexperiential dimension, we do not, of course, preclude the idea that the Absolute can enter into the field of experience, or that the contents of consciousness can bear truthful witness to its descension. But we thereby acquire the criterion of a distinction. We are all, of course, experts at linking the name of God to experiential certitude; and we make use of a concept, that of "religious experience," to thematize this link. And yet the ordinary usage of this concept—and this usage is the concept's destiny—suffers from an irreducible deficiency. Who (or what) is involved when we authorize ourselves on the basis of an *Erlebnis*, of a "consciously lived through" experience, to utter the name of God? Is it necessary, moreover, for him who wishes to exist before God to commend himself to an *Erlebnis*? Our initial response must be negative. For, if we cannot declare in an a priori sense that we necessarily remain in inexperience as regards the Absolute or, more precisely, that we exist in the absence of any experience other than knowledge, we can, nonetheless, know that all experience that takes place within the immediate sphere of consciousness is necessarily bound up within a still greater inexperience. We are not investigating here the criteria for the veracity of experiential language, the experiential confirmation of true knowledge—which is not to say that such criteria do not exist, but simply that their interpretation belongs to another problematic. But we can emphasize the vulnerability of such a language, whatever the possibility of its veracity. The (historical) presence of God is not his Parousia. And yet this (patently true) proposition implies, among other things, that world and history shroud in ambiguity every appeal we make to this presence. Only the Parousia could provide us with apodeictic proof and bridge the gap between the element of knowledge and that of immediate certainty. Since we do not in fact enjoy possession of the parousiacal presence, the fundamentally nonexperiential character of liturgy permits us to criticize every theory in which experience governs knowledge [*connaissance*] of God, or in which the relation of man to God reaches its culmination in the field of conscious experience. Knowledge [*connaissance*] exceeds experience here, which it may confirm (this is the question of the "discerning of spirits")[3] or refute; experience must in this case always take knowledge as its measure. Exposed to the Absolute, and free to expose ourselves to its condescension, we have no experiential hold over the Absolute that is not open to critique (a critique, moreover, that is a priori). Although it can be legitimate (but theoretically difficult) to appeal to conscious experience, this appeal can dissipate neither the veiled presence nor the ambiguity enshrouding the God that consciousness believes it recognizes as having entered into its sphere of immanence. Experience is a function of our historiality. This poses no problem insofar as only realities (presences) that take world and history as their measure come to experience. But it does pose problems if we contend that the Absolute itself comes to experience. The sole solution to the problem (outside of the case of mystical experience, which can only be interpreted as a suspension in the government of the world, and as a glimmer of the Parousia in advance of itself in the chiaroscuro of history) consists in not silencing inexperience, to which everyone who enters into liturgy must consent.

§ 21 History Bracketed

The logic of liturgy unfolds within the limits of our historiality. It is in the world that we pray, even if we symbolically subvert our relation to this world. We pray within history, separated perhaps from our origin, and doubtless separated from the *eschaton* that our praise anticipates. This is a foretaste of what God's condescension may afford us here and there, but which shows through only vaguely, and whose comprehension requires numerous hermeneutic cautions. And yet we are employing here a phenomenological concept of history and historiality that is neither the only concept at our disposal nor the usage we most commonly avail ourselves of. According to this concept, being-in-the-world and historiality are coextensive; we could not exist within a temporality that was not simultaneously structured as a historiality. And, if time is thought as the horizon of Being, perhaps it is also necessary that the phenomenological concept of the world itself not be bereft of the historical; this concept encompasses therefore the I [*le moi*] and the world. There remains a second concept of history available to us, according to which history is grounded not only in the phenomenological reality of time and of being-in-the-world, and or in the coexistence of men (a co-being-there) inseparable from their being-there, but also in a participation in some certain dialectics superimposed on the primitive fact of our temporality, our worldliness, and the procession of implications following from them. According to this second concept, history is not what has natively taken hold of us insofar as we participate in the (neither protological nor eschatological) play of the world. It is something we make, or something that is made through us, and which, reciprocally, makes us what we are, on account of our involvement in the play of a network of interrelations inextricable from our being-in-the-world. Our participation, albeit marginal, in the Hegelian dialectic of the master and slave, for example, is historial: in terms of the post-Hegelian philosophy of history developed by Gaston Fessard,[4] our (rarely marginal) participation in the dialectic of man and woman, or in the theological dialectic of Jew and pagan, is historial. But if the requests of ethics have their roots in a law that eludes the rule of history by virtue of its own principle—Levinas, of course, says that the exigencies of ethics are already inscribed in the elementary grammar of phenomenological historiality,[5] but we have difficulty in conceding this (see § 28)—then it is very much from within history, such as this second concept thinks its reality, that they take effect. It appears, then, that liturgy represents, on the one hand, a symbolic exodus out of phenomenological historiality, but also a certain, more real exodus from "dialectical" historiality, on the other. We will speak first of this second exodus because it will actually enable us to speak with greater clarity on the first.

a. One enters into liturgy through the passage to the limit traversed by those who recognize in the world a closed region of experience, but who then break through this closure by choosing to subordinate their opening onto the world to their exposition to God. Liturgy does not cease to be historial (in the phenomenological sense of the term) by virtue of this breaking through. If liturgy loses all interest in the spectacle of the world, it does not thereby become a foreigner to the world, or a foreigner to the phenomenological play of the world. It is remarkable that it contains a (provisional) annulment of the dialectics that constitute history (of our participation in "universal history"). He who prays is either master or servant, to put it briefly (and without supposing either that the complexity of historical becoming is reducible to the reign of the master-slave dialectic or that the relation between master and slave must be thought solely in Hegelian terms). But if the master and slave should pray together (which is outlandish in the eyes of whoever confines himself to viewing the problem exclusively in Hegelian terms, but which must not be ruled out if the work of thought partly consists in disrupting previous arguments), then their relation ceases to be the dialectic we have come to know, or becomes a more complex version of the dialectic. Bracketing history does not amount to annulling it (and we should not exempt ourselves from our responsibilities toward ethical exigencies if we do not want relations of violence to be the insuperable horizon of our co-being-there). Liturgy proves the possibility of a suspension in a way that returns us to the world and to history: it symbolizes and realizes at once, within in its own interval, a peace and fraternity that, in terms of *Weltgeschichte*, are utopian or eschatological. We will not, of course, be satisfied by the reassurance given by way of an interval. If the master and slave can pray together, and if we admit that the man who prays takes hold of what is most proper to him and liturgically shows his true face, we will not resign ourselves to what his participation in the liturgical play leaves intact, that is, his participation in the life of the polis and in the history of the world, which are both controlled by relations governed by a certain violence or a certain injustice. Because liturgy, on this point, already realizes what it symbolizes, it gives particular force to the refusal to resign oneself. We are thus already in possession of a place where the tensions that pass for the secret to history are resolved. This does not guarantee that, after having prayed together, we would know how to absolve ourselves of complicity with violence and injustice. But it does mean that eschatological peace is not utopian. Liturgy permits us to conceive of a topos of the *eschaton*.

b. This enables us, then, to say a little more about the liturgical challenge to the phenomenological structures of historiality. We have seen in § 10 how liturgy is constituted by a logic of the "non-place." It does, of course, occupy the location it subverts, but it also presents itself as a practice in time, the coherence of which every phenomenology will recognize even if there are paradoxes to be discerned in it. The space and the time it opens up are, however, those of a disinterestedness [*désintéressement*],[6] of leave taken from the play of the world. The world obviously never ceases to lay claim to anyone, even when someone wishes to divest himself of all interest in it: facticity surrenders only to death. But for those who turn to face God during the time of being-in-the-world, time loses its essential power to organize itself historically and to derive meaning from this ordered relation. The time of liturgy is not time bereft of a past or a future. It does not claim to imitate the *nunc stans* in the world, the concept of which enables us to think the eternal divine, and which can also enable us to think the eschatological encounter between man and God. Its eros is to break through every diachrony that has the world as its necessary and sufficient hermeneutic horizon. Every present is constructed as presence, and this presence is constructed as the bracketing of world by the man who wishes to attend to affairs that do not have the world as their measure. One can perhaps recognize here the difficult attempt made by those who wish to take leave of the (historial) order of the "world" for the (eschatological) order of a "cosmos" in which the world rediscovers its primary destination or accomplishment, and in which (who knows?) the encounter between one man and another finds a meaning that the hermeneutics of facticity cannot express. (This links the liturgical critique of the phenomenological constitution of historiality to the liturgical critique of the dialectics that constitute history.) Liturgy certainly neither produces nor establishes the *eschaton*. It has during its meantime the privilege of ridding itself of the violences of history—but not of abolishing the constitution of being-there as being-in-history, or the dependence of the present on the future, or the restlessness to which contingent possibilities give rise in the present reality. It must, however, be proposed that it symbolizes this abolition and perhaps even precariously realizes it. We cannot wish for liturgy without wishing to surpass history, and what we wish for grounds in a certain way what we do here. It must therefore be said that liturgy thinks and renders itself marginal in relation to the phenomenological structures of historiality, and that the man who prays marginalizes himself in relation to the concepts that think the humanity of man as being-in-history, and which ultimately define being-there as being-in-history.

§ 22 Nonplace and Verification

If we are to accord to liturgy the status of an authority with the right to critique what underlies the movement of history, and the phenomenological structures of our historiality, it would undoubtedly be unwise to forget that this critique, though perhaps perfectly consistent, is not proved by any apodeictic verification—all that it can verify is the provisional appeasement of the violences of history in the liturgical congregation. One can, of course, use the convenient concept, forged by John Hick, of "eschatological verification," which enables us to avoid such and such a present content of experience being improperly applied as a criterion, and serves to remind us that inexperience, which exceeds experience, is the mark of man's relation to the Absolute. But we can in no way prevent history from making of itself a critique of liturgical reason and from doing so within the order of the verifiable. Even if we know of good reasons to pray, and even if the Absolute has previously given us proof of God's condescension, the liturgical transgression of historical reason must appear tenuous. Will not the man who prays inadvertently embody an impoverished figure of humanity, deprived of his world or his earth, or be a figure maintaining no more than an impoverished relation with them, properly alienated by the suspension of his historiality and the refusal to settle the questions history gives rise to within history? The suspicion must be formulated, and we cannot respond to it in the first instance without employing a negative conceptuality and without admitting the uselessness [*inutilité*] of liturgy. We will have to come back to this (in § 30). But the precariousness of recourse to eschatological significations (and, a fortiori, to realities) other than those engendered by history itself cannot be emphasized enough here. Liturgy interrupts the circular return of world to earth and of earth to world, and the historical closure (phenomenological and dialectical) of experience. It has its reasons for so doing, although no strategy of immunization could ever be founded on them. Who am I when I attempt to pray? The response formulates itself once again in terms of place: he who prays makes himself symbolically absent from the world and wishes to take definitive [*réelement*] leave of the dialectics that make up history. The nonplace prepared by and for liturgy delimits a space in which, in outline and in advance, man wishes to exist in the mode of the definitive [*définitif*] beyond his historiality. The emergence of the concept of a definitive, eschatological existence brings with it theoretical dangers, however. The lexicon used—that of assumption and anticipation—must not mislead us. History will always weigh up retrospectively, in the element of the verifiable, that which claims to be freed from its rule; the definitive is only accessible to us in the form of the provisional; and the only verifiable eschatology is represented by our death (or, in Hegel and Marx, by an end to "history," which only opens a new aeon in the world, the originality of which does not mean that we no longer exist in the shadow of death). The liturgical nonplace is well deserving of its name. Refusing to be defined solely by his historiality, and symbolically subverting his relation to world and earth, he who prays is symbolically nowhere. He is refused the parousiacal proximity of the Absolute; he refuses to participate in the dialectics that make up history; and he declares the phenomenological ground of his historiality powerless to determine what he ultimately is. Thus does he live the tension between the provisional and the definitive in his worldly encounter with the Absolute; only one term of this tension fulfills the requirements of verification. Is it not possible for us, however, to think that the inaccessible and the unverifiable can determine our identity from afar? Would not whoever prays, insofar as he is right to pray, redistribute the terms of every logic of ipseity, and do so while still lying on this side of death? It is to these questions that we must attempt to respond.

The Absolute Future: Anticipation and Conversion

§ 23 History and the Interval

The interpretation of liturgy cannot be founded on what occurs in the immanent sphere of consciousness: against every privilege accorded to conscious experience, man's encounter with God gives itself to be thought, according to inaugural and fundamental negations, as nonexperience and nonevent. As regards the dialectics that engender history and the phenomenological reality of historiality, it also gives itself to be thought within the order of negation as nonplace. If we are to prioritize the liturgical critique of "dialectical" historiality in our interpretation, and to accord to the master and the slave the right to pray together, we would have to be able to conclude from it, or provide ourselves with the means to conclude, that the historical nonplace of their liturgy presents itself to us as a space of anticipation of primary importance: as the space of a reconciliation in which we could not fail to recognize an eschatological symbolism. A twofold clarification is required here. (a) In the first place, we will allow ourselves to state what we have already put forward as a hypothesis, that there is an essential link between violence and history. The philosophies of history are probably either destined to nourish eschatological ambitions or to fall back into skepticism.[1] The moral philosophies, on the other hand, are perhaps bound to nourish such ambitions — Kant provides us with an example as clear as day. The philosophy of history and moral philosophy, however, come up against violence (or "ill will") as against an inalienable secret of existence in history: although nonviolence can take place in history, it will never be its principal determinant. (b) Moral problems and the urgency of what they require us to do remind us, however, that if history cannot bring about the *eschaton*, it is incumbent on us here and now to reject the reign of violence and ill will. This obvious aim must, at the least, serve to refute the cynicism that liturgical experience would epitomize were it to amount to nothing more than an eschatological symbolism exempting us from historical tasks whose accomplishment, if it would not reconcile everyone, would at least prevent violence from claiming to rule the world. Morality can establish itself as an authority with the right to critique history because it knows how to demythologize its dialectics, reminding us that goodwill can be a creative force in history. It is an authority with the right to critique liturgy because it knows that no one truly has the right to bracket *Weltgeschichte* if he has not, on the stage of life, first acquitted himself of his duties, which is perhaps itself deserving of being called "liturgical" (see § 28). This must never stray far from our minds.

To its dismay, it thereby falls to liturgy to have in history the status of what might be called an "entr'acte." Is it, for all that, ethically responsible and theoretically illusory to signify a beyond to history (and to consign the reality of this beyond to the margins of history)? And would what we do here and now "between acts" ["*entre actes*"] be an act of divertissement? Would the moment of truth for liturgy be the morning of our relation to the Absolute, when the Absolute attracts us, sparks our interest in it, and confides to us its law? Or would it be, rather than the midday of ethical exigency, the evening of our relation to the Absolute, when, all history having been completed, it would then be possible to exult in its presence? We have to respond to these questions, which are not rhetorical, and every theory of liturgy that ignores them condemns itself to futility and, as we have said, to cynicism. They nevertheless have—and this is the important point here—a blind spot. They cannot be posed without presupposing that our being has the present as its measure, and that what we are cannot now be determined by what we have not yet become, by the hold our future has (and, when it is a question of liturgy, by the disconcerting hold our absolute future has) over our present. And yet this is what we cannot concede: the temporal structure of existence already precludes it in the first place, as does the structure of liturgical experience.

§ 24 Existing from the Future Onward

We all know that our identity is, on the one hand and in the first place, an inheritance from the past. Who I am has not been established this day, but compels me, when I question myself, to delve into my memory: to the question "Who am I?" no one can respond without telling a story, even if it is not the only direction the response should take. No phenomenology of nascent consciousness can be undertaken. No logic of an existence bereft of a past can be elaborated. But we all know to a greater extent perhaps that neither a phenomenology nor a logic of existence can be constructed without perceiving the investment in the present made by the future, as in the exemplary modality of care (by which the future matters for the present) and in that of projection (by which we take control of the future). We cannot say who we are without acknowledging how we have become who we are. It is even more important, however, that we recognize how we appropriate what by definition cannot belong to anyone, the time that has yet to pass, or how this time governs our present, the most profound determination of our relation to time. Nothing is more commonplace than the stranglehold exerted over what is by what is not yet, or over reality by the reign of possibility.

This must not, however, lead us to believe that liturgical experience would only be one case within a broader logic of anticipation. As with care or projection, anticipation constantly leads us to exist ahead of ourselves. It prevents the closure of the present, and it prevents us from furnishing it with a "vulgar" concept in which present and presence would be equivalent. Although it can shed some light on it, the excess of the possible over the real, and the future's domination of the present, cannot furnish us with an interpretive model for liturgical anticipation. The present of liturgy is constructed in the same way as any present: it would therefore be illusory to claim to have extricated it from the temporal play of consciousness. The remarkable problem it poses for interpretation is different, however: it is not that of an annexation of time yet to come, but that of the superimposition or interlacing of two modes of being. To designate what I am not (yet), which I nonetheless represent liturgically, we will speak of an "eschatological I [*un moi eschatologique*]," and understand by it the figure of the ego in which the relation to the Absolute is his lifeblood and suffices to define man. This figure is entirely possible, as are all things in God, if he has promised them. But its reality is only that of a sketch or a nascent reality; it is not as entirely real as the "empirical I [*le moi empirique*]" whose (utterly real) relation to the Absolute is caught up in the worldly network of local and temporal relations that determine it, where God is not "sufficient," and where the world interposes itself between God and man. Does it not follow, though, that the eschatological possibility is nothing but the (hoped for) horizon in which we experience empirical realities and our empirical reality? The logic of the liturgical nonplace points to other questions here. Does the man who prays exist within the horizon of his absolute future while also manifesting the proleptic hold this future has over his present? Does the eschatological I alone permit the interpretation of the empirical I, on account of its being, not only a higher possibility, but a possibility endowed with an inchoate reality? We should not be overjoyed that the paradoxes of liturgy enable us to enter into such lines of questioning; indeed, they compel us to do so.

Several remarks are called for here.

a. If it is trivial to state the law that the possible—the future—bears on the real, the modes in which the absolute future liturgically lays hold of the present lead to less trivial statements. The time that is not yet is constantly preoccupied with the time that is, and, as designated by care and projection, this constitutes the ordinary play of temporalization. And yet we can wonder, apparently quite justifiably, whether liturgy does not in fact enable us to live in a present that, as such, suffers no deficiency, and which can close up on itself without embodying an impoverished figure of temporality. We have already given a reason why we believe this to be so. Liturgy conjoins expectation with the recognition of a presence. The world is the kingdom of the non-Parousia, and it wishes for the Parousia. However, the delimitation of the liturgical nonplace gives itself to be interpreted as the bracketing of world and of history. Liturgy does not, of course, bring about the Parousia. It does, however, represent a certain power to consign to irrelevance everything that separates man from the Parousia or, to put it another way, to live in a presence as if—but only *as if*—this presence were the Parousia. It is important, therefore, to note that liturgical temporalization, at bottom, loses interest in every future that takes our being-toward-death as its measure (even if it is obvious that one does not take leave of the world, or of one's being-toward-death, and thus of the bearing they have on temporalization, simply because one thinks of the Absolute as one's sole preoccupation). It is of the utmost importance to note that the absolute future is not the *horizon* of liturgical experience, which must be thought of, not as manifesting the interstice separating the historical and the eschatological, but rather as its abolition. Thus the *eschaton* does not appear as this higher possibility which would ordain itself the real of a worldly present, and which would detach us from this present more radically than care could ever do. On the contrary, it appears as a present from which nothing is lacking: a present that is saturated with meaning, but which also may live in the joy of presence — of a present whose reality is not called into question by possibility because the final possibility, the *eschaton*, is no longer at a remove from it, because the distance that defines it finds itself neutralized. The worldly destiny of temporalization will always be able to reintroduce itself into a precarious, liturgical temporalization. We will, moreover, have to integrate the "parousiacal moment" of liturgy into the general economy of a time in which man's absolute future makes every present "tremble" [*"inquiète" tout présent*] (see § 32). Liturgy intends nevertheless to open the field up to its fruition. And, as we will see in § 73, joy has the first and the last word (even if, in between them, the man who prays must learn a strong lesson in sobriety and guard against exaltation). This ambition (and its consistency) is of greater importance than whatever it may realize. The logic that compels one to turn to face a presence as if it were parousiacal is what is of greatest importance here.

b. The concept of a plenary present is not that of an eternity, and liturgy exercises no power over the *eschaton*; liturgy can only precariously transmute the worldly reality of divine presence, and welcome it as one would welcome the Parousia. There is, however, no theoretical exaggeration in saying of him who prays that his liturgy's hermeneutic site does not first lie on this side of death, and that, in a certain sense, he has already survived his death. We do not pray in order to forget that we are mortal. But liturgically, we are prisoners of a certain logic — that of praise — over which our death neither has power nor casts its shadow. Our liturgies bring our being-before-God and our being-in-the-world together, but the (precariously) subverted constitution of a present, in which the Parousia does not critique the historical presence of the Absolute, does not efface the very real distance separating the historial from the eschatological. This distance and the world's presence between man and God is precisely what praise nullifies, however. We may not know very well what praise means, and we know that we also pray for other reasons. But the present of liturgy, in which we wish for God to "suffice" for us, eludes being-toward-death's every possible determination of the present; and the system of presence it presents us with, even if it gives more than adequate testimony to our historiality, establishes between the today of history and our absolute future a continuity stronger than any discontinuity. Liturgy does not ignore the sole verifiable eschatology represented by our death. On the contrary, it contains an acute critique of being-toward-death. In liturgy, death ceases to be the final reality to which we can reconcile ourselves by making of it our highest possibility, as Heidegger believes. The present of liturgy is the present of a mortal. But constitution of the present of liturgy exceeds every temporalization over which death reigns. Whoever exists in a present thus constituted gets ahead of himself more decisively than care or projection ever could.

c. We can then propose, but only in a very precise sense, that he who prays exists from his own future onward. We are not basing this on the work of anticipation, which is a conscious act: the intention is rather to extract from liturgy the secrets man does not have to know explicitly in order to pray. But it is grounded in the distinction between the empirical I and the eschatological I as the conceptual means that enables us to recognize in liturgy the intrinsic structures by which the absolute future takes possession of the present in advance. Is the definitive reality of what we are to be found here? In the worldly order of verifiable knowledge, death alone claims to embody the definitive—and that is why it can seem necessary to subject it to a Heideggerian hermeneutics and make of it our ultimate possibility. Yet liturgical experience is precisely the experience of a dimension of our being indifferent to every eschatology that subordinates itself to the reign of death. We cannot prove (within the worldly order of verifiable knowledge) that an absolute future other than death is promised us. (Beyond the "eschatological verification" already mentioned, we can only appeal to the resurrection of Jesus, understood as a promise.) When we attempt to pray, we nevertheless prove that our being exceeds our being-in-the-world; and this renders pointless the maneuver that takes possession of being-toward-death in order to make of it a being-for-death.

The *eschaton* is not available to us, and the definitive is given only in the form and under the conditions of the provisional. We cannot, however, ignore the tension between the "empirical I" and the "eschatological I" without losing all means of interpreting what is at stake in liturgical experience. This tension does not make of the man who prays the battlefield where two principles collide. It constitutes, rather, the sole conceptual instrument that permits us to comprehend not only an excess of "meaning" over "fact," but also the element in which the "fact" delivers all its significations. It is not for liturgy to prove that we have a right to exist beyond our death. It does, however, fall to it to prove, should such a right happen to be accorded us, that we already know how to think an eschatological modality of existence because such a modality, even though it contradicts the strict laws of being-in-the-world, is nevertheless capable of implicating itself in the margins of our relation to the world here and now. The logic of the *eschaton* liturgically interferes with that of our being-toward-death. We no more possess any future than we do our absolute future, which is all the more reason why it must be understood within the order of the promise and the gift. It is, nevertheless, this future which governs liturgical experience. It is certainly possible to pray while ignoring it. But no intellection of liturgy is possible if we do not recognize in it the clearing in which the Absolute's eschatological claims over us are substituted for the world's historical claims—not, of course, by abolishing the facticity of the world, but by taking possession of the liturgical nonplace and enabling a certain overshadowing of our facticity that does not amount to an act of divertissement. It is in this regard that the *eschaton* is, not the horizon in which the man who prays lives, but already the hidden *present* of our prayers.

§ 25 Consciousness and the Soul

Whoever prays is not himself and an other. Liturgy reveals, however, that we do not enter into it without making manifest a tension (between the empirical I and the eschatological I); and this tension can assume the form of a contradiction. The present of liturgy is at the crossroads of the historial and the eschatological. But by delivering us to the hold definitive realities have over us, liturgy does not remove the hold world and history have over us. It is thus perfectly clear to us— and is, moreover, an obvious given of experience—that the liturgical opposition between historical reason and eschatological reason precludes conceiving liturgy solely in terms that provide a speculative account of a possible eternal beatitude. The misinterpretation confusing the presence of the Absolute with its Parousia would then arise and be imposed on liturgy, which would be misinterpreted as the worldly place of the greatest happiness. But whoever exists from his own [*propre*] absolute future onward is ever mindful that he lives nowhere other than in history, however much liturgy might subvert historiality. Because it is primordially comprehensible only eschatologically, liturgy is also capable of revealing our historiality. And in whoever sees the world—in terms of care, of a lack of evidence for God, and so on—reinvesting itself in the time and place that he would like to take away from its control, liturgy can occasion the greatest feeling of helplessness. The laws that govern the life of consciousness in the world cannot be transgressed; the I [*le moi*] cannot cease to be determined as an opening onto the world; we cannot therefore make use of the concept of the "eschatological I" as though it signified a transfigured existence here and now.

For the purposes of conceptual clarification, it will be necessary to make a terminological distinction. Thus we would say that it is for the historial or empirical I to exist liturgically in the mode of *consciousness*. As regards the eschatological I, we would say that it lies less within the order of consciousness than within that of the *soul*. Let us be precise. There is "spiritual life" and a psychology of liturgical experience. Even quietism cannot speak of consciousness being absent from man's encounter with the Absolute. Prayer commonly lets itself be defined as an act of directing one's attention, or as "consideration" in the Bernardian lexicon, and this usage is not illegitimate. But we remarked earlier (in § 19) that an interpretation conducted primordially in terms of the contents of consciousness can lead us astray from what is truly at stake in liturgy. It belongs to the logic of liturgy and to the inaugural negations that mold its specific character that liturgy's experience eludes—if not totally, then at least in its innermost core—the jurisdiction of consciousness. We have already touched on why a conceptual system in which consciousness plays the central role does not do justice to the world's investment in us: this investment is a condition imposed on consciousness. We have also said why our relation to the Absolute does not rest on the same "opening" that determines our relation to the world but on an "exposition" that conjoins our being originarily available (but which is almost overshadowed by the structure of experience that the world is) with a freedom that consents to making itself available, which thus makes of it a complete actuality. We can now, therefore, take another step, and speak the language of the "soul" to designate that domain of life, more profound than that of consciousness but capable of rising to the surface in the sphere of consciousness, where the relation between man and God takes shape. Contrary to the meaning traditionally attributed to the concept, the soul does not therefore have the same dimensions as life, nor does it bear the entire theological meaning of life: our body also does so. But it must be said, finally, that the soul does contain all the coherence of liturgical experience. It is not alone in bearing the claim the Absolute makes over man (the body and consciousness also do so), although the soul alone tells us that this claim exceeds all that experience can comprehend of it, and that liturgy must accommodate itself to this excess if we are not to fall back into psychologism. It is in this sense that the concept of the soul overflows the historial and empirical determination of the I and is unquestionably linked to that of the "eschatological I."

In the chiaroscuro of the world and of history, liturgy, if we must speak of it in terms of consciousness, is that experience in which consciousness encounters a veiled Absolute and cannot take leave, if not from perpetual ambiguity, then at least from the necessity of a perpetual interpretation that is by no means infallible. No one enters into liturgy without wishing for God to visit him. But no one experiences liturgy without comprehending that God is never there present to consciousness in an entirely obvious way. We know God to be present. We even pretend to assimilate his presence to the Parousia. But we know just as surely that, in the immanent sphere of consciousness, we can demonstrate our attentiveness to but cannot give apodeictic proof of a visitation. In dislodging man's liturgical relation to God from the sphere of conscious life, we are not, of course, claiming that the Absolute denies itself entry into consciousness. We are not claiming that an eschatology of consciousness (in which, freed from the chiaroscuro of the world, consciousness would confuse neither the Absolute with the sacred dwelling in the world nor its self-presencing before God [*présence à Dieu*] with the presence of God) is unthinkable. But the historial modalities of conscious life certainly do not permit such an eschatology to fulfill the hermeneutic function. Because these modalities cannot be transgressed (or because their transgression in certain forms of "mystical experience" obeys no law other than that of an arbitrary divine benevolence), liturgical experience cannot be interpreted as a conscious experience without the logic intrinsic to liturgy collapsing. If liturgy involved only what lay within the sphere of consciousness, the condescension and the presence of God would have what reaches consciousness and, ultimately, feeling as their measure, and would be susceptible to all the critiques of religious feeling. But in the element of the a priori as in that of freedom, it is our exposition to the Absolute—our "soul"—that constitutes the site of the liturgical experience. We are sufficiently free to open up the space for a divine visitation, and our freedom thereby establishes a transcendental possibility that it disentangles from its ambiguity. As we have said, divine visitation falls within the logic of the nonevent and not within a logic of *Erlebnis*. It is very much necessary, then, that we cease to define whoever wishes for liturgy in terms of consciousness. Liturgy would otherwise become what must be considered its other, the place determined for religious experience in all its ambivalences, or it would lead to the disappointment felt by those who had been promised the joy of a sensible presence, with no possibility of this promise being kept. This does not tell us that consciousness, deprived of every privilege and ceasing to be valued as an ultimate authority, ceases to possess any liturgical signification whatsoever. But it does tell us that, by virtue of the historiality integral to it, the eschatological reality of liturgy remains out of its reach.

§ 26 Dialectic of Duplicity

He who prays is not himself and an other. The tension rightly identified between the life of the "soul" and conscious experience does not lead to a splitting of the I, although it does enable us to account for the way in which the historiality that affects every conscious act does not subject the liturgical nonexperience to its law. This tension compels us to comprehend at the heart of the present, when this present prepares a place for the Absolute's encounter with man, what we will allow ourselves to call a "duplicity": a native difference between the hold the provisional or historial and the hold the definitive or eschatological has over man. Consciousness and the relation linking it to the body, to history and to the world, do not suffice to define our identity (and this still applies if one has ceased to speak the language of consciousness in order to speak that of the "opening" onto the world). Symmetrically, liturgy affirms the excess of the I over its historial reality only by confirming that reality. The provisional refers us to the definitive, which takes hold of it inchoately in the margins of experience. And the definitive refers us to the provisional, which furnishes it with its current shelter. But if the border between the provisional and the definitive passes through our present, their reciprocal relation provides us neither an all-encompassing concept with which to take account of what we are in the element of this present nor any univocal measure of our humanity. The *quaestio de homine* must therefore reckon with conflicting significations, which is to say, with a conflict of dimensions. Liturgy contests our being-in-the-world and subverts it. The empirical eschatology represented by our death dashes (within the empirical order) the eschatological hopes that nourish liturgy. We can, of course, refuse to think that the eschatological is at all implicit within history, and we can think of the eschatological, when we consider it as a kingdom, only as a beyond whose rationality is indifferent to the worldly logic of existence. But we would thereby succeed only in proving our misinterpretation [*méconnaissance*] of this logic: the true relation between the historial and the eschatological presents itself not only as a relation of linear succession but also as an intertwined relation. According to our interpretation, liturgy entitles us to reject the simple identification of the definitive with what lies beyond death. The "beyond" liturgically takes [its] place [*a liturgiquement lieu*] on this side of death in an anticipatory and subversive mode. But the difference expressed by the subversive style of such anticipation is irreducible here and now; duplicity is thus a characteristic of our worldly being we cannot rid ourselves of.

Neither the provisional nor the definitive nor being-in-the-world nor being-before-God suffices to tell us what we are. At the beginning of experience, at the initial, lies the possibility of their difference. We are defined, in other words, by a facticity and by a vocation, by being and by an ability-to-be inextricable from it. It is by virtue of this ability-to-be that liturgy enables us to play with our location, and that it permits us to exist from our absolute future onward. The possible, which is grounded in the promises we attribute to the Absolute (and we envisage here, in a restricted way, the promise of a relation that could be offered only by an Absolute that is a subject) is not, of course, the contradictory logic of the real constituted by our being-in-the-world. It is a possibility that comes to be realized. But if there is a place in experience for a worldly inchoation of the great eschatological peace whereby the world would no longer be interposed between man and God, and in which the heavens unambiguously sing to the glory of God, such that being-in-the-world organically unfolds into being-before-God, and that liturgy seems to pass for the ultimate dimension of our facticity, then such an inchoation would mark a rupture with the rationality presiding over our worldly existence, and could only have the character of a grace beyond the universal. Our duplicity actually maintains an essential link with the chiaroscuro of the world. The facticity of our being-in-the-world is not the night when God is absent and where death alone would have the last word, but neither is it the great day when the presence of God would become clear to us: it is the primordial difference between the "clear" and the "obscure." This difference can be regulated by a compromise; the concept of the chiaroscuro, by precluding the possibility that the world is a theophanic place and that it is destined to know the Absolute only as the Absent, reflects this compromise. Nevertheless, the liturgical experience also demands that the difference between the "clear" and the "obscure" remain irreducible. The world is not only darkness, and our historiality is not only atheism, although the shadow of death does threaten all light. But liturgy is precisely the margin of the world and history in which what the Absolute requests of us gives us the power to dispel this shadow. The chiaroscuro of the world tells us that we can indeed exist in the presence of God, but without this presence annulling the rule of death. Liturgy proposes a mode of experience in which death is no longer the secret of life. Are we to exist for God or for death? Despite the light that death does not extinguish, our presence in the world confirms the empirical eschatology represented by death—within the order of fact; this cannot be falsified. Liturgy denies, however, that death has the last word on life—and it has its reasons for this denial. But so long as liturgy remains in the margins of experience—and that is its historial determination—the difference between being-toward-death and being-before-God must remain. Our duplicity thus precludes, not only the response to the *quaestio de homine* that simply consents to an imperialism of "fact," but also every response that would limit itself to a superficial refusal of facticity.

§ 27 The Liturgical Unhappiness of Conscience

Here we must take up our problematic again. We have already said (in § 23) that liturgical experience courts more than one danger, not least of which is the alibi it can furnish those who dwell on the world without respect for liberty, justice, and their promotion. We pray between acts, even though we can form the idea (and the project) of a liturgy coextensive with existence. But no one should risk this without fearing that or wondering whether, when he thinks of himself as absolutely devoted to the Absolute, it will render him deaf to the call of men (or make him forget that ethics itself has eschatological implications few would contest). How can we then justify, and by which order of finalities, the time apparently stolen from the urgent tasks of morality and politics [that should be] subject to no delay (other than that required for their interpretation)? Why call upon an absolute future, and call upon it to invest itself in our present in advance when we are so obviously unable to face up to those very exigencies inscribed in the logic of our presence in the world? We will respond to these questions below by remarking that the liturgical "entr'acte," should one recognize in it a symbolic economy, is not time prized away from our everyday affairs, but time gained through the "vigil," time that is not intended for the work of ethics (see §§ 30–31). But it is already necessary at this stage, before objections are made, the formulations and stakes of which we know well, that we admit to having no choice but to confess to a certain liturgical "unhappiness" of consciousness. No consciousness in Hegelian phenomenology knows greater unhappiness than the consciousness still ignorant of the consequences of the Christological reconciliation of the finite and the infinite, of heaven and earth, which lives off an "endless nostalgia" for the "unattainable beyond,"[2] and thus finds itself incapable of existing in the "peace of unity." The "peace of unity," let us recall, is the existence of a consciousness that, through its experiences, has traversed every possible history and represents an achievement of humanity every bit as eschatological as "absolute knowledge" (we will return to this in §§ 45–46). In the exacerbated form it assumes in Christianity, the unhappy consciousness is also in possession of a definitive knowledge. It knows that the reconciliation between Absolute Spirit and human spirit has come to pass. It knows that the true nature of man is to be found, not at the beginning, but at the end—and that man is most profoundly defined as a "citizen of the Kingdom." But to its unhappiness, it ignores that the Kingdom has no reality other than that of this world and no time other than when history has been completed in the world. Thus representing the *eschaton* as a beyond, and the Kingdom as other than this world, the unhappy consciousness cannot but live within a dilemma: either the world or the Kingdom; either history or the *eschaton*. But this representation is mistaken, and it forgets that the resolution to all the tensions between the Absolute and man, by now a fait accompli, opens the doors of definitive existence up to whoever has understood this. Failing to recognize in his worldly existence the conditions that could justify happiness, the unhappy consciousness can attempt to divest itself of all interest in the world. But to try to live somewhere other than the world in order to find the Kingdom is in fact to live nowhere. Or to put it in other terms: its unhappiness, in contrast to that of whoever knows how to interpret the event of Good Friday, lies in its unawareness of the fact that being-in-the-world and being-before-God are thoroughly intertwined.

Hegel's unhappy consciousness does not only encounter explicitly religious problems. Nor is religion, which Hegel repeatedly calls "the Sunday of Life,"[3] the cause of any unhappiness for those who concern themselves with the eternal rather than the temporal. Such a form of unhappiness must nevertheless be thematized when liturgy appears to be [a form of] dwelling within the margin — when it is considered not only as a critique of being-in-the-world but also as a careful precarious bracketing of the pressing exigencies born of our presence in the world. Although that world, of which liturgy occupies the margins, is not destined to futility, liturgy cannot claim to encompass all that is serious in life. Liturgy actually suffers from being in the margins and at a distance in two ways. It is removed from definitive realities, which it at best represents inchoately. And it is removed from all that which, in the domain of the provisional, justifiably demands that we take care of it. The first case reminds us of the limits within which the eschatological exercises its hold over the historial: it compels liturgy not to confuse the plenary present, where it tries to live as though the Absolute were present to it in the mode of Parousia, on the one hand, with the eternal present of a realized eschatology, on the other. The second case is of greater importance here. Whoever lives in the margins of the world between acts does not thereby take leave of a place where it would be impossible for him to be truly human or where he is not required to be. Despite the theoretical ambition animating his project, the marginality of liturgical experience must reckon with a real renunciation for which nothing that could come into his possession could compensate. Whoever divests himself of his interest in the play of the world between acts does not thereby enjoy possession of the eternal goods [*biens*] of the Kingdom; this lack of interest does not signal a turning away from a kingdom of vanity, but rather amounts to a temporary refusal to assume the gravest responsibilities inscribed in the logic of our historiality. We need elaborate no further for it to be understood that we do not delimit the nonplace of liturgy without endangering the unhappiness of those who claim to represent the eschatological measure of humanity, but who, for all that, are not in possession of their eschatological identity, and thus, one might suspect, are incapable of existing in the world humanely. The unhappiness that can arise from this is most certainly not the fundamental mood of liturgical experience. But if we really want to know what we are doing—and what we are not doing—when we pray, we cannot fail to feel this unhappiness or, at the very least, to concede that it is a logical possibility.

There is no conflict between the historial and the eschatological for those who claim here and now to be definitively and fully human. But do we exist here and now, throughout experience, such as we will always be? For Hegel, the response is yes—but we will need to examine this thesis more closely. For Hegel, it rightly follows that perpetual discomfort is not an insuperable modality of existence. But if the response is no (which we assume, subject to certain clarifications and elaborations that will need to be made), then the dissatisfaction befalling the man caught between the history in which he lives perhaps less well than others and an absolute future that does not entirely transfigure present experience gives a better account of what we are factually than the eschatological peace thematized in Hegelianism. It is necessary, then, to claim for the scrupulous consciousness the right and the duty to be somewhat unhappy. The point could be contested, at the very least because, for so long as the unaccomplished defines what we are here and now, we are not prevented from wishing for and attaining the peace, *hēsuchia*, which is a primordial mark of plenary liturgical experience. It could also be contested because the Absolute gives itself to be known [*se donne à connaître*] as a God of mercy, by virtue of the forgiveness that, in spite of everything, grants to those who try to represent the Kingdom, but who admit to being poor citizens of the world (see § 36). But even if it is possible for these objections to overcome the liturgical unhappiness of consciousness, we cannot, for all that, take away its right to figure in liturgical theory and experience: in liturgical theory, because it represents an ineluctable moment within it, and in liturgical experience, because it is an omnipresent possibility. Moreover, the doubtless appeasable tension that causes this unhappiness will rightly pass for the situation most proper to the man caught between the ethical exigencies stemming from his presence in the polis and the exigencies born of his exposition to the Absolute. The liturgical unhappiness of consciousness is almost unknown to classical theories of the "spiritual life," and we are perhaps the first to recognize in liturgy the danger of a *theōria* capable of diverting us away from a yet more urgent *praxis*.[4] One would not be mistaken, however, in saying that a contemporary question brings to light a problem that went by almost unnoticed for as long as the encounter with God was the uncontested summit of every topology of human acts, but whose resolution nonetheless turns out to be necessary for an accurate interpretation of liturgy. If the Absolute is a subject with whom a relation has been promised, then liturgy is the place, symbolically and in reality, necessary for the accomplishment of existence. Liturgy does not uproot us, however, from an order of experience that need only be seen as a preamble to true human life: whatever decisions we make as regards God, the historial facticity of our being-in-the-world cannot be thought through to the end unless we decipher the exigencies of ethics in all their ambiguity. By revealing to us that, during the time that leads us to death, a crucial debate opposes the liturgical project and morality's urgent appeals, the liturgical unhappiness of consciousness demonstrates the risks that, despite its being impossible for us not to wish for the *eschaton* to come, all experience claiming to represent it is subject to. If this unhappiness were not to be thematized, the true status of liturgy and its exact relation to our being-in-the-world would fail to come to light.

§ 28 Distance and Conversion

The just objections brought against liturgical reason by moral and political reason must therefore be examined with a certain rigor: from the fact that the liturgical unhappiness of consciousness is an inevitable moment in the logic of the experience, it does not follow that the former must reign over the latter and that we are doomed to a frustrating oscillation between a historial service of the good for which we are not sufficient unto ourselves and a logic of the eschatological that is subject to the suspicions of cynicism. Is liturgy a form of divertissement? This remains a sensible question even if we know the requests the Absolute makes of man. Do these requests require of us an exodus out of the world or a marginal dwelling within it? Because the world, when it is a question of God, is not only the place where we are, but also and especially a place to be what we ought to be, the space given to the freedom capable of doing good—which could not provide better proof of its dignity—would it not be more right and just to propose that these requests completely confirm our inherence in the world? We will present a thesis here, the reasons for which we will have to make clear: the diversion that liturgy has as its task is perhaps alone in permitting us *to rigorously ground the ethical meaning of our facticity.*

Being-in-the-world is primary, and liturgy secondary. Liturgy is, moreover, a possibility we can always reject. Moral and political exigency, after all, maintain in their genesis no obvious link with liturgical experience. But what link does this exigency maintain with the facticity of our inherence in the world or our presence on the earth? This question is open to more than one response. The most remarkable—because the most extreme—is that given by Levinas: moral exigency is actually inscribed in the immediate (phenomenological) givens of consciousness; natively surrounded by others [par d'autres moi] (by "the face"), the I [le moi] can establish no distance, no caesura, between its worldliness and the order of duty; ethics is first philosophy. The strength of such a position cannot be concealed: by annexing the prescription (the primordial duties that bind me to the others [aux autres moi] as soon as I open my eyes) to the domain of elementary experiences, and thus to a domain that we do not have to construct, it erases at the stroke of a pen the arbitrary law that Hume and his posterity brought to bear on morality ("no prescription from a description," "no 'ought' from an 'is'").[5] Description, such as Levinas approaches it, includes prescription; the world of life is the world of moral obligation. One cannot, however, conceal the weakness to which this thesis is susceptible. By granting to ethics the status of first philosophy and to its exigencies the status of immediate givens of consciousness, Levinas is condemned to passing over in silence everything that does not constitute our being-in-the-world as moral obligation. One could certainly not accuse this philosophy of being ignorant of the violence woven into the fabric of the history of the world: on the contrary, it is written against barbarism so as to deny that relations of force alone must alone and ineluctably reign over relations between men. But one would not misinterpret it were one to affirm that, written against the violences of history, it inscribes its protest by attributing to things an evidentiality they do not possess in the world. It claims—and this is the classical ambition of phenomenology—to (re)capture the originary or, at the least, the initial. It is at the dawn of experience, before violence has taken hold of the world and its history, that it proposes its alternative to the imperialism of violence and the reign of war. One should not concede too hastily that the phenomenological morning of experience lets moral exigency shine forth for all to see. One readily concedes to Levinas, against Hume and his followers, that moral prescription does not superimpose itself on the order of fact as though they were two distinct universes. On the other hand, one must never forget that, if the world keeps the Absolute veiled over, it maintains the requests of the good in its chiaroscuro. Amoralism does not govern our being-in-the-world. But nor is morality imposed on us in the way that the existence of the world is. And even though, from the dawn of experience, the human faces we meet with can be those of brothers to whom we are completely indebted, this possibility exceeds the facticity of our co-being-there; it is a free and charitable overdetermination of it. Yet the mute call that renders me "hostage" to others places no obligation on me that would emanate solely from the a priori conditions of my presence in the world.

Ethical exigency is not in evidence in a primary way. Heideggerian admonitions on this point, if they can seem excessive, are not lacking in importance. From *Mitdasein*, which constitutes in *Sein und Zeit* the fundamental relation between each I [*des moi*], to "liturgy" and "diacony," a word that appears in Levinas's writings in order to take into account the exigencies that others [*autrui*] bring to bear on me,[6] the distance is great. Although moral consciousness (*Gewissen*) is not absent from *Sein und Zeit*, its play (its "call") represents but one dimension of being-in-the-world, a dimension that is neither the first to manifest itself nor that which bears the entire meaning of our being. (We will leave aside the contents proper to this call and its incontestable poverty.) One might be astonished by how little the names of "good" and "evil" appear in a systematic interpretation of our facticity.[7] But we should try to see why this is (and not pass over its almost trivial character): no relation to the world is given whereby, at once, we would be in an ethical situation and an other I [*l'autre moi*] would necessarily appear to us as a brother. How are we to find such a relation? It is at this point that we should let liturgical experience intervene and elicit one of its characteristics that we have until now passed over.

Liturgy is the remarkable regional experience in which we do not simply engage one characteristic of our being-in-the-world, but its reality in its entirety. It is the symbolic space of definitive existence in the margins of the world, and the subversive space of its inchoation. Of even greater importance, liturgy is the experience that reveals to us most exactly how far away from the *eschaton* we actually exist. It completely diverts us away from the world such as it is—but it does not deprive it of significance for existence and does not mean that we are absent from it. One exists liturgically from one's absolute future onward. World and history are not consigned to the past for those who liturgically anticipate a beyond to history and to being-in-the-world.

One might even propose the contrary: the existence of the world and of history is never felt as acutely as when one attempts to elude their control; never is the exigency of human dwelling within the world and history felt as strongly as when their provisional reality is measured against the definitive. Liturgy is in possession of more than one element of knowledge. It knows, first of all, that the world does not have in its possession the conditions by which it can or ever could bring about the *eschaton*. It also knows, one would at least hope, the fragility of the gestures it makes within its order and the suspicion in which it can be held. It knows, finally, that the world from which it diverts itself is not handed over to the rule of violence with no possible recourse, but can be the shelter for insuperably human conduct. And yet this cannot but lead to a considerable reversal. Liturgy is diversionary or causes us to be diverted. It diverts us from urgent tasks. But it admits—without this admission imposing itself imperiously over every region of experience—that, though these tasks are indeed urgent, on the one hand, it is actually diverting us from what we ought but fail to do, on the other. The suspicions that ethical rationality raises with regard to the liturgical diversion cannot then be allowed to stand. We have better things to "do" than to pray, and when we pray, we actually "do" nothing. But the world from which liturgy diverts us is not a world over which goodwill reigns, and, at bottom, it is this world from which we must take leave, in a meantime, so as to discover our responsibilities in the world. This is a remarkable paradox. The world keeps the injunctions of the good veiled over; it is when we subvert our being-in-the-world in an attempt to implicate modes of being worthy of definitive value that we discover what precisely these injunctions are. There are experiences other than liturgy (games, leisure, etc.) that, between acts, remove us from the field of moral exigency, which should therefore give rise to "unhappiness." But the liturgical unhappiness of consciousness reveals, not only that liturgy prevents us from doing good during the time of the entr'acte, but also that we have ignored the ultimate (though veiled over) stakes of our being-in-the-world, and that we can *no longer continue* to do so.

We are not claiming that the radical nature of moral matters can only emerge from liturgical experience. But it must be recognized that liturgy and the diversion in which it engages open up a determinable path to the exigencies that the "daily" play of being-in-the-world obliterates (which is a truism), and to those in particular which do not derive from our immediate exchanges with the world. Distance is necessary for a true vantage point. If such a distance must be taken—for neither "world" nor "earth" offers us a place to demonstrate our exposition to the Absolute—the liturgical interstice lets us imagine our native place, no longer as "world" or as "earth," but as a place for another type of liturgy: a place where moral consciousness can be freely accomplished, and where, once again, an overdetermination of our being-in-the-world occurs. It is not by means of an improper use of language to say that we are thereby led to speak of our secular responsibilities in terms that serve to thematize our confrontation with the Absolute. Neither the relation to God nor the relation to goodwill is an element of our facticity: they are superimposed on the transcendental limitations of our facticity. The totality of experience can be governed by care for the good, which derives its incisiveness from the universal reconciliation for which liturgy is the symbolic and the inchoate space, but which cannot be confined within the limits of the symbolic without perverting it in the process. Thus, by returning us to "world" or to "earth" after its entr'acte, liturgical experience actually provides itself with a hold over this totality. Because of the eschatological surplus provided by liturgy, the dialectic of world and earth sees itself enriched by a third term, that of the Kingdom. Neither world nor earth, the Kingdom is the eschatological place that the man who exists before God claims to represent. If, in the end, ethical reason also reveals itself to have a liturgical meaning, it is because it can bring about a subversion within the world analogous to what liturgy, in a restricted sense of the term, is capable of in the margins of the world. It was necessary for those who wished to exist before and in expectation of God to open up the nonplace of liturgy. But it has become clear that this nonplace is not the only homeland we make use of in the time that leads us to death: it is also in the world that the eschatological homeland—the Kingdom—is implicated inchoately (and thus in a nonsymbolic way) in the world as soon as men see themselves as brothers, not only in the entr'acte of liturgy, but within the limits of their co-presence in the world. Liturgy, as we have said, exacerbates our not-being-at-home in the world and is a critique of our relation to the earth. But this should not be cause for distress. This exacerbation and this critique reveal to us, therefore, that it is only truly possible to respond to the question of our place in eschatological terms; they preside over the opening of the worldly nonplace in which the eschatological contents of signification proper to the humanity of man are unveiled. We must, finally, dare to say that liturgy enables us to dwell in the world and on the earth by superimposing on our facticity the order of an ethical vocation that alone authorizes us to let the Kingdom invest itself in world and earth in advance.

The ethical dimension of our facticity can thus be brought to light. Amoralism does not rule over the beginning. Rather, as is shown in exemplary fashion by the Heideggerian conception of a conscience that "calls" without our knowing exactly to what we are "called," ethics is in fact involved within the chiaroscuro of the world—how could it be otherwise? The austere and patient labor of morality is to liberate the "clear" from its links to the "obscure," and no one can claim this work to be doomed to failure. It nevertheless represents a victory for reason or the will, which is of little import here, over the immediate conditions of experience (and it represents in Levinas, if you like, the victory of a look [*regard*] capable of dissipating not only the superficiality of the everyday but also the chiaroscuro of the world itself). We cannot deduce the entirety of moral experience from our opening onto the world; nor would we know how to make the foundations of our moral experience foreign to our facticity. The ethical order as much as the liturgical is thus the order of a "call": a vocation. The rationality immanent in ethics enables us to discern the eschatological meaning of this vocation. This is all the more the case if the liturgical unhappiness of consciousness redirects us from the Kingdom we anticipate in the margins of the world to a hold that, with the grace of goodwill, the Kingdom can exert over the very fabric of historial existence.

§ 29 The Relation between Ethical and Liturgical Reason as Circularity

We can therefore challenge every interpretation positing that ethics and liturgy maintain no relation other than that of tension or even contradiction. Caught between its empirical identity (its "consciousness") and the eschatological vocation (the "soul") it attests to in liturgy, the ego sustains an ineluctable tension. But the tension between the historical and the eschatological is one thing, the relation between liturgical and ethical reason quite another: this becomes clear as soon as we recognize the work of liturgy and the labor of the ethical as the two poles of a unique structure, which is that of the definitive's hold over the provisional, and the Kingdom's hold over world and history. Setting itself up as a diversion, liturgy gives rise to a justifiable anxiety [*anxiété*]. But the distance that it creates in relation to the world establishes no ulterior world. It is likely that, on returning to it, liturgy affords even greater proximity to, or a greater concern with, world or earth, where man is neither away from home [*à l'étranger*] nor left any longer in the company of numinous forces foreign [*étrangères*] to God since he can let God reign there as well. Leaving aside the question of a vocation, it is through facticity, first of all, that the world concerns us; and this concern is not abolished even when, liturgically, it finds itself bracketed. Liturgy redoubles this first concern, to which we need not respond, with a second concern, to which liturgy does respond. Having taken measure of the world, and taken note of what constitutes its worldliness—the chiaroscuro and what separates it from the *eschaton*—and having thus taken note of the difference between the world and the Kingdom, liturgy knows what is at stake in it and in ethics, for the stakes are the very same: challenging the provisional in the name of the eschatological. Here and there, this challenge does, of course, take on different forms. Liturgy is the bracketing of being-in-the-world. Ethics is the step back that enables us to take hold once again, prior to the violences of history, of a relation to the real in the element of praxis that anticipates the eschatological reign of God. But this difference cannot conceal the identity of a critique: the circle that unites liturgical reason and ethical reason is the fundamental rhythm of existence, which, transgressing its native conditions, desires the accomplishment of the human beyond what can be derived from our facticity.

Existence as Vigil

§ 30 The Nocturnal Site of Liturgy

To have learned that the ethical and liturgical each participate from within their own orders in contesting historical reason does not entitle us to forget a fact we have continually repeated: liturgy has as one of its elements the unverifiable, and its critique of being-in-the-world cannot withstand the objections of every school of thought that gives itself world and history as ultimate horizons. The lifeblood of ethics, should it wish to think itself radical, and whether or not it knows it, is its eschatological ambition; and it can claim real success even though it does not have the power to ensure the reign of the good and of peace. Goodwill is at work in the world in a demonstrable way. By linking the destiny of liturgy to that of ethics, are we not thereby providing ourselves with insufficient means to grant to liturgy a legitimacy that within the world can only be granted to ethics? We did, of course, respond to this objection by discerning in the liturgical distance, and in the "unhappiness" to which it can give rise, the possible condition of a limitless concern with the ultimate (but natively veiled over) implications of being-in-the-world. But if the liturgical unhappiness of consciousness is to be interpreted and resolved, it is patently clear, and must become a conceptual certainty to us, that liturgical experience eludes the network of *bonum utilis* by virtue of its essence, and that we would not do justice to liturgy were we to fail to understand its uselessness [*inutilité*]. Liturgy has the prestigious task of attending to the highest work [*travail*]: *opus Dei*. As a "*work*" ["*œuvre*"], it is in sharp contrast with every other, however. It is not a *labor* [*labeur*]: it has no relation to the grueling confrontation with nature man must undertake to ensure his survival. We must correct the lexicon we have just used and say that liturgy is not a *work* [*œuvre*]: it produces nothing that could possibly be handled, admired, sold, or given. It is utterly foreign to the logic of *action*: it does not set itself up so as to furnish a solution to the problems of the polis, even though it resolves, in a symbolic manner which demands that the limits of the symbol be surpassed, the contradictions of political and social experience.[1] This requires, then, that we specify by what logic liturgy can resist modernity's equation of Being and doing [*de l'être et du faire*] in order to appear as the rather remarkable figure we will call "inoperativity" ["*désœuvrement*"],[2] the refusal to enter into any logic of production in the name of a logic bound up with more urgent stakes. From negations that preside over the opening onto the liturgical field, we must therefore proceed more precisely to the affirmative practice represented by liturgy. And we will determine it, first of all, by specifying in a new register where its symbolic place lies: in the night and the vigil.

By precariously distancing himself from history, the man who prays signifies and anticipates the accomplishment of this history. In this state of anticipation, he can neither forget nor deny the exigencies of practical reason: were he to forget them, he would thereby betray his ignorance of what he is doing. That is why one might be justified in affirming that the attention he devotes to and his expectation of God [*son attention et son attente de Dieu*] symbolically assume the nocturnal character of the vigil in which, every ethical duty having been honored, man gives to the Absolute the time (and thus the being) he might otherwise have given to sleep. The image of the vigil is anything but rhetorical. We live by day and by night. Although sleep, from which the freedom and the intentional acts of consciousness are absent, is not a part of life where we manifest who we are, that we live in a lesser mode of existence during the hours we devote to purely physiological operations is nevertheless essential to what we are. Behind the banality of this casual remark, we thus come up against a practically insuperable limit whenever the question of sleep is evoked. Only the angels ignore sleep—the Aramaic name for angel is "one who keeps vigil" ["*veilleur*"]. But we do not exist perpetually in the mode of consciousness keeping vigil; and sleep, as being-less and as a figure of being-less in general, of nonexistence, teaches us that we are not masters of ourselves: "life," in this case, has power over "existence." What, then, makes a man not sleep so as to gain time for the vigil? In this most common experience (for who has never kept vigil?), there is much at stake: to use the same lexicon, it is thus a question of the protest of "existence" against "life," a protest that is victorious. The animal can be prone to sleepless nights and can stay awake simply because he is hungry or because it is afraid (and I can certainly remain awake for the same reasons). But there would be no sense in saying that an animal is capable of keeping vigil: keeping vigil cannot be the object of an obligation; it is something that can only be the object of a desire. The philosophical importance of the question should not make us forget that we do not necessarily invest ourselves in the vigil for the most laudable reasons: though we see nothing but futility in his actions, the reveler also keeps vigil. He nevertheless has his reasons and the refusal to sleep conceals therefore a powerful affirmation. We can set ourselves up against the exigencies of "life" so as to "exist" a little longer: the time of the vigil is truly our time, that time which we gain at the expense of nonfreedom and nonconsciousness, or in other words, pure biological necessities. We are not accountable to any authority for this time. To deliberately deprive me of sleep, or of the sleep necessary to my good health, would be tantamount to abuse; I have the right to expect that the State or the company, except in cases of emergency, leave me sufficient time to sleep. The act of keeping vigil appears to us then as the purest form of the self positing itself, as the epitome of an affirmation of our freedom. Once our inevitable allocation of work, whose distribution is necessary, foreseeable, and commonplace, has been completed, and once our daytime duties have been fulfilled, the decision to keep vigil proves that we remain in possession of a fundamental right: that of proving, by the content we give to our vigil (which we can spend doing philosophy, writing poetry, or praying—and many other things besides), the surplus of meaning we give to our humanity.

The vigil does not reveal myself as I have to be, but as I would wish myself to be. One thus sees that it can provide us with a conceptual code with which to think the time that, removed from *bonum utilis*, we consecrate to liturgical "inoperativity." Liturgy is the absence of work [*œuvre*]. But no work is required of us in the vigil simply because no exigency bears on it. Liturgy can, for this reason, find itself in bad company. It is not only the vigil that can commend itself to no work [*œuvre*]. The man who prays must initially accept that he belongs to a class among which must be counted the reveler if he is to convince us that his inoperativity is in fact a critique of "doing" [*du "faire"*] and of "work" ["*de l'œuvre*"], and that the nonutility of his praise must not be interpreted as uselessness but as a beyond-to-utility. But with the means he has at his disposal, he can convince us of this.

§ 31 The Necessary and the Surplus

The vigil is neither a time of salaried work (*negotium*) nor a time appropriate for leisure (*otium*), for which "free" days would be better suited than sleep-deprived nights. Anything can of course give us the desire to keep vigil, to start with the pure desire to keep on "existing" a little longer. But if we wish to pray, it must be said in all seriousness that we see the vigil as the time most favorable to liturgy, its *kairos*. This is not to say that we only have the right (and the time) to pray at night, much less to invalidate the possibility, classically acknowledged by the ascetic tradition, of "constant prayer" and of an existence made wholly liturgical. But it does enable us to spell out a little more clearly the conditions under which ethical "work" [*œuvre*] can be distinguished from liturgical inoperativity, and under which the two maintain a circular relation. If we admit, and we do so unreservedly, that ethics occupies the most impregnable position of power within the topic of experience (both as an authority with the right to critique historical reason within history itself and as an eschatological profession [*protestation*] of the possibility of the ethical being concretely inscribed in the fabric of the world), then we must also admit, and again we do so unreservedly, that liturgy occupies no such position of strength. Its logic of diversion is certainly not a logic of divertissement, but of conversion. If, in addition, liturgy is itself an authority with the right to critique historical reason, it can do so only from within the margins of history. And if it is a profession of the eschatological, it cannot appeal to an advent of definitive realities we would be obliged to concede; and the "eschatological I" is measured against an "empirical I" that it cannot itself verifiably measure. On the other hand, we have refused to restrict the thinkable and the real to the domain of the verifiable (if we had not, why would we be showing an interest in liturgy?). If we assign to liturgy the vigil as its "favorable time," it becomes possible for us to think the bond that unites the daytime work of ethics and the nighttime inoperativity of prayer as a relation between the *necessary* and the *surplus*.

It is no small matter to have recognized in the liturgical distance the condition for a concern with the history of the world in the name of the reign of God—we will come back to the matutinal light that it thus projects on experience (see § 36). But just as being-in-the-world is primary and being-before-God secondary, so, too, the *kairos* of liturgy comes, as night follows day, after we have completed our duties, whose noncompletion (or, more precisely, nonrecognition) would indicate our powerlessness to understand that the meaning of our humanity resides in prescriptions more than in an empirical reality offered to description. We pray between acts. But the vigil prolongs this entr'acte. The day, which will return us to the care of things secular, is still far off. We do not have to account for the time we gain to devote to praise. And yet this very much amounts to saying that liturgy appears here as a surplus. Thus, if it is posed in ethical terms (and it is impossible not to do so), it appears after we have testified to our humanity—and at a time when it seems possible for the *disputatio de homine* to be brought to a conclusion. We must nevertheless ask how we are to understand the meaning of this surplus. Liturgy is not, in the strict sense, necessary. But the mode of this nonnecessity is the *same* as that in which *the Absolute is itself not necessary.*

We should clarify what we mean by these terms. We are not claiming by this that the Absolute is not a sovereign good, and thus in possession of the conditions of the beatitude; nor are we saying that liturgy does not unveil a "desire" for the sovereign good inscribed in the innermost depths of man, should the power the world exerts over man have covered it over or enshrouded it in ambiguity. We are saying, however, that it belongs to the logic of being-in-the-world (or of "earthly" existence) that man can, without committing theoretical suicide, embody figures of his humanity that require no divine guarantee, and which make liturgical experience supererogatory. We are stating, in other words, that God is not the ontotheological foundation of the world, and that liturgy is by no means the clear and distinct secret to life. From the fact that I can only exist in the form of Dasein or of a "mortal," or in the form of "goodwill," it does not follow that the nonnecessity of the Absolute and of liturgy must be interpreted as what language ordinarily dubs "contingency," accessory and unimportant. Let us suggest here that this nonnecessity must in fact be thought as a beyond-the-necessary.[3] If the concept of the necessary, within the logic of experience, amounts to being that without which we cannot exist, the Absolute and liturgy are not necessary for us. But we will define the beyond-the-necessary as possessing the conditions of an existence that exceeds the measure of being-in-the-world. The beyond-the-necessary lies beyond all measure. It ruptures the closure of experience, which does not, of course, encompass the plenitude of Being, but constitutes rather the native determination of existence. It is the eschatological or its promise, understood as a surplus. Liturgy will perhaps be able to offer us the bread necessary to life. But it first offers us the wine of the Kingdom.

§ 32 Care and Restlessness

We can now ask how the time devoted to the beyond-the-necessary — the time of liturgical inoperativity — is fundamentally structured. If it is true that we cannot know who we are without asking where we are, it is just as true, as we have already said, that we cannot shed light on ourselves without interpreting the time that is the horizon of our being, and without interpreting our relation to time (see § 24): our identity is a question of both place and of time. On the question of time, we acknowledge Heidegger's response: temporalization manifests a privilege of the future over the present and the past (the philosopher will never recant this), and is manifested in the exemplary mode of *care* (which disappears, however, in the "later" texts, where death, without ceasing to be the object of an existential conjuring trick that actually makes of it our highest possibility, enables us to exist serenely). The essence of care is the way the I perpetually gets ahead of itself, whereby what is not yet (and what it is not yet) is concerned with what is (and what it is). Care steps outside the present; it is dependent on something of which we are not the masters, on what we attempt to make ourselves masters of in the strategies at work in projection. There are nevertheless limits to the existential reign of care: the act of remembrance and the joy which lets us dwell in a present that no future can disturb and which takes the form of insouciance. Care, however, can no more be annulled than can our being-in-the-world. But we have learned through our topological interpretation of liturgy that it has the power to subvert the localized reality of being-in-the-world — it is not unreasonable to wonder, therefore, whether it might have a similar power with regard to its temporal reality.[4] We already know that man is capable of existing from his absolute future onward (see § 24); we can now elicit in a more precise way the structure of the present lived in the shelter of the *eschaton*.

Here as elsewhere, let us first take note of what is self-evident. It is from within the world that liturgy takes its distance from the play of the world. If it wishes to delimit a pure space where it can be attentive to the Absolute, its challenge to being-in-the-world is fragile, if it can be said to exist at all. The man who symbolically thwarts the hold that place has over his being does not, as we have said, free himself from the claim place holds over him. One can only imagine that this will also be the case with time. Care apparently makes up part of what liturgy challenges. It is not that the man who prays is indifferent to his future; if liturgy offers us the plenitude of the present, it does so by virtue of the absolute future from which his experience gains its structure. But it is a question here of an absolute future that eludes the worldly order of temporality, and which liturgical experience also wishes to elude. Liturgy is a nonplace. If care reigns over the time of being-in-the-world, it must also be said that liturgy is symbolically constituted as a "nontime": a time we no longer wish to be governed only by the eschatological vigil, and in which we wish to nullify the self's preoccupation with itself in favor of an expectation and an attentiveness [*d'une attente et d'une attention*] that divests us of our concern with ourselves and in every future we have made our *own* possibility. But it is a question here of liturgy's ambitions, of the meaning it gives itself and not of its empirical reality—the man who prays never ceases to be all alone and to see the worldly logic of temporalization exert its power over the time he would wish to extricate from the play of the world. Even the nontime of liturgy is perhaps as fearful of care investing itself in it as it is of its own project [*projet*] appearing to lie beyond all worldly measure.

It is a question here of grasping what is most obvious: to believe ourselves extricated from facticity on account of the opportunity we have to subvert it symbolically, on the one hand, and to overdetermine it ascetically, on the other, would be theoretically irresponsible. But this should not deflect our attention from the originary modes in which liturgy attempts to thwart the worldly laws of temporalization. The vigil is time gained, and thus existence gained, and this time is that of a marginal or parenthetic experience. From the fact that this time is gained, it does not follow that the question of temporalization is simply a matter for our freedom to decide upon willy-nilly; and from its hermeneutic site being in the margins of our being-in-the-world, it does not follow with any certitude that we thereby violate the a priori modalities of our inherence in the world. The interpretation of liturgical temporalization must recognize these restrictions. But, if liturgy can ground itself by setting itself up as a project that goes beyond the human (and we take it to be axiomatic that it can), these restrictions do not mean that the grammar of this temporalization is no more than a slightly exotic variation on the temporalization that takes our inherence in the world as its measure. What, then, does the "nontime" of liturgy consist of? Several elements need to be taken into account in our response.

a. Liturgical time manifests itself, first of all, as the time of an inchoation. We perhaps always exist in the mode of beginning, of return to the initial, and of nonaccomplishment. To interpret what we are in terms of the beginning, we will always be forced to pose the question of the *eschaton*—to an authority to whom we grant the last word on the matter. That the beginning provides us with the first concept with which to think liturgical temporality presents us with a paradox. Is it not the end that liturgy symbolizes and anticipates? This is true. But one need not be overly attentive to liturgy's system of anticipation to understand that, given that the day's work has been done (whether well or not), liturgy's nocturnal inoperativity does not put the seal on this achievement, but simply exposes the distance separating history and eschatology. We do not need to pray in order to experience the beginning. When we do attempt to pray, however, this experience takes on a radically new form: it teaches us, on the one hand, that history is, as a *totality*, only the place for the beginning of existence and, on the other, that between the beginning and the accomplishment of what we are, there is the greatest distance imaginable. If one understands liturgy to be our highest possibility, the beyond-the-necessary order of liturgy is of the order of the accomplishment. But it is of the order of the inchoate if one comes to realize—and how could one not?—that liturgical praise sets before man an infinite task, and that if he who prays gets ahead of himself in a way that care never can (because the limits of care are those of being-toward-death), no experience would be able to reduce the "eschatological reserve" the Absolute shows toward man. It must be said that the attitude of the liturgical vigil is eschatological: nothing interposes itself between man and God in it, and we can praise God as if he were already present in the mode of Parousia. But it must also be said that this attitude attempts to bracket care only so as to let the *eschaton* disrupt [*inquiéter*] the present more violently still—restlessness [*inquiétude*] prevents every development that could lead to a state of satisfaction by reminding us that the Absolute, which we are free to encounter, is never close to us without this very proximity sheltering a still greater distance. For whoever exists "onward from" his absolute future exists before this future empirically.

b. How, then, are we to exist within the horizon of an absolute future that is not our death, and that we can anticipate only by admitting the most radical of disparities? Liturgy wishes for the *eschaton*. It proves this by endeavoring to disqualify every temporalization governed by being-in-the-world and (thus) by our being-toward-death: by endeavoring to subordinate care to restlessness and facticity to vocation. It is nevertheless patently obvious that it does not bring about the *eschaton*, or to use more rigorous language, that the Absolute does not invest itself in the nonplace and the nontime of our liturgies so as to realize the *eschaton*. But by making our present tremble [*en inquiétant notre présent*], it must be recognized that the Absolute enables us to effectively infringe on the laws governing worldly temporalization. A temporalization contradicting one governed by care can only be as fragile as everything that breaks through the closure of the world. But this neither refutes the consistency of the arguments underlying liturgy, nor authorizes the misinterpretation that would see in restlessness [*inquiétude*] only a pious name for care. For if care and restlessness are empirically almost indistinguishable,[5] restlessness can nevertheless do what care cannot: enable the present that it structures to close up on itself again without falling back into a "vulgar" conception. God's presence is not his Parousia, and restlessness enables consciousness to grasp this knowledge experientially. But if the liturgical vigil waits for the dawn of the last day, it is also the field of experience where the chiaroscuro of the world is dissipated and where man can at intervals enjoy [*jouir de*] the presence of the Absolute as if he were enjoying his Parousia. Restlessness does not prevent definitive peace from reigning over our present in advance [*par anticipation*].

c. We must take a further step and ask whether the fundamental and intrinsic structure of liturgical temporality does not reside precisely in the dialectic that unites eschatological tension and the anticipated fruition of the *eschaton*. We probably never have a pure experience of the liturgical vigil. But that does not prevent us from providing it with a concept. On the other hand, if we attempt to do so, we cannot but notice that in the liturgical vigil we exceed the opposition of a time governed by expectation and a time governed by a gift of presence. The world no longer interposes itself between the Absolute and the I in the nonplace of the vigil. History is provisionally left behind. Its structures no longer have any bearing on me or on the relation I maintain with the Absolute. The fecundity of the paradox of liturgy lies nevertheless in the fact that the time we have symbolically freed from our historiality can remain a time of tension or, if you prefer, that restlessness is not only intelligible in the way it contradicts care, but in the way it can constitute a definitive characteristic of our being. Liturgy asks us not to choose between the representation of an eternal path of the soul toward God and that of a repose of the soul in God. Although it cannot free us from the concrete hold the world exerts over us, it can nevertheless offer us the joys of definitive peace here and now. And although it symbolically leaves the world behind, it cannot exclude restlessness as if its limits were those of our being-in-the-world. The Absolute, which promises us unending peace, can provide us with it within the time that leads us to death, and liturgy is the power to accept such a gift. It is, of course, banal to say that the Absolute intervenes in present experience in order to divest us of our concern with the world and to present us with its more than necessary offerings [*biens*]. It is perhaps less banal, but hardly intrepid, to propose that the Absolute that disrupts [*inquiète*] us during this time actually promises to "disrupt" us for eternity—and that liturgy is the power to accept such a promise.

§ 33 Doubting Facticity Philosophically

Nonplace, nontime: the paradox of these negations is the philosophical paradox of liturgy, and we must turn briefly to stakes that have lain hidden beneath the surface throughout our analyses. It may come down to one principal question. By bracketing the logic of place, understood as the dialectic of "world" and "earth," and by bracketing the logic of care, does not liturgy represent a particularly rich and systematic form of divertissement? It must be conceded that the suspicion is easily formulated and is not terribly original for those familiar with the terms in which the question of man is posed today. But the consistency of liturgical experience itself contains a symmetrical suspicion, which, if less easily formulated, is not so commonplace but is deserving of our attention: liturgy suggests that the facticity it overdetermines may in fact be the *true face of divertissement*, and that divertissement may have its roots in the *existential reality of what we are*. Instead of being a lesser relation to ourselves and the world, might not divertissement be our native condition? One cannot pose such a question without admitting that our inherence in the world and the government of care over us are unquestionably "fundamental," and that the philosophies that have continually employed them unquestionably speak of what we are: we have not allowed the Heideggerian questioning to haunt these pages so as to make use of it as a foil, but rather because the logic that it brings to light is indeed the logic of the authority that the world exercises over us. Liturgy, such as we have interpreted it, fulfills a function of diversion. What it diverts us from in the first place is not (even though it certainly does so as well) the "everydayness" in which Dasein loses the precise meaning of its being: this is very much the native reality of our being. Dasein is without God in the "world," and it is in the company of "deities" and not in proximity to God that mortals dwell in the "Fourfold." One might hastily conclude from this that neither Dasein nor the "mortal" justifiably occupy the position of lieutenants of man in philosophical theorizing. And yet it is another—more radical—conclusion that liturgy enables us to reach. If Dasein or the "mortal" were imprecise figures of our humanity, liturgical experience would cause us (and by no means in a small way) to reject the conceptual systems to which they belong. But, if liturgy presents itself to us as the power to subvert, it only does so by confirming the reality it tries to subvert, which it subverts either symbolically, inchoately, or both. Liturgy contests more than concepts: it is against the real that its protestations are directed. By its precarious dissipation of the chiaroscuro of the world, it reminds us that the chiaroscuro is an essential characteristic of our worldliness. By subverting our "earth" and "world," it entirely confirms that "earth" and "world" are the native structures in which our relation to place unfolds. By affirming that our being is to be understood in the final analysis as an (eschatological) vocation, in terms of an exposition to the Absolute rather than in those of an opening onto the world, it confirms the historial order in which this vocation can "exist," but it has no hold over the native conditions of experience other than that which comes in the form of a restlessness (theology would speak here of a "natural desire for the beatific vision") that does not yield all its meaning to a hermeneutics of facticity. One thus understands how we have come to form the suspicion that the divertissement is at the beginning ("at the *beginning*," which is not to say "at the *origin*"). Liturgical logic is almost foreign to our facticity. On the other hand—and this is the most acute problem—is what is at the beginning, the initial, the definitive truth of our being? In suspecting that at the beginning there is an interstice from the origin, and that the power of this interstice makes itself felt within the limits of the time that gives us passage to death, liturgy enables us to doubt that this is so. Its diversionary intention is thus the negation of an initial divertissement. If this divertissement is inscribed in what we are, it should come as no surprise that liturgical reason achieves major theoretical victories, but cannot govern experience as world or earth govern it "locally," and as care governs it temporally.

§ 34 The Hermeneutics of the Initial and the Heuristic of the Originary

By mastering the terms of the question, it thus becomes possible to ask whether the liturgical vigil enables us, with all the necessary cautions, to speak of the origin, and if one must not recognize in the fundamental structures that liturgy subverts an erasure of the originary. Must the overdetermination that liturgical reason imposes on being-in-the-world and the eschatological horizon it deploys be understood solely in terms of an excess or surplus, in terms of the overstepping of a limit, or do they not also signify that liturgy deciphers a primitive logic of experience buried over in the palimpsest, the forgotten depths of our being? We know that nothing opens the floodgates to myth more than recourse to the originary, and all the more so when the originary is not available to us in the beginning, when one is attempting to comprehend the interstice between the origin and the beginning. The interpretation of being-in-the-world as divertissement nevertheless compels us to pose the question. It is absolutely necessary to recall that *Geworfenheit* (thrownness), the "dereliction" or "projection" that, in Heidegger, assigns Dasein its residence in the world, is not a return to a *status pristinus* (the text is perfectly clear on this point, and needed to be, so as to rule out any hasty theological usage that might be made of it).[6] Nonetheless, is not the initial the originary? The arguments for liturgy enable us to rigorously doubt that this is the case, and to appeal to the originary rather than the initial without invoking superfluous entities.

A common concept in ascetic literature indicates the nature of such an appeal: the concept of the "remembrance of God." This remembrance is not a memorial to the passage of the Absolute in history, such as it is organized in the theology of the sacraments or in the *lectio divina*. This remembrance concentrates on nothing that has taken place in the world and its time; it is another name for the time and attention we devote to God. It is nevertheless a question—and this is what prevents us from believing the term "remembrance" to be employed here in an utterly equivocal manner—of an attentiveness gained at the expense of an inattentiveness that is entirely deserving of the name of "forgetfulness." One does not, of course, forget the existence of God once one has acquired such knowledge. But this knowledge is not immemorial, and this obvious truth gives rise to a real difficulty. What, then, does the transcendental ignorance in which we find ourselves in relation to the Absolute signify? Liturgical reason provides a response when it discerns in our facticity the transcendental ground of a divertissement. But it can only provide this response because its lifeblood is the "remembrance of God" and the violence that this remembrance does to the native modes of experience. We have thought this violence in the form of an overdetermination, which nevertheless presents itself as possessing the conditions of a plenitude of Being: liturgy implicates the eschatological in the historical. And yet it is precisely the necessary introduction of the eschatological motif that forces us to have recourse to the originary and to dissociate it from the initial. The beginning is ambiguous: it is neither the practical atheism of Dasein nor the paganism of "earthly" experience, but the circle that unites the two, in which it matters little whether one enters through one or the other, and on which restlessness cannot impose its rationality. This beginning is what liturgy abolishes in the element of experience (and what the affirmation of God abolishes in the element of knowledge). This abolition turns away from the initial, diverts itself away from the transcendental power of divertissement in the name of a vocation that transgresses the conditions of being-in-the-world. At the beginning, it is precisely a question of the self. But it is not at all a question of an ipseity that, in the mode of beginning, holds the secret to eschatological accomplishment: the ambiguity of the beginning must be negated and liturgy must live on an inaugural negation. It is for this reason that the liturgical hermeneutics of the beginning, by perceiving in the I [le moi] a native capacity for divertissement, enables the "remembrance of God" to speak the language of the originary to us. The originary is not what is proper to a time before time, to an archi-beginning. It is—more modestly, but without theological *protologia* finding itself disqualified—this relation of the I to itself which enables us to think the *eschaton* as an accomplishment rather than as an annulment. The ascetic and speculative function of the "remembrance of God" is to respond to the scandal of our transcendental ignorance and inexperience of God; and it does so by suggesting that the liturgical overdetermination of our facticity elicits the conditions of our being inextricable from our vocation. The originary is the identity of being-in-fact and being-in-vocation. It is what liturgy gives us access or perhaps returns us to: the existence over which the *eschaton* stakes its claim in history. (What it does not show us, only because we systematically refuse to know enough about it, is how to represent and think a pure before [*en deçà*] and a pure beyond [*au-delà*] for history.)

The lessons we thus learn from liturgical reason are not lacking in importance. The originary is not the initial. But it remains accessible both in the inoperativity that frees us from the logic of "doing" [*du "faire"*] and in the subversion of the worldly modes of location and temporality. However, even though the mediation of the accomplishment is conceptually indispensable for gaining access to it, the originary is not the *eschaton*; the liturgical vigil, whose lifeblood is the "remembrance of God," also lives on a desire; and it thus conjoins, but must also distinguish, the originary site that it occupies and the eschatological restlessness that discerns in the origin a provisional order of reality. The origin is not the Parousia. (If the truth be known, the concept of the Parousia can reveal itself to be singularly inadequate to think what unites the originary and the *eschaton*—the noninterpositioning of "world" or "earth" between God and me—and what separates them—the infinite journey that marks the relation of man to an always greater God, and which prevents us from conceiving the eschatological reality of this relation as [the possibility] of enjoying possession of an omnipresence in which God would cease to dwell in an "inaccessible light").[7] But, by giving or returning us to the originary, the liturgical nonplace provides the conditions in which to think our vocation as [the possibility] of enjoying possession of the Parousia. Owing to this, the liturgical vigil, in concluding our historial tasks, also manifests itself as the symbolic place of an absolute beginning, of a beginning freed from all complicity with *divertissement*.

§ 35 Patience

To both the embarrassment and the fecundation of liturgical theory, whoever prays is no longer nowhere; if the rationality at work in the liturgical vigil enables us to speak the language of the originary coherently, it in no way masks the fact that neither the gift (nor the restitution) of the origin nor the tension that ordains the absolute beginning an absolute future makes the Absolute available to us: liturgy does not cease to be determined as a nonexperience because the philosopher uncovers its rationality. In attempting to bracket the claim the world makes over him, whoever prays achieves a great deal but does not annul the world's irrepressible intrusion into his relation with God—and it must doubtless be said that forces of historiality appear more vividly to those who know (whether thematically or not) that although their being-in-vocation exceeds their being-in-fact, their access to the originary will always be mediated by the native conditions of experience. But how then can restlessness exist in a present between the origin and the accomplishment, in a meantime that is removed from the time of the world only in the eschatological symbolism of the vigil, and in which at bottom we merely pretend to be witnesses to the Parousia, knowing all the while that the Absolute is present to us in a historical rather than parousiacal mode? We can respond by uttering one word: "Patience."

Liturgy is inoperativity, which means that its logic is not that of the great theurgical work, of the force the religious man brings to bear on the divine. This is not to say that the one he expects is the Absent. But because it concerns itself with a presence while hoping for a beyond-to-presence, and because it hopes as one hopes for a gift rather than for the payment of a debt, its expectation must reckon with the possibility of perpetual frustration. It may be expedient here to recall that liturgy engages one as a "soul" more than as a "consciousness." No theoretical marginalization of consciousness can result in time not being a matter for consciousness. Whoever prays must learn that Hegel was right and Schleiermacher wrong on a point of major importance: man's relation to God takes place, not in the element of feeling (*Gefühl*) or of immediate "knowledge" ["*savoir*" *immédiat*] (*Wissen*), but in that of "knowledge" ["*connaissance*"] (*Erkenntnis*).[8] He must nevertheless also learn (though Hegel makes no contribution to this teaching) that no rationally acquired knowledge [*connaissance*] prevents the liturgical (and thus experiential) relation of man to God from being governed by a logic of inexperience, and that the liturgical vigil is the time, not in which man enjoys his theological knowledge [*connaissance*], but in which he awaits the morning when the experiential will confirm the conceptual contents of knowledge [*connaissance*]. But this wait ignores all the delays involved in the Absolute coming to experience—whether it comes on this side or the beyond of death. Thus, for consciousness, if we must speak of it, patience is a major liturgical virtue. The patient consciousness knows that its attentiveness and expectation [*son attention et son attente*] give it no hold over God. It is a confession of powerlessness. Impatience is undoubtedly not a fault. We should, for example, impatiently desire the good to come about immediately, without delay. It is neither senseless nor probably unjustifiable for man to impatiently wish that "grace comes and that the world passes."[9] If we admit (and it would be irresponsible, both experientially and conceptually, not to do so) that the liturgical vigil provides the conditions for the hospitality man wishes to extend to the Absolute—but also that the guest will come in his own time; that he will, or perhaps already has, come incognito; and that no visit he makes to us in the time that leads us to death will grant us the definitive intimacy in which the immediate would be the nondeceiving and insuperable element of our relation, then impatience must yield to patience (for it is simply a question of respecting the logic intrinsic to liturgical experience).

(This is confirmed for us by knowledge that we have not wished to call upon thus far—the theological knowledge grounded in divine self-manifestation—and which teaches us the good usage of faith. Theology knows and declares that, if the world is interposed between God and us, and that if there exists no clear alternative between a chiaroscuro omnipresence and the Parousia, it is because the world shelters a third presence by which the Absolute participates in the logic of inherence, namely, what Christology and the theology of the sacraments teach. And yet even the gift of the Eucharist, in which the Absolute occupies a place here and now, is made to us only on condition that the world interposes itself, and that a so-called "real" presence does not render it diaphanous and theophanic. This interposition is ontically the most tenuous there is: the breadth and tenuity of the Eucharistic species, of bread and wine. But these tenuous realities bear within themselves all the ontological density of the world; and if they are the place of a presence that constitutes the joy of believing, they also constitute for him a constant reminder of his historiality. That is why this presence does not absolve us of the duty to be patient.)

What do we do when we are patient? We do not have to wait for the question of liturgy to be posed to know what it means to be patient. We can be patient while waiting for a train, for a visit, or for the mail. But the nocturnal patience that liturgy requires of us tells us more about this figure of consciousness. Liturgy never ceases to tell us that being-in-the-world is not the definitive, and that it represents the initial and not the originary. Moreover, the restlessness that is associated with knowledge (and which learns from this knowledge what it itself is), in order to guide the liturgical subversion of being-in-the-world, constantly reminds us that we have not freed ourselves from the government of world or earth when liturgy has overdetermined being-in-the-world. Whoever is patient "does" nothing. Moral consciousness, if it radically wishes for the good, also wishes for the Kingdom (whether or not it knows it), and can—asymptotically—hasten its arrival. And yet it is to the asymptotic character that "doing" assumes when hastening the arrival of definitive realities that the inactivity proper to patience responds. We can go some way to assuming our responsibility to the *eschaton* by consenting to the call of the highest moral exigencies (on condition that we do not forget that our finitude tragically contradicts the infinite task set for good-will). But the work of man will not bring it about; and between God and us the world remains that which we can neither leave nor abolish. It must be understood then that, in being patient, we *renounce* [nous nous démettons] *all pretensions to being the project managers of the definitive, and put ourselves in God's hands* [nous en remettons à Dieu] *as the giver of all that does not pass away.* We are free to open ourselves up to the Absolute's design. We are free to offer him our hospitality. But this hospitality can be accepted unbeknownst to us, on the one hand, and history maintains us far from the eschatological reversal by which the Absolute will offer us definitive hospitality, on the other. Our time must thus be lived in patience [*Il faut donc donner notre temps en patience*].

§ 36 Freedom at the Initial and at the Origin

The debate between liturgical reason and ethical reason can now receive some final clarifications. Ethics wishes for the Kingdom but cannot institute it. When its time comes, ever-patient liturgy declares the contradictory character of such an institution. But there is more. For, although morality can strive for the Kingdom, whose undeniable importance is not to be discounted, it can only do so asymptotically. The theoretical ambitions of morality cannot conceal from us the shortcomings of our practice; the world that liturgy brackets is the very one in which we have made pacts with violence and evil. If conversion is an obligation intrinsic to liturgy (see § 28), it is inaugurated by the admission of such past pacts, in Kantian terms, by the admission of the radical nature of evil. Whoever takes the risk of praying does not ask for God to bring to perfection a work already nearing completion: the liturgical vigil is not an offertory for the good we have done; it allows us to raise up nothing but empty hands at the hour of the evening sacrifice. And yet this shows us exactly how liturgy resolves the debate on the nature of evil. Is it an (excusable) error or a wrongdoing [*faute*] (which calls for forgiveness)? Is it the blunder [*faux pas*] of whoever has not known exactly what to do in order to do good, or the option contrary to the good, more or less deliberately taken, which we can always be held accountable for, and which calls for mercy? The most elementary grammar of liturgy tells us immediately: the freedom that makes it possible for our patience to be put to the test is also the freedom that can desire to exempt itself from doing good: prayer comes after doing wrong; the first request that must be made of God (if what we know of him authorizes us to do so in theory—but would we persist in praying if we thought that mercy was not a divine attribute?) is for forgiveness. It is for this reason that the liturgical night must be interpreted, not simply as a last act, but—just as the last morning heralds the Parousia—also as the dawn of a new day and the resumption of our worldly tasks. To put it another way without using metaphor, liturgy participates in a logic of beginning or renaissance [*du commencement ou du recommencement*].

We were able to think the originary such as it differs from the initial, but also such as it can be given or returned to us (within the limits that the world imposes on this gift or this restitution). Is the origin what we can recapture by ascertaining the primitive givens of consciousness? Or does it constitute the unattainable par excellence, which the *eschaton* may perhaps return to us, but whose mere mention is not, however, sufficient for the interpretation of our facticity? Although the reasons why we deciphered in liturgy a symbolism of the originary and a critique of the initial need not be repeated, the admission of the radical nature of evil and, correlatively, the liturgical request for forgiveness, enable us to be more specific on this point. We thus come up against the radical nature of evil as against a facticity. World or earth is not only our place in a general sense; it is also the place of a native compromise with evil (which means, to repeat a point of some importance, that there is no equivocation between the phenomenological concept of world and the theological concept of a world that differs from the creation, on the one hand, and that a denial of creation governs, on the other).[10] Morality must doubtless recognize a kairological character in every situation that falls within its domain. Goodwill does have a place in the world, and good can and must be wished for here and now. But morality cannot live on illusions. No *kairos* can destroy the moral I [*le moi moral*] during the time of its construction; although this construction is not simply a violence done unto what we are initially, such violence never-theless constitutes an essential moment within it. These remarks, which we readily admit are trivial, set out the ontological or existen-tial problematic (or aporetic) on which moral philosophy is built. Whatever thematization of the origin we arrive at, we cannot think morality without recognizing an ambiguity at the beginning that, within the order that presides over our being-in-the-world, authorizes morality but does not exclude immoralism, and which contains no express obligation to willing the good and the doing of good deeds. We are no longer, however, at the beginning—and are perhaps fur-ther away from it than ever. If the accessibility of matutinal certainties of consciousness is an article of faith on which phenomenology lives, and which gives it access to a pure phenomenon of the world prior to everydayness, prejudice, and habit, this access cannot absolve us of what we are because we have become that way. The world can unfold before us once again such as it is originarily, or at any rate, such as it is in the beginning. We can gain access to the morning of conscious-ness, to its discovery of the world and of itself. But this access cannot free us from the past in which we have made our own decisions by willing and, in particular, by not willing the good. Our past wrong-doing bears on the present of moral experience as a destiny: the kairological meaning of moral experience cannot therefore be abstracted from this destiny. What we are is thus constituted by a twofold distance: a distance in relation to the origin and a distance in relation to the beginning.

This twofold distance is what liturgy enables us to traverse. The man who prays provides himself with access to the originary: carefully bracketing world or earth, he is granted or has returned to him the grounding sense of his ipseity. We can now propose that the beginning—the matutinal freedom of willing for and doing good—is returned to him, and simultaneously (what is more) that the liturgical restitution of the originary dispels the ambiguity that natively enshrouds his being-in-the-world. Being-in-the-world is at a distance from the origin. The present of moral experience is at a distance from the beginning. But liturgy annuls the distance, in the first case, by subordinating our commerce with world and earth to our relation to the Absolute and, in the second case, by proposing the field of signification that Kierkegaard contemplated in the concept of "repetition." This is deserving of our attention. Night follows day and heralds the dawn. But if, after having considered the liturgical vigil as a postlude, we consider it as a preparation for the day—if the man who keeps vigil is not only a man who delays his sleep but also a man who rises before the break of day—we may perhaps see in it the strongest possible denial of moral fatalism. Our past compromises with evil are not only a characteristic of our past; their importance makes itself felt in our present, and they can predispose our future. The freedom that chooses ill will and bad deeds seals its own fate. And yet this destiny becomes irrelevant in the interval of the liturgical vigil. Led toward the origi-nary, we can recognize that we are unambiguously promised to good rather than to evil; and if the Absolute is known to us as a God who forgives, this symbolic irrelevance can find itself combined with an absolution of our past pacts with evil. It is the reality of this absolution that must now be debated: beyond the fecundity of its symbolism, and the anticipatory meaning of the gestures that constitute it, is not the liturgical vigil also the time when the Absolute comes or inter-venes [*vient ou inter-vient*] between our wrongdoing and ourselves?

Let us suggest then that in experience the liturgical nonplace or nonevent can play the role of the "loose screw" ["*case vide*"] without which, in phonological systems, neither the movement [of significa-tion] nor originality would be thinkable. For whoever prays, it may be that nothing happens that makes manifest the grace of God—the most rigorous theoreticians of the spiritual life have taught us that what does happen can, in any case, distract us from what is essential. But the nonevent or nonexperience is a condition of possibility. The Absolute is not asked to come to experience in the immanent sphere of consciousness; but if it does come, and we can discern that it is indeed the Absolute who has come and that we have not confused it with our own exaltation, the liturgical vigil confronts us, first of all, with its incognito. One might attempt to conceive of a God who is not a God of forgiveness. But this possibility, if we investigate a little further, is of little importance once we have recognized the presence of the Absolute at Golgotha. The God who intervenes incognito in the nonplace of liturgy can easily be recognized, by those for whom this nonplace opens up a space for his intervention, as he who can grant the wonder of a new beginning [*recommencement*]. Liturgy can-not compel him to do anything. His grace does not have to come to consciousness and become an affective certainty. But whether his presence is sensible or not (this is of absolutely no import whatsoever), the guest of the liturgical vigil can—alone—resolve the unhappiness caused by the tension between the eschatological I and the empirical I and by the failure to be human made manifest to us when, in the nocturnal inoperativity of prayer, we confess to not having borne the burden and the heat of the day. Freedom cannot liberate itself. Although liturgy does not confer on us the grace of a transfiguration, it is nevertheless the exemplary site of an existence reconciled both with itself and with the Absolute. The new day that concludes the liturgical vigil must be understood as the gift of the beginning given once again: the symbolism of the origin leads to the reality of a starting point, to the reality of a space opened to a freedom capable of willing, and indeed of doing good.

§ 37 World, Earth, and Kingdom

What, then, is man's place? We have caught a glimpse of how liturgical experience doubly contradicts our inherence. It contradicts the *Unzuhause* that determines being-in-the-world primordially: what is signified here is the originary; the liturgical nonplace is a symbolic figure of the dwelling place. And it contradicts the earthly logic of existence: we feel at home there only ahead of time [*par anticipation*], for what gives substance to this anticipation does not derive from the numinous treasures of the earth, and it is not essential that we enjoy [*jouissons de*] an intimate relation with God here. It is not enough, however, for liturgy to rupture the dialectic of world and earth only between acts. If it is in the mode of an interval that it allows our "nocturnal" relation to the Absolute to subvert the historial laws of our inherence, is it not conceivable that the "diurnal" time of our worldly toil could be subverted in the same way? If it is obvious that being-before-God does not abolish the facticity of our being-in-the-world, is liturgy, then, the sole space in which the latter can be subordinated to the former? Or to put it another way, by posing in the form of a question what we have already stated in passing, would liturgy, which we have interpreted as a region of experience, doubtless the richest in theoretical paradoxes, ultimately be able to render itself coextensive with life? There is time enough for everything: to work and to rest, to write philosophy and to pray. But we would perhaps overlook the ultimate significance of our interpretation were we to confine ourselves to the contradistinction between place and nonplace or between diurnal work [*œuvres*] and nocturnal inoperativity. It is not solely in the meantime that the *eschaton* makes our present tremble [*inquiète notre présent*]. Even though a worldly time that restlessness [*inquiétude*] alone invested itself in and freed entirely from care is scarcely thinkable, one cannot conclude from this that a complete liturgical overdetermination of being-in-the-world is unthinkable. It is only for the saint, if there is such a thing, that being-before-God constantly subverts his participation in the play of world and earth and the ambivalence that this play imposes on whoever participates in it. We have ourselves all made pacts with evil and forgotten God. But if liturgy opens up for us as the time favorable to absolution, these pacts and this forgetfulness are not omens of a destiny to come: our days can be lived in remembrance of God; and if the world cannot bring about the *eschaton*, it can nevertheless shelter the paths that mark out its inchoation. Our absolute future thus tells us today who we are and what our place is. The "world" is not given to us as a homeland, and we must reject the notion that the "earth" can pass for our homeland. Only the Kingdom can be a homeland for us, and we do not live in the Kingdom, even if its order is not simply transcendent to that of the world and death. We can attempt to make the dimensions of our lives conform to those of liturgy, or at least will that they do so. This possibility should not deflect our attention from the fragility of eschatological anticipation, nor from the ambiguity in which our facticity is enshrouded. It is nevertheless the desire presiding over this anticipation—if we have not gone too far astray in our interpretation, and on condition that we clarify our position further—which most accurately signifies the meaning of our humanity. Liturgy, understood in its broadest sense, is the most human mode in which we can exist in the world or on the earth. And it is in the world or on the earth that it responds, once and for all, to the question of the place proper to man: beyond the historial play between world and earth, man has for his true *dwelling place* the *relation* he seals with God or that God seals with him.

PART II

Fundamental Experience

The Disparity with the Initial as a Hermeneutic Principle

§ 38 Return to Questioning

In thematizing liturgy as an overdetermination of our native relation to world and earth, we assure ourselves of a considerable theoretical benefit: we liberate the relation between man and the Absolute from all the opacities with which immediacy and the obfuscatory rule of religious feeling encumber it. The conceptuality put in place does not open up a way to the "philosophy of religion," but puts forward a certain redistribution of the terms in which the question of religion is commonly posed. "Religion" is commonly understood, in the philosophies that treat of it sympathetically, all of which are inscribed in Schleiermacher's legacy whether or not they know it, as a native dimension of the humanity of man, as an essential capacity for ecstasy or a fundamental capacity for affectivity. And yet its transcendental status becomes remarkably fragile as soon as we perceive in the dialectic of "world" and "earth" the dominant feature of our facticity. What is religion, if the oscillation between an existential atheism and an existential paganism, which conceals the eschatological tension to which restlessness bears witness, is the primordial rhythm governing existence? It is obvious here that neither being-in-the-world (as a matter of course) nor even the earthly reality of existence makes us a priori capable of experiences that can be interpreted only by introducing the name of God. Initially, the Absolute is either unknown to us or we fail to recognize it [*nous est . . . inconnu ou méconnu*]: it is perhaps only with the sacred and the deities that we maintain an immemorial relation. It remains unknown or unrecognized for every form of thought that assumes the initial logic of experience to be the ultimate horizon. This follows from consequences we have already glimpsed, but which it may be worthwhile to shed a little more light on, and which may enable us to specify further the terms of the *disputatio de homine.*

§ 39 Phenomenology and Liturgy: "Life"

The first problem that demands our attention is thus that of a certain distance: the liturgical logic unfolds at a distance from the immediate realities of life. Let us understand here by "life" the sphere of antepredicative evidence, such as Husserl thematizes it in *Experience and Judgment.*[1] The aim of this work is to gain access. Prior to the world that has already been constituted by consciousness, and prior to the world that knowledge [*le savoir*] has already judged, phenomenology attempts here (in its greatest attempt to be faithful to its original project) to comprehend the real in the very act of its appearance, before predicative judgment has completed its work: a real that no knowledge precedes, to which no foreknowledge [*nul pré-savoir*] can stake a claim, and that is given without any mediation between itself and the consciousness comprehending it. "Life" thus has as its place the morning of experience, recaptured by philosophical ascesis, whose thinking is necessary to us if we truly wish to understand the high noon of experience and the mediating role of knowledge. Life is a perpetual dawn, the eternal youth of the beginning. Each perception, each appearance opens up the horizon of the world anew, and within this domain, previously acquired knowledge must not affect the reception [*accueil*] we reserve for the present: the element of life is naïveté, and the project of philosophy is to restore to man this naive perspective.

This schematic reminder should suffice to indicate the point that bears on our interpretation here: the leave that liturgy takes from immediacy and from life understood as total and uninterrupted immediacy. In stark contrast to the initial manifestation of the "life-world," the field of liturgy is governed by knowledge. Only a fundamental presupposition—that the Absolute is a subject, with which a relation has been promised—enables it to open itself up and organize itself. The logic that presides here is not that of primitive acts of consciousness and the raw appearance of phenomena: on the contrary, it unfolds within the order of mediation, and this mediation is a critique of the antepredicative evidence of life. The immediate thus keeps the Absolute veiled over [*dans l'inévidence*]. Things show themselves to us in the plain light of day, and every mode of objectivity possesses its own correlative mode of proof. But if, as a matter of protocol, we do not rule out the possibility of the Absolute granting itself an objectivity and a clarity in the world, it is nevertheless obvious that the fact that it is veiled over is primary, and that the function of liturgy is to overturn this. Between the world of life and the liturgical field there is, then, a *cognitive delay*. We have no immediate way of knowing what would grant legitimacy to liturgy: according to the Husserlian concept, life is atheistic. And, in a way, the world of life is what must be overcome so that man can face God. The evidence given first in life must surrender to the secondary evidence that authorizes liturgy. This secondary evidence will perhaps install a secondary immediacy that will enable us to perceive in the world, such as it is presented to us, the clear and distinct reflection of the divine glory. But we must never forget that this perception is the offspring of the work of interpretation, and projects onto phenomena a light and a univocal meaning not actually given in conjunction with the phenomena. Liturgy is born of interpretation, whose greatest success would be for it to become so implicit that we would believe ourselves to be living in a theophanic world—indeed, it is essential to liturgy that it simulate the joy we anticipate in the Parousia. Manifestation is not, however, the work of the world because the world manifests only itself and the phenomena that appear within its horizon. To the consciousness that brackets all knowledge, phenomena show only themselves and the milieu of their appearance. God must be named beforehand for the heavens to sing his glory. The secondary immediacy or secondary naïveté of liturgical experience presupposes the work of critique. One might say (though Husserl would not) that it is a question here of a new mode of living, where things appear to us in their most secret truth, and that the perception that lays hold of them is capable of penetrating to what is fundamental. But for this to be true, it must be accepted that life escapes the *initial* conditions bestowed upon it, and that the phenomenological quest for the beginning actually enables to us to accede to what must be transgressed in order to comprehend what is ultimately at stake in experience. What comes along first in life is the veil that the self-giving immediacy of things draws over the Absolute; this is undeniable. Liturgy compels us to admit that antepredicative experience maintains us in a state of nonknowledge [*inconnaissance*], or keeps us from the originary. Not only does it not suffice to question the immediate so as to know [*connaître*] what is ultimately at stake in experience, it is the immediate that veils what is most important.

§ 40 Phenomenology and Liturgy: Facticity

The dimensions of the lifeworld are certainly not those integral to experience: the Husserlian theory is foundational, and (needless to say) leaves no room for experiences that would abolish antepredicative evidence, or rather that would assimilate it into the element of judgment and knowledge. The atheism of life, if one traces the path followed by Husserl's interpretation, is incontestable—but the interpretation in no way denies, nor does it pronounce upon, even by paralipsis, our right to know more of life than it teaches of itself: all that it teaches us is where we need not search for the Absolute. The debate becomes more contentious, however, when we consider that liturgy not only suspends the immediacy of life, but also establishes itself far from any a priori logic of experience. To return from 1938 to 1927, and from Husserl to Heidegger, one can formulate within a hypothesis we have already explored (see § 32) the problem that arises here: the liturgical play appears to be almost foreign (the "almost" here designating the discrete presence of restlessness) to the logic of facticity. The central (but not exclusive) intention of *Being and Time* is to unveil the fundamental structures of experience such as they are everywhere, always and for everyone. These (so-called existential) structures are indifferent to the particularity of my experience or to the experience of my neighbor. They define and make manifest what we all are; particularity understood as such (the "existentiell") is of only anecdotal or psychological interest—what is of philosophical importance is the way in which my neighbor and I occupy the same situation within Being, the situation of the being for which the philosopher reserves the name of "being-there," Dasein. It is not only the immediacy of life, then, that is in question. The logic of facticity is not simply that of the matutinal appearance of phenomena to consciousness; it is also a logic of knowledge, of questioning, of the utilization of things, of the occupation of the world. The texts and concepts are well known, or so one hopes, and are mentioned here for the record. But, if one admits that the project of a hermeneutics of facticity is a valid one, and if, moreover, one admits that the native or transcendental conditions of experience are those which make man appear as Dasein (while granting, should the need arise, the dialectic we have proposed that perceives in the "being-there" and in the "mortal" two alternative but harmonious conceptual figures of human reality), then one must also admit that facticity leaves the liturgical relation of man to God indeterminate. The atheism of being-in-the-world and the paganism of earthly existence correspond here to the evident atheism of life. Liturgy has, therefore, no existential status other than that which a "restlessness" totally absent from Heidegger's text, concretely involved in the play of care, and unaware of what keeps it silent can precariously offer it. This raises certain questions. Is man initially nothing but his own beginning? And is what is most proper to him concealed from him? As a corollary, can we conceive of an existence that, strictly abiding by the laws of facticity, would remain foreign to what is ultimately at stake for man? These questions are not rhetorical. Liturgy is not, in fact, one possibility open to me among others (as is the love of music or cats), which would serve to define me but not determine what it is that makes me human. If one admits that what it proposes is an existence in possession of what is most essential to it, it must be granted that what is most essential is absent from the beginning, or at least that the beginning keeps it wholly veiled over. The initial conditions of experience are certainly not inessential, but neither are they inescapable: in the time that leads me to death, what I am never ceases to be defined by a relation to death, by a relation to place, by my co-existence with others [*avec d'autres moi*], and so on. But if it is necessary to recognize liturgy as man's ultimate act and the highest demonstration of his being possible for him, it must be conceded that the initial, facticity, keeps silent and conceals more than it reveals and declares. The disturbing [*inquiétante*] hypothesis of a humanity satisfied with existing "without God in the world"[2] must therefore be taken seriously. Atheism is neither simply nor in the first place a theoretical problem: it is first what is a priori to existence. It is for this very reason, and not by virtue of the reasons that might lead us to deny God after he has been named, that we must concern ourselves with it. Only a certain violence enables man to exist before God. Man liturgically exceeds what he is initially; the limits of the existential are not the limits of his humanity. But where can we learn how to break through the limits of the existential? The question gives rise to an obvious response: whatever we cannot account for transcendentally, we can only account for categorially; what is absent at the beginning of history, and from the logics that make this beginning available to us, must be given in history. Denied a place in the morning of history, knowledge [*connaissance*] of God is proper to the midday, or perhaps to the evening of history. Atheism cannot be refuted by grounding its refutation in what comes to experience always, everywhere and to everyone. One must question, therefore, what is so particular to the coming to light of God.

§ 41 Contingency and Manifestation

Philosophy, the saying goes, is born of awe. And yet, if it is right in the first place to be in awe that being is, one should be as acutely in awe that it is intelligible to us, on the one hand, and that we possess an intellect to understand it, on the other. The intelligibility of the world is an elementary given of experience. We are not only questioning and interpreting animals who cannot live without wishing to understand: the real is also given to us as something we can acquire and that organizes knowledge [*le savoir*], as something we can question and to which we can respond correctly. Before us, we find a cosmos and not chaos. The facts are ordered by laws. We always encounter an order. If we can always form the notion of the unintelligible, of things devoid of meaning, of totally anarchic entities, this does not enable us to think the reality of something we would be able to encounter. From intelligibility to intellection, the passage is not, however, a necessary one. Although we live in a world where the work of knowledge is in all its forms a fait accompli, this fact cannot conceal from us that this knowledge almost always bears the mark of contingency. The intelligibility of the world is not imposed on us. There is doubtless knowledge that we cannot avoid possessing. No one can be unaware that he is mortal. No one can be unaware that there was a time when he did not exist. Nevertheless, we have been well able to exist while being ignorant of the earth's roundness or the atomic structure of matter. But beyond such ontical ignorance, we may well have misunderstood ourselves philosophically and have overlooked the most decisive of questions. Ignorance is, after all, the circumstance proper to whoever is posing a question: if we already know, we do not question. The reality of ignorance, as with that of misinterpretation [*méconnaissance*], tells us that we will not remain forever more "in truth." We are destined to desire knowledge since we naturally wish to know. But its possession is promised to us only on condition that the work of interpretation is brought to a conclusion. It is certainly not inscribed within the a priori limits of experience that this must be the case. Intelligence only encounters the intelligible (be it in the form of positive or philosophical knowledge) — but this does not imply that the reasons behind the real are given in all transparency.

The generality of these remarks, and their trivial appearance, should not conceal how much they bear on our discussion. The liturgical play presupposes certain knowledge, but we do not possess this knowledge of necessity. Only a fool would deny his birth and death or that he exists corporeally. But the Absolute remains transcendentally unknown to us, on the one hand, and our daily relation to the world does not enable us to acquire distinct knowledge [*connaissance*] of the Absolute, on the other. World and earth keep it veiled over. If it must be said that man can only accede to what is most proper to him when this veiling has been annulled, and is able to subordinate his being-in-the-world to his being-before-God, it must also be said that this annulment can only be the nonnecessary act of an unveiling, or of penetrating through ambiguity. One can understand this in either of two ways: as the divine grace of a manifestation of his self or as the human work of the logos. We will not broach here the questions raised by the "natural knowability" of the Absolute (to every book its own subject matter), and the link it maintains with the divine self-unveiling, for, whatever the debate and the issues surrounding it, the same contingency is to be found in the self-unveiling of the divine Logos and the unveiling in the element of the concept for which man himself has been responsible. We could never be successful in rigorously articulating who God is; but God will not have departed from his inaccessible light. What is at stake in the question of contingency should therefore give us more to think here than elsewhere. It is man's destiny to come face-to-face with his death, but it is not his destiny (on this side of death, in any case) to encounter the Absolute. Even when the Absolute has been unveiled to us, this does not for all that become inevitable.[3] We are free to name God (whether this naming returns us to a human power to shed light on God or it is our response to a divine process of self-unveiling), just as we are free to sleep, or to carry out the work of thought poorly, or to satisfy ourselves with what world and earth teach us. The contingency of the unveiling is redoubled by that of its reception and its appropriation.

§ 42 The Manifest Absolute

The disconcerting hypothesis of a humanity that contents itself with existing in the world without God, or on the earth solely in the company of the deities cannot be taken lightly: prior to their historical destiny, atheism and paganism are inscribed in the initial structures of existence. Furthermore, the hypothesis of a history in which the Absolute would remain unknown must be taken into account for what it can show us: that it is right to be astonished that God ceases to be a priori veiled over. But neither the nonknowledge [*inconnaissance*] proper to the beginning, nor the forms by which this initial nonknowledge perpetuates itself, can conceal that the unveiling or self-unveiling, whose contingency we admit, demands to be thought in the mode of the real rather than the possible. Atheism and paganism reign over the starting-point of history, and even if it should not definitively determine it, this starting point is always present to us because our belonging to world and earth is essential to our identity. It is nevertheless within our power *to abolish* this starting point. We will not inquire here into the genesis and profundity of the reasons authorizing us to speak of God. We would do well, however, to recognize that these reasons precede us and that every withdrawal into our transcendental ignorance of God is in many respects anachronistic. From the fact that God has already been named and—something we take as a given—that he has been named with sufficient rigor for our liturgies to make sense, one cannot, of course, deduce that his existence is as obvious or manifest to us as the heavens above. Because the question of God has entered into philosophy's terms of reference (a topic we will not discuss here), and because philosophical knowledge does not have the cumulative character of ontical knowledge, thought undoubtedly has the perennial task of demonstrating whatever or whomever it is that world and earth veils over. We could never be satisfied with what we know [*savons*] of God in the way that, for example, we are satisfied with the knowledge [*nous nous satisfaisons . . . de savoir*] that water boils at one hundred degrees. It remains that every attempt we make to improve on how we speak of the Absolute is radically preceded by a veiling that it must presuppose, and which constitutes its horizon. God has been named before I name him. A light, which we believe to represent a theophany, that has come in the sole element of the concept has been shed on an event of divine condescension, or on a self-manifestation and its interpretation that coincide with each other. If, therefore, we can continue on methodologically as if this light had not been shed, in order to dissipate the chiaroscuro of the world once again, and if, on the other hand, the manifestation calls for rather than compels our assent, it is nevertheless perfectly justifiable to consider our a priori nonknowledge [*inconnaissance*] of God or every return to this nonknowledge as strictly archaic. We are no longer at the pagan or atheistic beginning of experience. We can always be seduced by immediacy and our facticity. We can live only according to the conditions that world and earth bestow upon us, and we find in these conditions the limits of the thinkable. The right to experientially exceed these conditions and to think beyond these limits is, however, engraved in history where the Absolute has been disentangled, or has disentangled itself from the ambiguities of the initial. It must be seen, then, that the theoretical problem of atheism is for us in the first place regressive.

One can thus better perceive the liturgical redistribution of the terms in which the question of our historiality is posed. Initial historiality defines us as living in the world within the horizon of time, and this is a characteristic inextricable from who we are. We can, however, believe in the existence of God without this belief leading to the establishment of a new modality of experience. Although we cannot, in all likelihood, know [*savoir*] that God exists as we know a purely factual piece of knowledge, such as the roundness of the earth, we can certainly know that he exists without his existence affecting ours. But when the affirmation of God is sealed in liturgical experience, nothing can conceal from us that the initial is not the definitive, and that its conceptualization is not sufficient to tell us who we are. The problem, at the beginning, is not that we are alienated in existence; it is that we, ourselves, are in question. A stipulation is nevertheless necessary here. It is we who are in question, but in a mode of existence still removed from what is ultimately at stake for us — in the mode of being-in-fact over which being-in-vocation as yet holds no sway. The contingency of the manifestation of the Absolute (whether the Absolute itself brings this about, it comes through the human work of concepts, or both) is thus an act of redefinition. Liturgy does not annul the a priori laws governing existence. But it does prove that transcendental forms of experience do not constitute the entirety of our capacity for existence, and that the humanity of man does not let itself be determined exclusively by what comes to experience always, everywhere, and to everyone. The manifest God provides a future for man.

§ 43 The Human and the Definitive

The field of our problematic can now be broadened. Because a specific historical process (the manifestation of the Absolute) opens up access to a figure of experience that can in no way be deduced from its initial figure, and because this figure is, not one existentiell possibility open to us among all others, but the possibility of an existence that takes hold of what is most proper to it, it must necessarily be admitted that the project of phenomenology, in its classical form, specifically prevents us from ascertaining what is proper to man. What it does enable us to do is to ascertain a beginning that cannot close up on itself without becoming enshrouded in ambiguity or giving rise to a meaning only partially unveiled. We cannot dispense with thinking the beginning and its underlying presence in all experience — but it is not at the beginning or in fidelity to it that man exists in truth. A question arises here, however. Is it not at the end of history, more than at its dawn, that we will have to question the rationality of the humanity of man? Is not the logic of the initial in actual fact a logic of existence in bare outline, awaiting the accomplishment of history for it to be entirely self-identical, where meaning would no longer be dissimulated, and where the definitive advent of the essential would have taken place? Because it possesses no clear and distinct transcendental status, liturgy compels us here to assume the care that propels every historicism, and to assume it up to its final implication, the hypothesis of an eschatology of existence. From the fact that man has a history — or, to be precise, that his humanity is a becoming — it most certainly does not follow that this becoming is destined to come to a conclusion: it may be that incompleteness entirely determines what we are, and that the idea of humanity reaching its accomplishment is but an idea. And yet, if this suspicion possesses an evident legitimacy insofar as the future of man has for its limits those of the world — insofar as the concept of history is that of the history of the world — the problem of eschatology cannot but arise when the question of man is inextricably linked with the question of God. It is, of course, first posed in terms of a symbolism or of anticipation, or in terms of the tension that unites and opposes being-in-fact (the "empirical I") and being-in-vocation (the "eschatological I"). It can nevertheless be posed more radically still as a question of the realization of the *eschaton* — of the worldly realization of the absolute future of man. Could the logic of existence at its beginning leave room for a logic of the accomplishment of existence without being contradictory? Within the conditions that the world bestows upon experience, would man be able to face God in a properly insuperable mode? Would we then have to say that the tension between "fact" and "vocation" gives way to an identification of the one with the other, whereby the hold that definitive realities exert over everything is total? We have been satisfied with knowing little enough about God for the purposes of interpreting liturgical experience, and with knowing it abstractly, without alluding to history or to histories (the history of divine self-communication, the history of philosophy, the history of theology) that enable us to utter the name of God without confusion. We cannot, however, persist with such abstractions. It was justifiable for us to speak the language of the *eschaton* as soon as it was possible to speak of the God's person unequivocally and without error, and thus as soon as we were able to exceed what we are at the beginning. But this in no way presupposes that the histories that made the Absolute manifest are finite histories, that we no longer have to wait for another manifestation, that our encounter with God has assumed its definitive form, and that we are now in possession of a humanity that wants for nothing. But is it incongruous to suppose that these histories are actually finite and that man's humanity is such that no becoming could ever affect it? The question requires more than a brief response. It announces and demands a debate with the sole philosophical eschatology that exists safe in the knowledge of God: Hegel's eschatology.

Hegel and the *Eschaton* This Side of Death

§ 44 The End at the Beginning

It is significant for the present inquiry that, at a time when the West's metaphysical endeavors were deemed to have been brought to completion, the first volume of a philosophy that saw itself as more recapitulatory and definitive than any other put itself forward as a "science of the experience of consciousness." The *Phenomenology of Spirit* is that very book which, by simultaneously following the private path of every consciousness and the public path of humanity throughout its history, claims to lead up to the point where, history finding itself properly completed (i.e., no longer promising ontogenesis), man is fully, absolutely, and eschatologically himself, and neither fears nor hopes that this identity will be called into question or that a new questioning will emerge, either of which could be brought about by the continuation of history.[1] Philosophical reason, in its classical forms, almost always wishes to manifest the truth by conferring on it the status of the definitive: the figure of man fully in possession of his humanity is not an obviously Hegelian creation. But if every philosophy, or almost every philosophy, classically acknowledges that all that is, insofar as it *is*, goes hand in hand with the definitive (spirit as such, Being freed from appearance, the idea, etc.), Hegelianism is alone in proposing, first, that the definitive had been absent and unattainable and, second, that it is no longer only the secret of the provisional, but the already reached conclusion of what had been played out in the provisional. What is involved in history before it reaches its accomplishment is no less real. The master and the slave are not human in appearance alone. The unhappy consciousness and the beautiful soul are real figures of experience. The provisional exists and is intelligible, and makes up a real part of the unique history in which the Absolute becomes what it is (which is of no import to us here), manifests what it is, and is reconciled with man, and in which man acquires the knowledge of this reconciliation. The moment is therefore within its rights in revealing, in the mode of a fragment, the reality of Being and of consciousness, or of spirit. But the moment, or the fragment, only makes sense within the dialectical totality in which the part takes its place amid the whole, and the provisional amid the definitive before which it effaces itself. No man, while history still awaits its accomplishment, is definitively at one with his humanity. In the master as in the slave, in the unhappy consciousness as in the beautiful soul, participation in the dialectics that make up history implies a want of being [*un manque à être*], a partial and deficient modality of existence: the provisional aspects of consciousness are all inadequate to express the true humanity of man.

The nature of man has a history: and the end, the *eschaton*, alone enables us to take measure of its beginnings in such a way that the end actually constitutes the true beginning within the speculative order. This thesis might be thought to put off all interpretation of an absolute future, which may be thinkable but which undoubtedly exceeds the present, until the horizon, by definition out of reach, is attained. And yet one learns in fact from Hegel (not, of course, from the letter of his text but from the coherence that governs it) that history, at the very moment when he provides it with systematic intelligibility, is well and truly complete. The "science of the experience of consciousness" is to be a vesperal knowledge and the last word on the matter, and coincides with the gift of the ultimate facts and the ultimate reasons. For all the undoubted abruptness of this declaration, it would be wrong to tone it down. It is easy to subscribe to the proposition of a retrospective historical knowledge [*connaissance*], of a memory that comprehends what has taken place and discerns in it the genesis of what is taking place today. On the other hand, the idea of an eschatology that has already been realized can only seem scandalous to those who perceive that history, to all appearances, continues on after Hegel—which is all the more scandalous for those who discern in this continuance of history the threat or the promise of a new future for man. If one reads Hegel accurately, this scandal is unavoidable, however. No apocalypse, apart from the drama of the Napoleonic wars, accompanied the publication of the *Phenomenology*. But the disappearance of the Germanic Holy Roman Empire opened up, if not a new aeon, then a new epoch in Western history. And Hegel himself must have been witness to the collapse of the new empire born of the French Revolution and to the attempts to restore the old order (even though this meant offering the Prussian State privileges bestowed upon the Napoleonic Empire at the time of the *Phenomenology*). The aporia—or its appearance, at least—cannot be overlooked. At Tübingen, Hegel, Schelling, and Hölderlin were distanced from each other by a watchword: the "Kingdom of God." In 1807, there was certainly nothing to indicate that this kingdom had been established in the world.

§ 45 Knowledge and Eschatology

It is nevertheless important to be somewhat prudent and to perceive the exact aim of Hegelian eschatology. The perpetuation of history, of its violence, and of the "labor of the negative" provides an obvious objection to it. But Hegel does not conclude the *Phenomenology* with the vision of a rediscovered Eden, or of messianic times where reality would be transfigured in its entirety. He concludes with a theory of knowledge, which is very different. To completed history belongs, according to the philosopher, the "peace of unity," *Ruhe der Einheit*, or the "satisfaction," *Befriedigung*, in which every contradiction has been overcome, all restlessness assuaged, and every deficiency removed. And yet these concepts only recover a specific experience: the experience of reason that properly takes hold of the reconciliation of finite spirit and infinite Spirit, such as it is accomplished on Good Friday. It is no longer necessary to defend the clear theological ambitions that motivate Hegelianism, nor to prove that the Hegelians of the Right can claim to be the legitimate heirs to the master—recent research has established this beyond doubt.[2] Hegel's system presents itself in all its architectonic coherence as the articulation of three histories: the eternal history of absolute Spirit, the temporal history of absolute Spirit and the human history of spirit. At issue here is the last of these: the slow becoming of man. But it is only at issue if one presupposes the other two. If the *Phenomenology* claims to lead to and speak from the end, this claim, despite all the surprises to which it gives rise on a first reading, becomes perfectly consistent when one perceives, on a final reading, that human history is fully determined by the manifestation of God that reconciles him with man on the one hand, and by the human appropriation of this reconciliation, on the other. The Hegelian problem of the end of history is theological and soteriological. The Absolute has communicated itself and given itself to be known [*donné à connaître*]; and ever since Good Friday, peace can and should reign over the relationship between him and man. The problem, however, is that on the evening of Good Friday and the evening of Easter, consciousness is still unaware of what is at stake in this reconciliation, and will remain unaware of it for a long time. On the Cross of Christ, God uttered a final word, which one might imagine man to have grasped. The paradox on which Hegelian eschatology lives, and which enables it to delay the accomplishment of history for eighteen centuries, is then the paradox of a delayed interpretation. Reconciled with the Absolute, man has failed to recognize [*a méconnu*] the import of this reconciliation. Capable of knowing [*de connaître*] (and even understanding) God and of enjoying possession of this knowledge, he satisfied himself with what Hegel said preceded and was only analogous to true knowledge—"representation." The centuries that separate Hegel from the historical Good Friday, from the factual reality of salvation, are thus those in which Christian consciousness failed to recognize the true significance of its redemption, and this consciousness has congealed into a series of figures completely powerless to embody reconciled existence lived before a God made "manifest."

It should thus become clear (the texts are doubtless difficult but do not, if the truth be known, lack clarity) that Hegelian eschatology is not falsified by facts for the simple reason that it does not really speak of facts. Of course, no text, in the trivial sense of the term, is less idealist than the Hegelian. The spirit of the *Phenomenology* is no stranger to flesh and blood; the concrete does not remain unknown to it. But if the delay necessary to man knowing himself [*se connaisse*], to properly knowing [*connaisse*] God, to knowing himself [*se sache*] to be reconciled with him, and to living in this light has unfolded in pain and tears, the last of all the figures of consciousness—the consciousness in possession of "absolute knowledge" ["*savoir absolu*"]—is no longer determined by this fact alone but by the availability of a final and exacting knowledge [*connaissance*] that has received its ultimate articulation. Thus is it useless to assign to definitively human man a dwelling place other than the world, just as it is useless to expect the world to find itself thereby transfigured.

Knowledge thus encompasses (almost) everything, and actually represents a substitute for the beatific vision. What is ordinarily given the name of "history" can continue on after Hegel: it will simply be a history bereft of a theophanic and soteriological meaning, and as such, will be a history that does not call for the work of thought, whose contingencies have no bearing on the essential. The *eschaton* is access to absolute knowledge, and to the consequences that ensue from this. What survives after the acquisition of absolute knowledge, but which is not a consequence of it, is of no theoretical importance. The man who knows himself to be at peace with God lives at peace with himself. For one or the other reason, he exists in the mode of the definitive: he is destined for no future that would call into question what he is or which his being-more would depend on.

One cannot conceal the principal (but paradoxical) strength of this thesis. A thinker of finite history (of a realized eschatology), Hegel is no theoretician of the apocalypse; and the end sealed by absolute knowledge entails, not the annihilation of time and of all becoming, but the delimitation of a specific domain where man can be himself to the full and exist in complete authenticity. This last term is not employed inadvertently. If one judges by the received taxonomies, Hegel figures among the philosophers of "history" and not among the philosophers of "existence." The fact remains, however, that at the end of the Hegelian reconstruction of history we find ourselves confronted with a properly existentiell eschatology. History is, therefore, finished [*finie*] in a very precise sense, and in a very public way with the publication of a book in which the conditions of its end are recorded. In finite history [*histoire finie*], moreover, there exists a new city (about which Hegel has nothing to say in the *Phenomenology*, however) in which definitively human existence provides itself with institutions (see § 46). But neither the public and social reality of the *eschaton* nor the dialectics that inexorably lead to absolute knowledge can conceal from us that it is, finally, within our power to decide whether or not to exist eschatologically. To refuse absolute knowledge and the fullness of experience proper to reconciled existence is certainly irrational. To refuse to leave the field of "representation" for that of the "concept" is nothing other than a refusal to truly be oneself. This refusal is nevertheless possible. Since it is a refusal to attain what is most proper to man, it is perfectly justifiable to speak of it in terms of "inauthenticity," and to speak of eschatological existence in terms of "authenticity." The authenticity of existence, which survives the end of history, is not offered to everyone, always and everywhere, as is the case with Heidegger. Nor is it offered to everyone everywhere as soon as the Christian kerygma is formulated, as is the case with Bultmann: it is only offered (to everyone) at the twilight of a process, eighteen centuries of which were placed in the protection of the kerygma, but in which man could only exist in the mode of the provisional or the fragmentary. Obvious dissimilarities should not, however, cause us to overlook the real complicity. In Bultmann's eschatology[3] as in Hegel's, the future is totally neutralized: the present can completely house the definitive realities. For whoever enjoys possession of Hegel's absolute knowledge, just as for whoever shares Bultmann's experience of faith, history has ceased to fulfill whatever governing function of Being and meaning it may once have had. An "eschatological reserve" that would permit God to one day give more than we have today is unimaginable. Although the parallel must not, of course, be pushed too far, it does enable us to perceive under what conditions the *eschaton* can fully invest itself in the present. Hegel does not do away with the future, but he expects nothing from it, and his reasons for this are not lacking in coherence. God is an Absolute who "in its being-absolute wishes in and for itself to be close to us."[4] This presence is, however, already available to us. God is manifest, hides nothing of himself from us, and we are finally capable of comprehending the entire meaning of this manifestation, and the implications it has for us. It is therefore actually in the mode of Parousia (Heidegger does not hesitate to use the word in his commentary) that the Absolute is present to us. What has yet to unfold that comes under the name of "history" can no longer be of more than anecdotal value. It is possible to dwell in the world without history and the future continuing to determine our identity.

§ 46 The Definitive in Its Place

The excess of "existence" over "history" and the right to think of ways of being human beyond history are what every eschatology must grasp; and it would appear that Hegel's has not failed to do so. The mode of being in which this excess manifests itself is clear, or even too clear: whoever survives history enjoys the possession of his salvation (the reconciliation of finite spirit and infinite Spirit) in his total knowledge of the Absolute. But even if it is not false to speak in terms of an "existentiell eschatology," it would nevertheless be erroneous to reduce the Hegelian conception of the "last things" to the private fruition of knowledge (to a solipsist authenticity), on the one hand, and to the bracketing of man's relation to the world, on the other. We have nothing more to hope for from the future once the secrets of the divine life have been unveiled to us and once the relation between man and God is no longer governed by opposition. This does not, however, give rise to exaltation in Hegelianism, which would constitute the classic corollary to a realized eschatology. If the end of time really is here and we are in possession of our absolute future, as is shown in Gnostic exaltation, then the laws that reign over existence no longer apply. The age of morality and of politics is past. Man is no longer a citizen of the world, and the heavens have already taken possession of the earth. Christian monachism will provide an orthodox version of such a theory. The monastic community obviously exists in order to provide a privileged place for the purpose of conversion, and its foundation thereby proves that the believer stills remains at a distance from his eschatological identity. But it also exists in order to liturgically anticipate the definitive reign of God—the life that it wishes to live is no longer the life of man but that of the angels. Joachimism will, in the end, assume more than one of the features of gnosis. The age of Spirit is one in which every institution, right up to and including the ecclesiastical institution, will be shaken. It completely overturns the relations established between man and the world and God. The originality of the "eternal Gospel" breaks with ancient practices and disqualifies them. And yet, if there is one point on which Hegelian eschatology differs from all those which precede it, it is certainly in its refusal of such tendencies. Wherever absolute knowledge has been acquired, history has completed itself and inaugurates the new times to come. But this completion and this inauguration in no way imply that man qua definitive man takes leave of the world, or exists there in an especially unprecedented mode. When finally identical to himself, man belongs to the community of worship comprising those who do not content themselves with knowledge of who God is, and who offer him praise in spirit and in truth: this can easily be interpreted in eschatological terms or in terms of eschatological anticipation. But man does not, for all that, cease to be the citizen of a secular city, and this city is in fact presented as a space ideally suited for insuperably human existence. The degree of continuity outweighs all discontinuity. The practical exigencies of ethics and politics do not disappear with the completion of history. Even if absolute knowledge fulfills the function in Hegelianism that the beatific vision fulfills in classical theology, the eschatological experience of consciousness no longer has as its sole modality the contemplation of the now manifest mystery of God, but conserves the principal dimensions of historical experience. The Kingdom is thus of this world, and does not do violence to the world; the dwelling places of historical existence on its path toward itself are the very same as those of an existence arrived at its definitive self. Where and how is man to enjoy possession of his total and insuperable rationality, of his total and insuperable humanity, of the "peace of unity"? We know that Hegel gave more than one response to this question, and that he responded both directly and allusively. Man's definitive dwelling place is what Kojève called "the universal and homogenous State,"[5] the promise of which seemed to be represented by the Napoleonic Empire at the time of the *Phenomenology*, whereas at the time of *The Philosophy of Right*, it was incumbent upon the Prussian State to guarantee morality and meaning. But whatever the displacement, the important feature of Hegel's eschatology remains: the remarkable modesty of an eschatology that commits itself to no transfiguration, offers no new heavens or earth, and proposes only a mode in which to dwell in this—and no other—world.

We thus find ourselves confronted with a radical reorganization of representations and themes commonly associated with the *eschaton*. What persists after absolute knowledge has taken possession of the reconciliation between God and man is the definitive, which cannot be reintroduced into any dialectic. No surplus of meaning can be given, and there is to be no new or other existence. The evidence provided by the "facts" is surely that the negative continues to "labor" and to engender history. This, as we have said, does not undermine the consistency of Hegelian theses, although, faced with this evidence, one is at least certain that Hegel's eschatology demands little from the advent of the definitive. On the other hand, to suppose, if we adopt the Hegelian reading of the real, that today we are the citizens of the Kingdom, we would have to concede that the reality of this Kingdom is highly inconspicuous [*discrète*]. The *eschaton*, according to Hegel, is not present in the form of an incognito: the end of history (its theological end) is an objective given. Its presence nevertheless defies all the categories in which we ordinarily think it. The object of every hope and the goal toward which history tended was therefore nothing but this: the right to an authentically human existence in the world and, as we will see (in § 49), in the shadow of death. Although this is no meager right, we know that theology ordinarily wants, or at least promises, more than that.

§ 47 From History to Nature

The hardly spectacular eschatology that absolute knowledge opens up is not indicative of a speculative fiasco, but actually reveals the philosopher's measured ambitions. Since Kierkegaard, we have grown used to considering Hegelianism as a paroxysm of intellectual immoderation—and it is true that whoever knows God's thoughts before the creation of the world does indeed know quite a lot. Nevertheless, the lack of ostentation with which the *eschaton* is realized in Hegel gives us the task of thinking it. To do so, one must say with still greater insistence that the end of history actually represents in Hegel what is ordinarily (i.e., outside of the "philosophies of history") found at its beginning—"nature." History arouses the interest of modernity because it is that which produces Being. It does not appear as a becoming extrinsic to Being, but as the becoming itself of Being or of spirit. Its function is not only ontophanic but also ontopoetic. It is for this reason that the philosopher, when concerned with thinking history, can truthfully say that he concerns himself with the essential. And yet, if this is right, it must therefore be said that the real is still absent from the beginning, or that it is only there in impoverished or "abstract" forms destined to be annulled and taken up in richer and more "concrete" forms that will come forth over the course of time. The true beginning—the real identical to itself, man identical to himself—will have the end as the place proper to it. Or more precisely: it will take place at the end if the end ever comes. It does not actually follow from the presuppositions of historicism that historical ontogenesis must have a conclusion. History can be thematized without contradiction as the perpetual call of the future, as the perpetual horizon of Being; Being can never find itself freed from the laws of becoming; and the humanity of man can always possess a future. The problematic question posed by Hegel's interpretation is thus clear: what will become of Being if the end should truly come to pass, if, therefore, it comes to pass and signals the end of all ontogenesis, and if it leaves intact, having provided them with their definitive form, the permanent conditions of experience that are time, the world, society, and so on? To this question, we have already provided a response, which we need only develop: under the auspices of the conclusion of history, the state of nature will then be established. With the conclusion of history, reality is finally given to us. History was the process of creation, and this creation is now complete. Becoming no longer has a hold over Being. No longer is the future one of promise, or one of menace for that matter. One can probably understand, then, the status Hegel grants to the grammar underlying his eschatology. It is undoubtedly true that time survives the *eschaton*, and that this time is to all appearances the time of history. But its survival is only intelligible as the time of a history now devoid of any ontopoetic secrecy; and if one admits that the ontopoetic function is essential to the definition of history, it must be spoken of as a pseudohistory, whose true meaning is to guarantee an immutable dwelling place to man finally become human. This is not to say that nothing of import comes to pass now that man has come to possess his nature definitively: Hegel would agree with those who refer to facts that deny this (how could it be otherwise for the author of a system in which the eschatological point of view coexists with an ethics and a philosophy of right?). On the other hand, it does imply that everything that comes to pass, if one scrutinizes its most profound logic, occurs only in the mode of perpetuation or repetition. The "history" that continues on after Hegel is deprived of the privilege that constitutes history in the proper sense, which makes what has not yet been come into being. In a sense, absolute knowledge dominates every future, and nothing essential eludes it. The unexpected is no longer capable of exciting the least fascination. It is useless to philosophize on the future when the totality of meaning is within our reach today; what will be cannot but reiterate what is, and no possibility holds reality in abeyance.

These theses surely stand or fall on theology's approval. The true "nature" of man appears in Hegel, at the twilight of history, when man consents to his salvation and recognizes all the consequences this entails. It is most certainly Hegel's doctrine of salvation—of a reconciliation, whose entire reality can be manifested in the world on this side of death—that accounts for the discreteness of his eschatology (see §§ 49 and 52). Man's final self-identity is not the product of forces immanent in history, but is finite spirit objectively reconciled with absolute Spirit on the Cross of Christ; the task, then, is to then take rational possession of this reconciliation and to live it out. One might attempt an interpretation of the *Phenomenology* that entirely respects its eschatological ambitions while denying its theological intentions. This attempt—which Kojève undertakes—probably represents the most fruitful misinterpretation of which Hegel has ever been the object. Its results are clear: Kojève's reading compels us to admit that Hegelianism is unintelligible unless one perceives that this philosopher thinks and judges history from its end, and that he presupposes the realization and universal attainability of this end. Kojève's cut-and-dried judgments must be considered both as critique and as the expression of a debt, but his violent misinterpretation should be just as clear. The anthropogenesis for which history is the field becomes for Kojève a theogony. At the end of history, man is God; the possession of absolute knowledge is the apotheosis of man. The violence done unto Hegel's text is thus not insignificant. Kojève understands perfectly well that if man must remain living when history has finished, this life will only be thinkable as the reign of nature: there will no longer be any history because there will be nothing historical at stake. On the other hand, he fails to recognize [*méconnaît*] the strictly theological meaning of the natural state thus attained. By permitting us to exist in the mode of the definitive, absolute knowledge and reconciliation make possible the unity, rather than the identity, of man and God. God is other than man at the beginning, and he remains other than man at the end. At the beginning, this alterity has the character of an opposition; but at the end, it has the character of a conciliation. At the end of history, man is at peace with, and exists face-to-face with God. Man—Adam—finally exists.

§ 48 Existence after History

One problem remains, which Hegel does not pose explicitly and to which he responds only obliquely, a problem the interpretation of his eschatology cannot but confront. After history comes nature. It comes about as the definitive order of things, as what cannot be criticized or abolished. And if Hegel is right, I am today—a man reconciled with God, who knows himself as such—the possessor of all that I can be, a survivor of history. One major characteristic, therefore, distinguishes Hegel's realized eschatology (and every eschatology related to it) from every theory that entitles us to hope. The *eschaton* in Hegel (and this is also true for Bultmann) is not only thinkable but also there for all to see. Definitive existence is no longer an object of speculation but has entered into the domain of description. How then are we to exist after history? This is an acute question. Every tension between the provisional and the definitive disappears at the end of the *Phenomenology*, and partiality no longer affects conscious experience. "Peace" has been acquired, and nothing in principle can disturb it. The mode in which we know the Absolute [*l'Absolu est connu*] is insuperable. Man no longer wants for anything: neither for himself nor God. He knows that the finite and the infinite have been reconciled, and can thus overcome all the contradictions and existentiell aporias capable of giving rise to the unhappy consciousness. No one could thus be more human than he who, henceforth freed from every alienation, finds at his disposal communities — civil society and the Church — in which to enjoy possession of what he is, and what he knows, without the present depending on a future. The definitive has taken its place in the world. We must be more specific, however. What is there to "do" after the completion of history? The relative discretion of the Hegelian text does not hide that the fruition of knowledge and the exercise of morality are the definitive modalities of existence. Two lines of questioning arise from this.

a. Hegelianism is not simply the philosophy that has learned most from theology (or, perhaps, the philosophy that has brought down the barriers separating the philosophical from the theological in the classical organization of knowledge): it is the thought that supposes the work of theology to be complete. It is of little import that Hegel loftily ignored the history of theology, and considered himself to be, more or less, the first theologian, that is, the first to think what religion propunds when brought to conceptualization beyond the element of representation. It is, however, of great importance to our problematic that he also conferred on himself the rank of the final theologian, and that absolute knowledge brings all interpretation to an end. It is almost banal to declare that the God manifested in the history that culminates in Good Friday and Easter Sunday has spoken his last word; Hegel is not alone in defending this thesis. It is nevertheless less banal to declare that the manifest God demystified himself for us, and is just as remarkable to declare that from this revelation, we henceforth possess, after eighteen centuries of Christian history, a complete and immutable knowledge. Yet these last declarations are at the heart of Hegel's theological system, and they actually constitute the justification for his eschatology. By reconciling itself with man, the Absolute has made itself manifest; it has unreservedly ceased to be a hidden God. The Spirit that "searcheth the deep things, yea, the deep things of God"[6] communicates all its knowledge to man; it is therefore in the plain light of day that the Absolute faces man. To the manifestness of the divine that leaves no room for negative theology, is added, on the other hand, the certitude that the human work of theology is itself complete. In the evening of history, the divine Logos and the human logos have completed their work of unveiling and of interpretation (and it is the evening of history because they have completed them). There is nothing more that man can know, nothing he cannot know better—the classical distinction established between the theology of mortals (*theologia viatorum*) and the theology of angels or the blessed (*theologia comprehensorum*) disappears, and absolute knowledge is, as we said above, the substitute for the beatific vision. This calls for a critique. It must be remarked, perhaps somewhat surprisingly, that the post-Hegelian destiny of thought, and fundamentally of theology, constitutes a more serious objection to the realization of his eschatology than the objection constituted by the ongoing spectacle of history, or of what resembles it. Of this ongoing history, it is always possible, and by no means illogical, to say that it is only a simulacrum of history, a history of no essential consequence, a nonhistory, therefore. One would, on the other hand, have greater difficulty in dismissing as pointless every theological question posed and every response proffered after Hegel. If Hegel is right, the attainment of absolute knowledge consequently abolishes every questioning: only those on the path toward this knowledge can pose questions, and whoever enjoys possession of this knowledge has nothing greater to desire. But if Hegel is right, the elementary logic of existence must necessarily be transgressed on a major point: man must cease to be defined as a questioning animal. The idea of plenary knowledge [*connaissance*], proof of which would leave no room for questioning, is not a pseudoidea. The experience that it wishes to provide an account of—the eschatology of knowledge—is nevertheless only thinkable as an erasure of the modes by which being-in-the-world is organized in the form of a presence that questions Beings [*êtres*] and things. We know the God who has communicated himself to man well enough, of course, for us to attend to his contemplation today, and for our liturgies not to be suspended on account of incomplete hermeneutic tasks. Is this to say that all theological work is behind us, and that only the didactic task of the transmission of acquired knowledge remains? The ongoing reality of our theological questions (it must be conceded, at the very least, that Hegel has not posed every question possible, and that the recent history of theology is not that of a series of footnotes to Hegel) should sufficiently demonstrate that enjoying possession of absolute knowledge does not satisfy us—or that the knowledge at our disposal is not "absolute." The legitimacy of these questions, moreover, is sufficient to indicate that in posing them we do not refuse to approve of pre-existing and definitive responses. But the desire for the knowledge [*connaissance*] that would silence this questioning suffices in turn to indicate that the Absolute is not truly obvious to us and that it remains known and unknown [*connu et inconnu*] in a mode that we cannot truly call eschatological. One can, after the historical manifestation of the Absolute, pose questions that it renders obsolete, and one can, after Hegel, pose questions to which Hegel has already responded. But this does not authorize us to grant to absolute knowledge the status of the last word on theological knowledge [*connaissance*]—nor even to claim this status for some system to come, whatever it may be: being-in-the-world implies an excess of questions over responses. Understanding, in the precise sense of the term, is not a mode of being-in-the-world.

b. A second difficulty arises when one notes that contemplation is not to rule over the eschatology placed under the auspices of absolute knowledge exclusively, and that the Hegelian end to history is the conclusion to all questioning, but not to all praxis. Morality is essential to definitive existence. Everything continues on as before as though the only questions that remain, when every speculative question worthy of the name has been settled, are the practical questions of ethics and politics. The Kingdom, for Hegel, is nothing other than the city. The city is, of course, the dwelling place of a theological community that finds its joy and peace in knowledge, and which also exists as a community of worship entrusted with the task of giving thanks to the manifest Absolute. But this community lives in the time of the world, and the difference between Church and State remains: liturgical worship and liturgy celebrated in the element of conceptual knowledge are not the entirety of eschatological existence, and the conditions for action are therefore still in place even though the *eschaton* has been realized. The praxis that survives history should, of course, (at least in principle) avoid the pitfalls that would lead to the reinstitution of history. At the end of the *Phenomenology*, we should know enough to avoid a resurgence of the dialectics that govern history. We no longer have to become ourselves, and we should be content simply to be. One issue still remains obscure, however. So long as the *eschaton* does not remove us from the labor of everyday existence, and we remain responsible for the common good, the threat of the return of history cannot really be considered to have dissipated. This threat is that of a fall outside the rational—but this makes it no less real. Past history is, in true Hegelian fashion, overcome and retained—*aufgehoben*—in the present of the *eschaton*. From the view-point of absolute knowledge, the less than whole figures of conscious-ness grappling with their historical becoming could only reappear illogically. This illogicality is nevertheless the first reality with which an ethics and a politics must reckon. Knowledge does not vanish into thin air. But it does not follow from this that the man reconciled with God, who knows himself as such, necessarily transcribes this knowl-edge into fully rational and (therefore) fully eschatological action. Is the possibility of a resumption of the power of historical reason in fact inscribed in the tasks that await man even though history is suppos-edly at an end? Does the continuance of praxis at the very heart of the *eschaton* compel us to think that definitively human existence, such as Hegel thinks it, cannot be an object of definitive possession? To these questions, the answer must be in the affirmative. If Hegelian escha-tology were only a theory of completed theological knowledge [*con-naissance*], these questions could not be posed. But it is also a theory of totally rational practice. It can easily be seen that this all-encom-passing rationality cannot be instituted in the world, even if it is found to be present in institutions.

§ 49 *Oblivio Mortis*

The most surprising characteristic of Hegel's system is not therefore its relative lack of astuteness in assigning to man in the world the concrete modalities of definitive existence over which the provi-sional no longer has any hold. Nor should it come as a surprise that Hegelianism, for this same reason, if indeed it is the thought in which all is recapitulated, lends itself to a distortion that would hold the key to a philosophy of hope. To Marx's critique, Hegel had, of course, responded in advance that the time of the transformation of the world and the coming of man is past, and that it is henceforth possible to oversee and let be the final natural order of things. Even if the interpretation had to precede the realization, and history after Hegel benefited from a reprieve necessary for everyone to be able to live in reconciled existence, this reprieve would still confirm the rad-ical worldliness of Hegelian eschatology, and the questions to which it gives rise. It is possible that the anthropology born of the recon-ciliation of the finite and the infinite, and of the knowledge that lays hold of this, thought what had yet to become fact, or rather what was still only the case for a small number (or for Hegel alone), but that it had thought it correctly. The world is definitively our dwelling place, and we can exist there in an insuperable mode without waiting for graces from the Absolute other than those we have already been granted. "The Sage," Kojève remarks, "realizes in its concrete reality the *fullness* of human existence conscious of itself; *its* content, being *total*, is therefore *the* content. . . . The Sage thinks all that is *thinkable*, and at the time when the Sage is living, all that is thinkable has already actually been realized: the totality of his knowledge is thus truly established by the totality of the realization."[7] It is thus time to ask what status can be assigned to death in an eschatology that does nothing to dissipate the threat it poses the sage as much as the next man.

In Kojève's interpretation, finitude and its limitations do not contradict the process by which man appropriates for himself the divine at the conclusion of the *Phenomenology*—on the contrary, finitude appears as the condition of a concrete divinity. The sage "is therefore the Logos incarnate. But this is not a God who is born and dies, lives, eats and drinks despite his divinity, but who need not do such things. No, the being that Hegel has in view is the Logos because he eats and drinks, is born, lives and dies, and dies for good, without being brought back to life."[8] The commentator is mistaken, we said, in attributing to Hegel an atheistic eschatology. There is, however, one point on which he is absolutely correct: at the Hegelian conclusion of history, death ceases to be an issue. It neither bears any meaning nor disrupts the fruition of meaning. Its reality calls for no further elucidation; and the philosopher duly loses interest in it. But we should not be too hasty in accepting this. There are certainly clear reasons for overlooking the death to which Hegel's worldly eschatology bears witness. Blood and violence are omnipresent in history, which begins with the "fight to the death" where the one becomes a slave and the other a master. In the evening of history, however, nothing can come of death or its denial. Man can recollect his past, but he is henceforth deprived of a future. The present fruition of what he is and the present fulfillment of his responsibilities circumscribe his existence. He has nothing to expect from death, nor anything to fear from it—it is nothing more than a natural peripeteia, and it neither houses the promise of a beyond, nor challenges the abundance of meaning on this side of death. Does the vesperal reign of a state of nature nonetheless mean that there is no longer anything at stake in death? Can one remain mortal without death inescapably bearing down on all experience, even if experience is no longer determined by history but by its completion? This is what we must contest.

The reality of Hegelian eschatology is that of existence surviving history within the world. The world is the place of the definitive as it was that of the provisional, and it is as a carnal being that man comes to possess the *eschaton*: the elementary conditions that define him in history continue to do so after history. It is possible to lose interest in death, and to say that whoever has the highest knowledge at his disposal is no longer concerned with it. But can the worldly structure of existence be maintained without it implicitly maintaining the claim death exercises over us? The strange idea of a being-in-the-world that is no longer identical to a being-toward-death constitutes here (in a conceptuality that is not Hegel's, it must be admitted) a major aporia. No one knows better than Hegel to keep his distance from the initial realities of experience; this decision must be accepted if only because it leaves open the possibility of thinking that a relation to an Absolute absent from the beginning is what is "proper" to man. But if one keeps such distance, one nevertheless comes up against death, just as one does against the reminder and perpetual presence of the initial. The Hegelian end to history does not abolish the transcendental laws of experience, and nothing allows us to postulate that, by attaining the highest knowledge [*le plus haut savoir*], we can thwart these laws. Death—man's relation to his death—perhaps has a history in which man's relation to God introduces meanings to which the logic of being-in-the-world is indifferent; and perhaps there is, in some shape or form, an eschatological way of facing death. But it is important to recognize that this history does not annul the logic of being-in-the-world and its permanent validity, and it is important to recognize that Hegelian eschatology cannot radically call into question present concerns with the empirical absolute future represented by death. The end—reconciled existence and the attainment of absolute knowledge—is a critique of the beginning, and it is a powerful critique: what is given at the beginning can, after all, distract us from what is essential, and the mediation of knowledge can justifiably claim to be the condition of an authenticity. It is not, however, a totalizing critique. Hegel's eschatology finds itself powerless to neutralize death because it is in fact powerless to provide a logic of existence in which death would cease to bear on the present—such a logic could hardly provide us with a better example of a forgetting of the real. From the fact that death is not an issue when Hegel interprets the end of history, it does not follow that death *must* no longer put anything into question: it follows only that a certain problem is overlooked in Hegel's treatment of definitive realities, or that a certain reality ceases to be a philosophical problem—which is very different. But because no theory can spare the man who knows himself [*se sait*] to be reconciled with God and who knows himself [*se connaît*] as having no dwelling place other than this world the possibility of seeing in his death the collapse of all meaning, it must also be said that this oversight compromises the entire theory. At the Hegelian end of history, it is not certain that what lies on this side of death, even if it permits the fruition of supreme knowledge [*savoir suprême*], is truly the place of an imperturbable beatitude.

§ 50 The *Eschaton* and the Present

In Hegelian terms, nature comes after history; the essential is not the originary but what has come to pass, and finally self-identical man no longer has to worry about any future where his identity could again be called into question: he can therefore face up to the toils of the present by recollecting his own coming into being. The ethical and political work that accompanies the enjoyment of the highest knowledge is not without its munificent glory. The establishment of a city where morality concretely and fully reigns is a work worthy of man; and if morality is to be complete, it is only right that this work should have an eschatological dimension. Already in Kant, morality was linked to the *eschaton*, and his critique of Kant should not hide the fact that, for Hegel also, using different words, it is a question of wishing for "the kingdom of ends." There is, however, a major difference. Morality in Kant is an infinite work that, if it is to lead to the good, must break through the limits of the time that leads us to death. And yet the eschatological action that Hegel speaks of demands no such rupture: it is taking place right here and now, or can in any case take place in the world. We are thus led to ask what particular structure could house the time that (if Hegel is right) remains the unaltered horizon of our being within completed history, and thus to ask what problems will result from this. One of the serious problems every eschatology must tackle is that of the ways of being proper to whoever has escaped the laws of history, or the laws of history and the world, and who is henceforth subject only to the law of God or, in the secularized eschatologies, to the laws of a nature that has finally been conquered: as we have already said. If the *eschaton* is entrusted to God, it would ordinarily be a question of thinking an eternity in the measure of man. If, on the other hand, atheism can accommodate itself to an eschatology, it would be a question of thinking the plenary act of being man solely in the company of other men, a homeland finally attained, a universal joy of being that could not be provided by history. Hegel's eschatology falls under neither one rubric nor the other. The definitive confrontation between man and God is its primary content. But this confrontation, which for Hegel fulfills the function of the face-to-face encounter in classical theology, is a temporal and worldly event. How thus would time be able to house the *eschaton*, while respecting all its determinations?

To respond to this question, we must emphasize once again that this can only be the case if one grants to the present the right to govern this time, and if one disqualifies the future's hold over the present. Eternity might be defined as a perpetual present: *nunc stans*. It might also be defined as the "total and simultaneous possession of a life that knows no end."[9] This last definition is doubtless that of the divine eternity and not that of an eternity imparted to man. One major feature pertinent to both these definitions demands our attention. For time and the *eschaton* not to exclude one another, a condition is thus required: what is now, and which we can declare to be the definitive, must not give purchase over itself to something that is not yet; true life, life lived to its fullest, must be lived today; the present must be a plenitude of all time and the end of all time for us. And yet this alerts us once again to the paradoxical necessity of a dialogue (whose structure we are indicating here in only the most schematic way) between Bultmann's and Hegel's eschatologies. The Swabian philosopher and the professor at Marburg would appear to have nothing in common. But if one agrees to take Hegel seriously, and not to consider the ultimate implications of the *Phenomenology* (and of the entire Hegelian system) as an affront to good sense, which historians should have the courtesy to modestly pass over in silence, Bultmann's eschatology perhaps provides us with the conceptual means to combine temporal experience and definitive existence, and to read Hegel correctly. Bultmann's problem is certainly not that which confronts Hegel. In Hegel, it is a question of thinking history from its end and of discerning in it the path that leads to the *eschaton*, whereas, in Bultmann, the eschatological maintains no link with the historical, of which it is nothing but a critique. Instituting true authenticity and the veritable form of eschatological experience, faith is an attitude of rupture: it vanquishes the "world" (understood in its Johannine and Pauline sense, and interpreted as the sphere of inauthentic existence) and liberates us from the "world." It remains—and this is where Hegel and Bultmann intersect—that, on the one hand, the believer (obviously) does not cease to exist within the phenomenological totality of the world, but that, on the other, he can escape any disturbance that a future (his death or the hope of a beyond) might project upon the present: his time is thus nothing other than the *kairos* from which nothing is absent since man then receives the grace of God, and thus arrives at what is most proper to him. God will perhaps be able to give more than he gives today (Bultmann's text scarcely enables us to be more specific on this point). But, from today on, he most certainly provides us with the opportunity to dwell in a beyond to history. Thus can the present of faith close up upon itself. Nothing is lacking in it. It is *"tota ac simul possessio."*

It is probably in this vein that we should understand the temporality that, for Hegel, continues on after the completion of history. The Hegelian "sage" finds himself no longer in want of being [*manque à être*], but in definitive possession of himself. Time no longer demands to be thought according to any dimension other than the present; the entire reality of the past is given in this present, and the future cannot but accept this present, by way of perpetuation. The mediations of the moral and the political remain (they also remain in Bultmann, whose realized eschatology no more leads to states of exaltation than does Hegel's), the good use of time remains, but the future does not vanish, although the present remains independent of it, and the entire meaning of time is concentrated in it. In the eschatological events that are Bultmannian faith and Hegelian knowledge, the absolute future is the present reality. The present is thus an "absolute present" in which the definitive reality of existence is concentrated. It is sufficient for its own [*propre*] interpretation and can close up upon itself within its own riches.

§ 51 Religion, Mediation, and the Humanity of Man

The principal benefit of our necessarily too brief, but by no means ornamental, commentaries is that they ground still more clearly the disjunction between liturgy—religion in Hegel—and immediacy. At the beginning of the private path of consciousness, all that is given is sense certainty and its "abstraction," its powerlessness to integrate what it is certain of into an ordered whole. The private history of consciousness is itself bound up with the public history of humanity: there is no existence that precedes the history of the world. Man, in Hegel, does not, of course, concern himself with God alone. But this history is nevertheless a religious history. The history in which he accedes to his self is essentially driven by the manifestation and communication of the Absolute. This is not only the history of human beings in their own midst: it is the history of human beings and of God. It is, finally, a history that has reached its conclusion, and has been interpreted from the point of view of this conclusion. It is not necessary, of course, for the Absolute to be obvious, "manifest," or to have uttered its last word for man to maintain a relation with it. Religion already exists in a "determinate" form (according to the lexicon of the *Lectures on the Philosophy of Religion*) prior to divine manifestation engendering "absolute" religion. One thing is nevertheless certain, whether it is a question of "determinate" religion or of "absolute" religion, of Christianity correctly interpreted: its logic unfolds far from the immediate sphere of consciousness in the element of knowledge (whether it is rudimentary or fully organized). One can and should read the *Lectures*[10] as a blunt polemical accusation brought against Schleiermacher, who had published his dogmatic work one year before Hegel taught the philosophy of religion in Berlin for the very first time. On the other hand, the severity of the accusatory attack and of the critique of "religious feeling" teaches us nothing that is not implicitly or explicitly present in the sections of the *Phenomenology* devoted to "manifest religion" and to "absolute knowledge." Although the exposition differs, of course, depending on whether one reads the *Phenomenology* or the *Lectures*, whatever the path leading from "natural religion" to "aesthetic religion" to "revealed religion" (the *Phenomenology*), or from the "concept of religion" to "determinate religion" to "consummate religion" (the *Lectures*), one point predominates: what is of true importance is "revealed" or "consummate" or "absolute" religion. It is not until the end that man veritably exists before God; and the Absolute is not something he feels, but someone he knows [*connaît*]. It is legitimate to study the archaeology of the religious; indeed, it would otherwise be impossible to write the history of the world and its philosophy. On the other hand, it would be impossible to appeal to the beginning as an authority with the right to critique knowledge [*le savoir*] that is not given until the end. All of this we can attribute to Hegel.

There remains one question to be posed, which we have yet to tackle. When the divine process of manifestation and reconciliation is considered to have come to a close, when God is not simply known [*connu*] to us but is understood, and when speculative theology represents the highest experience man can have. Does the Absolute in fact communicate itself to knowledge alone? Is man's relation to God accomplished in the sole element of the *logos*?

The Hegelian response is clear. Manifest (or absolute) religion is certainly not absolute knowledge, and its "representations" have yet to be brought to "conceptualization." To repeat, it is more than possible that Hegel betrays an unfailing ignorance of the history of theology when he interprets the transition leading to absolute knowledge (i.e., to the knowledge he is the first to formulate systematically): whatever the highly idiosyncratic meaning of Hegel's notion of the "concept," the theologians were not waiting for him to think the contents of the faith they were living, and the Hegelian tactic of rejecting whatever he wished to overcome or rethink in the field of "representation" (the idea of the beyond, for example) owes more to the politics of the text than to strictly philosophical work. But the central point remains: the Hegelian theory betrays a consistent refusal to let the relation between man and God find its truth anywhere other than in the happiness of knowledge, in discursive knowledge, in a totally logical, nonaffective mode. If, in the evening of the history of the world, the *eschaton* must exceed the private sphere of consciousness and realize itself in the element of social existence, it is, in a sense, as a vast community of theologians that we should imagine a finally self-identical humanity, finally capable of fully rational ethical action. This community, of course, does nothing but devote itself to the work of thought or, rather, to enjoying possession of the fruits of this work. Knowledge does not annul the practice of worship. The God they think remains a God who is praised and to whom prayers are addressed. The Hegelian subordination of worship to the practice of conceptual knowledge [*savoir conceptuel*] is nevertheless incontestable and well known, and its consequences for the *disputatio de homine* are not lacking in importance. Philosophy debates what is proper to man and to the truth of his being, and theology cannot avoid debating these issues either. This properness [*propriété*] or authenticity is in Hegel an eschatological given and a present reality: one can bring what man is to light only when he insuperably embodies the entire truth of his being; but when Hegel has his say, he leaves us in no doubt that the conditions of this embodiment have been completely satisfied in the world. The mode par excellence in which human life is lived is that of theoretical knowledge [*connaissance théoretique*], which thus constitutes the supreme experience of God.

What we might think here to be banal betrays itself as being anything but trivial. Philosophers, for as long as there have been philosophers, have seldom failed to discern in their own work the highest activity to which one can devote oneself, the accomplished act of being man. Hegel, in this regard, says nothing new. Nor does he say anything new in thinking the *eschaton* as an acquisition of insuperable science (despite the obvious and surprising novelty of an eschatology realized within a world that annuls all difference between the *scientia beatorum* and the *scientia viatorum*). Is knowledge, or more precisely conceptual knowledge, sufficient to qualify experience as "eschatological"? To the definitive question of the *disputatio de homine*, "Who is to be considered as representative of humanity totally present to itself?" Hegel responds unambiguously: man proves that he has arrived at the fullness of his humanity when he has taken hold of definitively articulated theological knowledge. Yet it is worthwhile noting that the theologian, or whoever appropriates the knowledge elaborated by the theologian, has, as a general rule, the elementary humility not to present himself as the highest object of theological anthropology. If the theologian ceases to speak of God in order to speak of man, it is ordinarily the saint rather than the theologian who provides the most appropriate paradigm of humanity reconciled with God. The theologian can be a saint. But one is not a saint simply because one is a theologian, or a disciple of the best theologian there has ever been—if we accept that it is necessary to speak of sainthood (and Hegel does not), it must also be said that the most sublime mastery of knowledge is not sufficient to bring about man's accomplishment. These cursory remarks give us much to think about. Knowledge [*le savoir*] should certainly preside over religion if it is not to lose itself in [*s'abîme dans*] the ambiguities of feeling. Knowledge [*connaissance*] of God should, however, when the *eschaton* is left in God's hands, guarantee the definitive joy of man. But must it be that this joy has no modality other than that of speculative knowledge [*savoir spéculatif*], and that man's relation to the Absolute closes up on itself in the eschatological triumph of the concept? Hegel knows that paying homage through our reason is not the only way we can give to God, and that religion, the "Sunday of life," is irreducible to the happiness of knowing [*bonheur de connaître*] through concepts. It is nevertheless this happiness, and no other, which constitutes true beatitude. Although, at the conclusion of history, religion and its practices will remain, the sacramental institution will retain its rights (severely controlled, it is true) in the life of the Church, and the concept will, in a way, control the good usage of representation, no beyond to theological discursiveness is thinkable, and there is no prerequisite to the beatitude other than the good usage of reason. The eschatological perpetuation of moral and political tasks would certainly permit us to reject the disturbing hypothesis that might emerge here of a beatitude that could coexist with immorality, the possibility of which would not require the man reconciled with God to have undergone what the traditional lexicon would call a "conversion." This does not, however, prevent the reign of conceptual knowledge. This knowledge may not be coextensive with reconciled existence but it is indisputably the kernel essential to it.

§ 52 The Salvational Meaning of the Cross

One problem still awaits the precise determination of its terms. The eschatological is the definitive—this is nothing but a question of the definition of words. The definitive for Hegel, on the other hand, takes place in the world in the shadow of the Cross on which the Infinite is reconciled with the finite—it is a question here of a thesis, whose violence cannot pass by unnoticed. This violence is not the result of a lack of reflection. One cannot accuse Hegel of simply having ignored that according to its most common grammar, the thought of the *eschaton* forms one body with the representation of a beyond to the world and to death. One can accuse him even less of having actually elaborated a secular eschatology, in which God died on Good Friday and has remained dead. One can and one should notice, however, that there is a strictly theological reasoning behind the strategy by which Hegel renders the *eschaton* immanent in the world: the absorption of the event of Easter into that of Golgotha (or at the least) their indifferentiation.[11] Hegel's Christology is a Christology of the Cross through and through. On the Cross, everything is consummated, and even though classical Christology still awaits the lordliness of the Crucified to be manifested in his resurrection because the word of forgiveness pronounced on Good Friday has not established the entirely new creation, this new creation has, for Hegel, no dimension other than that of reconciled existence. According to Bultmann's formula as it appears in the heading to this section, the "resurrection" is nothing but "the salvational meaning of the Cross," *die Heilsbedeutung des Kreuzes*.[12] It is of the order, not of an event, but of interpretation; and this interpretation perceives a gift accompanied by no promise. The God who gave his forgiveness has nothing else to give man. The Cross shines of its own light rather than through the light of Easter. It is, therefore, the conclusion of every hope. Although the properly theological imbalance from which Hegelianism suffers is of no importance to us here, its consequences for Hegel's anthropology are of great importance. Because the reconciliation accomplished on Good Friday constitutes the entirety of man's salvation for Hegelianism, it is our absolute future. Thus, in contrast to classical theology, where the *eschaton* is simultaneously given in the element of the present (the reconciliation) and in that of the future (the resurrection), Hegel can think the realization of definitive realities exhaustively. Thus, too, the last article of faith finds itself eliminated from the Hegelian system. Hegel does not await the "life of the world to come": he contemplates its present reality.

The reasons for which the definitive and the real can coincide perfectly are thus obvious, and find here their strongest justification. Traditional theology has to do with memory and with hope, and conjoins the certitude of irrevocable gifts with the admission of the current unaccomplished state of man. But what remains unaccomplished can no longer occupy a position in a thought where man's future is his reconciliation with God and nothing but this reconciliation (a future that, of course, is not to be underestimated), and where the resurrection of Christ is not inserted between the forgiveness given on Good Friday and the gift of the Spirit on Pentecost Sunday thereby promising what cannot be offered within the limits of the world, an eternity that would take our carnal existence as its measure. On the evening of Good Friday, man does, of course, possess a future for Hegel: he will have to appropriate the reality of his salvation for himself. For that, he will need the long delay that leads to absolute knowledge. But when he has finally appropriated it, he has no more than a present and a past. Insofar as he is concretely reconciled with the Infinite, the finite has already been revived. At the Hegelian conclusion of history, man has certainly not become God. Here one can nevertheless recognize the most profound reason for which man has indisputably lost every future and "is in possession of" all that he can be. If the Cross is the final *fact*, and the resurrection the *meaning* of this fact, there can only be one conclusion. Once again, the eschatological point of view that dominates Hegelianism and the realization of the *eschaton* should not be considered oddities, but should be seen to possess a remarkable consistency, and a fundamentally theological consistency at that.

The Preeschatological Site of the Question of Man

§ 53 The Next to Last

The question of the humanity of man—of its provisional and its definitive reality—can now be posed in more precise ways, and we can never be too grateful to the thinker who has forced us to formulate them. Do I have a future that fixes the perspective by which to interpret my present, or does this future invest itself in my present from this day forward? To this question, Hegel's response is clear and rigorous—but it is less certain that it is entirely tenable. One will readily acknowledge what even a formal analysis of liturgy can confirm, and which can be confirmed by following other analytical procedures:[1] that the problem of ipseity is an eschatological problem. It will be admitted—and we have already done so—that this problem is linked to that of a history in which the relation of man to God is dependent on a contingent unveiling. It is not at the beginning (in the morning of consciousness and at the dawn of history) that man is truly himself. Authenticity is to be found at a distance from the initial: it presupposes the private history of man that annuls or overcomes his immediate relation to world and earth, and it presupposes the public history of humanity that has made the Absolute manifest, or for which it has been made manifest. In either case, meaning comes at the end. But from the fact that the Absolute has been made manifest, and from the fact that this manifestation bears on the very being of whoever grasps and consents to it, must we conclude that we are already at the conclusion of the becoming that defines what we are essentially?

The strongest objection to Hegel's anthropology that arises here appeared in the preceding section: Hegel could only be right, finally, if the resurrection of the Crucified did not have to be interpreted as a promise, and was nothing but the meaning of the last fact — of the reconciling Cross. The modesty of Hegelian eschatology should not give rise to astonishment when one considers that it has its roots in the minimalism of the theology of Easter or, what amounts to the same thing, in Christology's concentration on Good Friday. It is all the more possible to announce the realization of definitive realities when one expects little of them or, at any rate, when one expects of them nothing that cannot take place in the world. But if one admits (and we take it as axiomatic) that the Cross and the resurrection are two events, or at least two distinct moments within the same complex event, it would be difficult to maintain that the reconciliation between man and God is his absolute future, and that the reconciled man is his definitive self in the time that leads him to death. We must therefore argue against Hegel on the grounds of a *splitting in two of the end*. One would scarcely doubt (and it has scarcely been doubted in the history of theology) that the divine manifestation that culminates in the destiny of Jesus of Nazareth has the character of the insuperable, of the last word proffered in history. Nor should one doubt that the reconciliation inextricable from this manifestation redefines the humanity of man in a way that cannot be interpreted without recourse to the lexicon of the *eschaton*. Man exists "within" the alliance forged on the Cross more authentically than he exists in the world; and this alliance definitively determines the relation between God and man. Although history does, of course, continue on after the event of Good Friday, this event introduces a rupture. The man reconciled with God, who knows himself as such, expects nothing from history. He can justifiably claim to represent the Kingdom. The peace that reigns between him and God is not transitory. This does not, however, permit us to postulate the total realization of the definitive. For if it is true that the gift of reconciled existence is inextricable from the promise given on Easter Sunday, this promise itself remains unfulfilled. Although Christ is risen from the dead, Hegel is not, nor am I (except in the metaphorical sense of the term used to describe the eschatological meaning of reconciled existence, which is not lacking in biblical confirmation, but which is also a possible source of equivocation). In resurrecting the Crucified, God also puts himself in a position of debt to whoever has reconciled himself through his Cross, and promises him a future to which the concept of reconciliation cannot do justice, which implies that one can exist authentically and thus, in a sense, eschatologically, without being in definitive possession of oneself. Reconciled existence takes place therefore in an *interim between the eschatological blessings* [biens] *already granted and the eschatological blessings that still remain within an economy of the promise.* The logic of reconciled existence is certainly a critique of the logic of being-in-the-world and of being-in-history. But the fact that the last and highest promise has yet to be fulfilled indicates that man still has a future. The question of man cannot therefore be settled through a hermeneutics of the alliance lived within the transcendental limits of the world: so long as these limits are imposed upon us, our humanity remains in abeyance.

A conceptual and terminological stipulation is thus required here. It is *too late*, when man faces an Absolute that offers its alliance, *for the* disputatio de homine *to have dimensions other than those of a hermeneutics of facticity.* But it is *too soon*, when the man reconciled with God encounters care or restlessness, and all the concerns that being-toward-death projects onto being-before-God, *for us to believe him definitively at one with his humanity.* We will speak thus, in order to name the interim deriving from the splitting of the end, of "preeschatological" experience, or of a logic of the "next to last." The words denote a fact, which in turn gives rise to a new questioning.

a. Beyond every nondialectical contradiction of the provisional by the definitive and of the definitive by the provisional, they refer to the at once real and symbolic hold the *eschaton* exerts over the present, the horizon to which is provided by divine manifestation. We are no longer at the beginning if we prove ourselves capable of uttering the name of God and of existing in the mode of liturgy. Moreover, liturgy, which is grounded in divine manifestation, and which represents the play of the reconciled man before God, sets up within the world the greatest possible distance between itself and the initial — the presence of reconciled man before the manifest God [*au Dieu manifeste*] perhaps establishes, between the present and the a priori conditions of experience, a *caesura more considerable than that separating the worldly reality of reconciled existence from resurrected existence.* We have already explained why it is not necessary for the Absolute to have uttered its last word for man to be able to avail himself of the right of liturgy. But when this last word has been uttered, liturgy displays all the eschatological significations it can possibly assume. That being-in-vocation contests being-in-fact does not annul the latter. Man does not cease to be needed in the world. The debate between being-in-fact and being-in-vocation will always be settled by the facts (and who would be surprised at that?). The definitive transfiguration of every thing and every experience is denied to us today. In the time that leads us to death, no mode of being can be anything more than *pre*eschatological. But more than one emphasis is possible here. The time that leads us to death is also that of the reconciliation and of the alliance over which the definitive exerts its hold: within this, our modes of being can assume the character of the preeschatological.

b. These remarks, to tell the truth, do little more than open up the path to a new questioning. The next to last, we will later say, mediates the opposition between the provisional and the definitive. If we rigorously think the provisional and the definitive together, it enables us to think their distinction and conciliation at once. Its logic is a tierce logic: neither that of a realized eschatology nor that of a historiality the *eschaton* would leave intact. This teaches us nothing yet, however, of the concrete figures of preeschatological experience. Does it fall to the next to last to let the eternal splendor of the "end" shine through in advance? Or does it fall to it to submit this splendor to the chiaroscuro of the world, to be the *eschaton* present in the form of its contrary, and submit to the laws of the world? The definitively human man, despite what Hegel might say, is not within our grasp: we can speak a language cognizant of ultimate realities, but certainly not one that describes them. On the other hand, the man reconciled with God is not primarily an object of speculation for us (however reputable and factually based such speculation might be). His experiences take place on this side of death. This can—and "should"—be our experience if it enables man to lay hold of what is most proper to him. This is why we must undertake the task of description. We know of no other way of responding to the questions posed.

§ 54 Knowledge and Inexperience

To highlight the privileged position that knowledge [*le savoir*] holds within it, let us return to our interpretation of prayer. Whoever prays stands patiently before God. He does not stand there before the Unknown: only he who takes the risk of liturgical patience and the paradoxical attitudes that it presupposes can think what precisely the name of God means. This is all the more the case when one no longer appeals to elementary certainties that authorize liturgy, but to an insuperable historical manifestation. We are not, of course, saying that whoever prays must have brought to conceptualization all that God has communicated of himself, and that true prayer is the sole prerogative of the theologian. But it must be said—and this is no more than a platitude—that the act of presence that constitutes prayer is accomplished after Easter in the element of a knowledge [*connaissance*] that perhaps leaves room for nonknowledge [*inconnaissance*], but which is not endangered by this nonknowledge. To know [*connaître*] is not to understand, and it also belongs to what we should know of God [*savoir sur Dieu*], for our knowledge [*notre savoir*] to be consistent, that God give rise to thought without it ever being possible for its reflections on him to come to an end: he must continue to elude our grasp. It is nevertheless imperative that liturgy not be a confrontation with a mystery on which no light can be shed (this would deny the possibility of liturgy pure and simple), that it not deal with an absolutely other that it would have to praise without knowing [*connaître*] it (which would be a flagrant contradiction), that it not know enough of God [*en sache assez sur Dieu*] to justify itself—and that it be preeschatologically grounded in an unconcealment that no longer prepares a space for man to expect a resumption of the word of the Absolute in history. This is not the place to avail oneself of the contents of theological knowledge [*savoir théologique*]. It is, however, the very place to say that the man who prays, when he prays, thinks of God and has something to think. The contemplation of whoever thinks of God is not, of course, a theological endeavor (even though nothing prevents us from supposing that his prayer can facilitate the theoretical efforts of the theologian). Nor are we forced to affirm that whoever prays necessarily grounds his prayers in a theology that would have displayed the contents of divine self-unveiling in this world in an insuperable way: on the one hand, the idea of a definitively completed theology is properly aporetic (see § 48, para. a); on the other, one cannot demand of whoever prays that he have previously conceptualized all that the Absolute unveils of itself in the act whereby it reconciles itself with man. But although every schema that more or less assimilates the contemplative prayer to the Hegelian enjoyment of absolute knowledge must be rejected, the cognitive moment of liturgy cannot be neglected, however. Prayer now takes place after the logos has grasped divine manifestation, and it cannot be completely ignorant of this apprehension. Its logic is not totally independent of that of the theological thematization. It is also constituted as a certain experience of thought.

One cannot think of the manifest God without also being able to give some account of what the name of God means, and without prayer representing a certain practice of knowledge.

It is here that a remarkable paradox, which we have already considered (in § 19) reappears, but which is revived by the preeschatological necessity to interpret liturgy within the horizon of the divinity made manifest in knowledge. Whoever liturgically turns to face God obviously demonstrates thereby that he is not content with the pure enjoyment of knowledge. There is more than one reason to pray: we pray in order to engage in contemplation or praise, to ask for forgiveness for our sins or to ask for something else. But whatever the particular reason, we do not pray without presupposing that the experience of thought is not the only way to found a relation with the Absolute (without stating, therefore, that prayer is not an anachronism for whoever makes use of theology), and without presupposing in a more or less articulated fashion that the God who can be thought can also bear witness to himself in the immanent sphere of consciousness, and become for man a God "sensible to the heart" whose presence is guaranteed in the element of affectivity. And yet this presupposition meets more often with falsification than with verification. It will certainly not be denied that the Absolute can be the subject of affective knowledge [*connaissance affective*], on condition that a somewhat precise hermeneutics of the latter (i.e., a "discerning of spirits") can be undertaken. It will, on the other hand, be denied that this knowledge must confirm conceptual knowledge [*savoir conceptuel*]; and it will therefore be denied that it belongs essentially to the preeschatological structure of experience. Could it be that the highest knowledge [*le plus haut savoir*] overlaps with "nonexperience" or "inexperience," and even with the *highest inexperience*? And would this overlapping be, in fact, a primordial mark of reconciled existence? The suggestion must be examined.

The questions we have posed do not, of course, arise in Hegel, who readily admits that "religion" is not solely a matter for "pure thought," but who interprets "pure thought" as the truth of what is comprehended only outside itself in the impoverished order of representation and feeling. But these questions insistently recur when one is not satisfied with the joys of theoretical knowledge [*connaissance*], whenever liturgy confronts us with the alarming conjunction of knowledge [*du savoir*] and inexperience, and whenever he who prays can only appeal to his knowledge and experiential confirmation is refused him. Inexperience frustrates those for whom knowledge does not suffice, those who demand certitude and affective verification but who are refused such things. Intellectual knowledge [*connaissance*] appears to him incapable of embodying the greatest proximity the world can afford between man and God, but affective knowledge cannot embody it either—one thus perceives how liturgy can become a veritable tragedy for consciousness. We should become more precise in our understanding of what inexperience denies us; we should then recognize that it clearly exposes our incapacity to accede to an eschatological plenitude of experience (and therefore confers a genuine preeschatological privilege to knowledge), but that it also sets itself up as a judge of the worldly ambiguities of immediacy.

a. It must be suggested, against Hegel, that knowledge [*le savoir*] consecrates itself to the distance that separates us from the definitive fruition of the Absolute. Within its order, that of discursive mediation, it belongs to knowledge ("faith" being the case in point, the name given to the human apprehension of divine manifestation) to suffer no deficiency. One can wait for the eschatological "vision" that will render conceptual mediations obsolete, release us from the work of thought, and give us yet more to know [*connaître*] (without, of course, invalidating any of what we know [*savons*] here and now, which is true once and for all). But insofar as the initial conditions of experience apply to those who turn toward God (insofar as knowledge is a mode of being-in-the-world), there is no reason for us to require knowledge to ever undergo [*que le savoir connaisse*] an eschatological transfiguration here and now. It would obviously be an act of bad grace were one to deny the Absolute the right to confirm for affective consciousness what intellectual consciousness already knows [*sait*]: this would constitute an attack on its freedom and its omnipotence. But until such time as the laws that govern experience are suspended, the a priori field in which this freedom and omnipotence operate dictates to liturgy its elementary logic; but it is more important to consent to this logic than to recognize that it can also be suspended by way of an exception. Liturgy imitates the Parousia while acknowledging the nonparousiacal presence of God, and no experience that necessarily figures in liturgical grammar will annul what separates us, in the world, from the Parousia. The conjunction of knowledge and inexperience (our incapacity to introduce into liturgy experiential verification as a constitutive moment) cannot be torn asunder. Man wishes "to see" God, but everything he sees disappoints him (preeminently, to cite the most significant example there is, the "sacramental species," the bread and wine consecrating the Eucharist, under or behind which are given the most "real" of presences). He wishes for the sensible certitude of God's condescension but can ground it only in the objective reality of his reconciliation, in his knowledge/faith and the reasons that underlie it. Knowledge does not placate all his desires. But we should remember that knowledge does not deceive us, and that it should therefore give rise to happiness: if not the happiness that derives from the Hegelian apotheosis of concepts, then at least the happiness of the man who waits, not for an eschatology that calls what he knows into question, but for an eschatology that verifies what he knows.

b. The critical force of inexperience can be brought to bear on our desire for the *eschaton* and on the dubious seductions of religious feeling, even though or perhaps because inexperience exists in solidarity with it. Feeling presents itself as a source of certitude, and its certitude attempts to set itself up as a verification: as the origin or as the confirmation of knowledge. The grave problem of "religious experience," and indeed of every "religious a priori," is nevertheless lodged in the ambiguity in which the "earth" enshrouds them. The transcendental is the play of "earth" and "world"; and when the "earth" prevails over the "world" and is imposed on us as the present truth of place, the sacred can become familiar to man [*devenir le familier de l'homme*], and the god(s) can come to experience. And yet this tells us that the logic in which religious feeling participates is in fact never foreign to that of the initial. But this is not to say that the sacred, thematized in all the theories on the religious a priori since Schleiermacher, veils the Absolute from us absolutely. We are not confronted here with a pure equivocation. The function of the sacred is not to disguise the Absolute and give rise to idolatry. The sacred at once veils and unveils. The "deities" can bear witness to God just as they can establish an economy of experience (and of thought) from which God is excluded. But one thing is very much certain: insofar as we have not distanced ourselves from the initial, ambiguity remains, and religious experience, under whatever conceptuality we might care to think it, does not permit us to unhesitatingly utter the name of God. One thus sees why liturgical inexperience can disqualify, or at any rate declare itself indifferent toward, every recourse to the immediacy of feeling, and can present us once again with the prudent joy of knowledge. The immediate is not what liturgy and the knowledge that grounds it have annulled. It is, rather, what they have overcome. When the ambiguity of the initial has been dissipated, liturgy cannot appeal to the chiaroscuro of the religious a priori without it thereby marking a regression. It cannot deny the existence of this a priori. But it should know [*connaître*] its exact signification and its position within the logic of the initial. And, faced with the impoverished kinds of knowledge [*savoirs pauvres*] derived from the element of feeling, it should set its critical force to work. We know and do not "see." Our knowledge nevertheless exceeds and judges every experience of the Absolute falling within the measure of being-in-the-world. Liturgical inexperience must teach us to demystify our capacity for "religious" experience: to completely rule out the immediacy that precedes knowledge, and not to require too much of the immediacy that succeeds it, which may, but need not, verify it.

Between knowledge and inexperience and vice versa, there is a fundamental oscillation, and it constantly reminds us that we face the Absolute within the element of the provisional. This holds true as soon as we can speak rigorously of God, as soon as we intend to exist before him and do not require him to be "manifest." Nevertheless, what we will call a "preeschatological exasperation" can be visited on experience. Not only does the highest knowledge not suffice, and nourish a desire for immediacy that it cannot satisfy, which compels us to commit to liturgy, it comes up against an inexperience itself immutable. Whoever prays knows toward whom he addresses his praise and litanies, and he declares this. But although he remembers what he knows, and justifiably declares that he will not be able to know more in the time that leads us to death, he cannot fail to see the difference between knowledge and inexperience not only perpetuate itself but become exacerbated. Paradoxically, then, what separates the provisional and the definitive thus *appears much more clearly when the provisional is qualified as the "next to last."* Whoever lays hold of divine manifestation—which is not to say "enjoys possession of" his knowledge—feels the pain of inexperience more than those who only make use of the elementary kinds of knowledge [*connaissances élémentaires*] necessary to the birth of liturgy. We are never more aware that the definitive realities are not within our reach than when we exist within the order of the next to last.

§ 55 The Night

Let us return, then, to the interpretation of liturgy as vigil. The concept appeared (in § 30) when we had to coordinate the work [*œuvre*] of ethics and liturgical inoperativity; the nocturnal reality of liturgy

was then that of time gained at the expense of the nonbeing symbolized by sleep—a time for which we do not have to answer before any
authority. It takes on a second signification here: the night gives itself
to be understood as a space of nonvision and of nonfeeling, as the
index of a twofold interstice that separates us from the "earth" and
from the *eschaton* and returns us to knowledge [*le savoir*] (to faith)
alone. The night thus defined is not the only face of liturgy. Whoever
prays can also taste the proximity of the God with whom he knows
himself to be reconciled. The known God [*le Dieu connu*] can also
"touch" man and present himself to affective consciousness. We
would nevertheless suggest that the night is, at the very least, the
pure secret (and essentially the preeschatological secret) of liturgy,
and the "experience" in which its essence and its destiny are manifested
in exemplary fashion and by emphasizing the reasons underlying it.
Although there is probably a pagan happiness, where the familiarity
of the sacred and the enchantments of the earth suffice to fulfill man,
the promises made at Easter enable us to think a beatitude that
respects all the dimensions of our being, and which therefore exceeds
the joy of knowledge. Indeed, it is not inconceivable that a worldly
inchoation of this beatitude can, in the end, be granted to us. On the
other hand, the liturgical night warns us that the dubious charm of
the earth must no longer seduce those who assent to the divine manifestation, that we cannot demand guarantees from the *eschaton* (whoever would do so would, after all, risk returning to the initial and to
the lack of a distinction between the sacred and God). We have
already spoken of this at length. The highest knowledge, despite
what Hegel has to say, cannot be identified with the beatific vision;
but because we are in possession of this knowledge, the logic of the
initial ceases to exert its hold over us: we already know enough of
God for an urgent interpretation of the ambivalences of religious
experience, and the dissipation of the chiaroscuro in which the earth
maintains the Absolute, not to be necessary. The night is not, therefore, the symbolic place of doubt or of uncertainty, but of the pure
affirmation of this knowledge, or of the pure reiteration of consent.

The "purity" of this affirmation and of this reiteration, however,
calls for comment. The night thus radicalizes or schematizes the
conditions under which man now faces a God who has been made
manifest. The one who "knows" or "believes" can only appeal to his
knowledge or his faith. This last remark is less banal than it appears.
This knowledge, in effect, rests on nothing that comes to experience
in the present. On the one hand, it is in the element of memory that

he grasps divine self-communication: the God who appeared has withdrawn from the field of manifestation, and the present of the liturgical night reveals nothing of him. But, on the other hand, it is in the element of hope that he awaits his proper verification: the time of pseudoverifications issuing from our native relation with the sacred is past, and the time for an eschatological verification that alone could present the Parousia has yet to come. If it had to close up on itself, the present of the liturgical night would actually be atheistic. Having yet to experience the definitive reign of God and no longer having experience of the earth and of the sacred immanent in it, we can do nothing but make ourselves present to the "world"—and in the "world," man lives without God.

One problem is inescapable. The liturgical night is the paradigmatic place of knowledge (of "bare" faith) and of nonfruition. But, if it is a critique of every experience on which man's initial relation to the sacred bears in one way or another (including, one suspects, experiences in which one should not be too eager to recognize an anticipation of the eschatological), it nevertheless embodies this critique in a mode of being—of radical inexperience—that must appear to us to suffer from a real deficiency. Liturgy exceeds and judges every annexation of God to the field of affective knowledge, but this includes within it an important affirmation. The time given to man is, above all, that in which he can strive for what is most proper to him: to exist before the Absolute with which he is reconciled. No act testifies better to being-in-vocation (whatever might be the testimony that ethics also gives to it within its order). Nowhere in the world does man reveal himself more truly. And yet we should be warned that this testimony or this revelation at bottom only comes to pass *sub contrario*. There are justifiable eulogies of liturgy that discern in it access to the greatest happiness to be found on this side of death. However, these eulogies and the experiences that justify them come up against the nocturnal face of liturgy as what they have failed to think. Because knowledge is the lifeblood on which it lives (and the only lifeblood on which it can live), and because there is a joy in knowledge (and, a fortiori, in the knowledge that one is at peace with the God who offers this peace), the liturgical night is nothing but unhappiness. Nevertheless, man does not liturgically turn to God and take the risk of the night for the satisfaction of rigorously grounding liturgy only in knowledge. Radical inexperience, "aridity," the "desert"—although it enables us to specify with great clarity, to the pleasure of the theoretician, the distance at which liturgy is from the initial and the *eschaton*—does not exist without giving rise to turmoil and unease. The liturgical night neither proves the absence of God nor denies his proximity: on the contrary, it teaches how to think them better. But it thus proves that God can be present and near without giving rise to a joy other than that which derives from believing; and it thereby proves that the man who prays and finds himself returned to knowledge alone lives an empty present, a dead time [*temps mort*]—it proves that liturgical inoperativity, while removing the joys that the provisional can provide, does not necessarily open up a field of experience where the bliss of definitively self-identical existence would come to light in advance. The twofold critique the liturgical night conducts—the critique of eschatological anticipation and of the anachronisms of religious experience, on the one hand, and of the liaison between them, in the form of a critique of affect, on the other—thus pays a high price.

One can count the cost more precisely by furthering the interpretation of liturgical temporality, and by proposing that *boredom* can be a principal mood of nocturnal experience. Can man become bored with facing God? As provocative as it is, the question must be answered in the affirmative. It would doubtless be contradictory for man to be completely eschatologically satisfied with the Absolute. But the nocturnal nonexperience is not eschatological. Although the Absolute, for whoever reflects on the content of concepts, remains always greater and the object of a desire that will never be satisfied, the act of making oneself present that instigates liturgy could not fail to be affected by the distance, preeschatologically exacerbated, which remains between whoever prays and definitive realities. Inexperience has no hold over knowledge, and actually permits its rationality to unfold fully, while contradistinguishing itself as clearly as possible from every religious emotionalism. It does, however, have a hold over the form of the present, which is not therefore structured in the first place by joy. It is not primarily the impatient expectation to which a visitation has been promised, or which it has promised for itself. Because it is, first, the work of an ascesis, of making oneself present and of waiting for which no affect compensates, one can well understand that this time can be one of boredom. The time of liturgy is diverted time (the time of inoperativity) and time given. Boredom reveals more here by underlining that this time can also be experienced as wasted time; and it is thus that impatience is reintroduced here in an indisputably alarming way, but this should come as no surprise, as it is the impatience that wishes to put an end to this dead time (to devote it, if possible, to an indisputably more "interesting" activity, such as theological work). The bored consciousness wastes its time. It can, of course, compensate for this wasted time and transform the dialogue it would like to establish with God—which does not actually take place—into a soliloquy: it thereby retakes possession of this time. And it can, of course, attempt to overcome boredom by intensifying its vigil—the night is perhaps at its end and God will perhaps bring it to a close soon. On the other hand, if one concedes that the night is not simply one case among others, but an indispensable moment in the liturgical life, then one must also concede that the boredom felt before God is really part of the secret of nocturnal experience. Boredom neither claims to disqualify the happiness of contemplation nor to pass its concept off for a basis on which to provide an account of man's encounters with God. Its moment must not remain unthought, however. David's dance before the ark[2] is not the only image of liturgy we can provide, nor is it certain that it is the first we ought to provide. Although liturgical inexperience need not give rise to boredom, boredom is a constant and useful reminder to us that nonexperience is essential to the liturgical play—and that it can be intolerable to us.

§ 56 The Disoriented Consciousness

A question arises that we have already formulated (in § 25), but the liturgical night enables us to take stock of what is truly at stake in it. Do consciousness and what it bears witness to suffice to take account of the relation between man and the Absolute? Or, more radically, is it necessary to speak in terms of consciousness in order to take account of this relation? The urgency of the question becomes clear to us when we recognize that every description of liturgical (in)experience in which man is primordially a conscious being is necessarily an impeded and misleading description, leaving us incapable of thematizing more than a series of negations. This is not to say that such a description is impracticable: we can describe every experience, even inexperience, as the "experience of consciousness," and therefore in terms of intentionality. But, in the present case, this enables us to do no more than verify the presence of whoever is praying or is attempting to pray, and to verify the disappointment occasioned when knowledge coincides with inexperience. The description is impeded because it cannot connect whatever the content of consciousness might be to the presence of God. It is misleading, in particular, because it cannot accede to what it would like to enable us to think, the actual condescension of God toward man, and comes up against man's transcendence toward God as the limit of what it can describe. Inasmuch as it is in the modality of consciousness that man faces God, when he faces him in the night of generalized inexperience, consciousness can only attest to solitude. Only the tension within the man turned toward God can be described, and this tension is sufficient for its own interpretation. No content of consciousness can call God into question. Contrary to the ordinary system of intentionality, where the latter is only intelligible according to the correlative relation linking it to the self-giving [*autodonation*] of phenomena, the aims of consciousness lose every significant link with exteriority. The reign of immanence is established. If consciousness is to dictate the protocols of the interpretation, the liturgical night can only be interpreted as the I closing over upon itself [*comme enferment du moi sur lui-même*].

We should not conclude from this that the concept of consciousness is dispensable because to arrive at that conclusion would entail more than the regional analysis of the liturgical night. But we should conclude that liturgical (in)experience compels us to cast our description in other terms, and reciprocally, regionalizes every description cast in terms of consciousness. Faced with the liturgical aporia of consciousness, only one passageway through remains. The aims of consciousness are without power and have no rights before God. It is also urgent for us to reverse the order of aims, so as to put forward that the life of intentionality, when man faces God, is in fact subordinate to God's intentions for man, traces of which he does not necessarily leave in consciousness. This reversal can be expressed in two fundamental and interrelated ways.

a. Although man's most profound desire is perhaps to "see" God, we must try to understand the sense of these words. I "see," in effect, what appears to me within the horizon of the world. And yet the conditions necessary to seeing are also those which enable me to be seen. I do not only look, and I am not only this capacity to see. I exist objectively, carnally. I have a world, and I also make up part of this world. And, in a way, I make up part of the world of others, who appear to me, let themselves be seen, and I myself also appear to them. Moreover, I can be seen unbeknownst to me. I am exposed to others' sight, but I can give no reason for the looks cast at me. I do not exist solely in the mode of the I [*le moi*] that opens up the perspective by which the not-I manifests itself to it: I am also the potential object of [someone else's] gaze. As metaphorical as it is, the language of sensory perception enables us to comprehend one particular problem. Facing toward the Absolute, man can certainly make himself present, and the limits of this act of presence are those of liturgy. But when every "vision" is refused him who prays (when knowledge is the only foundation), he must in fact learn that he will never, before God, occupy the position of spectator (in the world, in any case, whatever the eschatological destiny of consciousness), and that he first makes himself present in order to open himself up to God. We wish to see: but do we need to learn to be seen, or at least consent to being seen without seeing ourselves? We do not need to elucidate liturgical (in)experience to know that God is not available to us, that he could not be "seen" unbeknownst to him, behind his back, and that we do not enter into a relation with him that would be thinkable without it being on his prior initiative. We do learn from its elucidation, however, that we can make ourselves available to God, and that, if it is necessary to speak of experience in order to interpret liturgy, God will in fact be the subject, and we the object. It is not therefore necessary, in this respect, to require an end to our inexperience.

b. To express the same inversion in other words, it is a question of dislodging the I from every position of centrality, and though the task is not really new, it becomes for liturgy an urgent one. When the humanity of man gives itself to be thought according to the privileged mediation of consciousness (of the concept of consciousness and to what it refers), the ego is the first and focal point. It does not enjoy (or suffer from) a transcendental solipsism. It is not only with things, but also with others [*les autres moi*] that it has immemorially shared its world. This useful stipulation does not deny—the words used suffice to demonstrate this—the fact that it is primordially as an I [*moi*] that the I is thematized, and in particular, that it experiences itself. I am certainly not only an I since I am a you [*toi*]. I am an other for others [*autrui pour autrui*]. Just as I can be looked at, I can be addressed as a you [*tutoyé*].[3] These remarks, whose banality does not deprive them of their importance, cannot rid themselves of a difficulty in which the same banality is easily recognizable: although being an other for others [*autrui pour autrui*], being a you, is not exterior or accidental to the reality of the ego, this does not mean that I also exist in the mode of the You [*Tu*] as originarily as I exist in the mode of the I [*Je*], or more so. Consciousness is not destined to enclose itself within the figures of the "transcendental I" [*le "moi transcendantal"*], of the "pure I," or of the "monadic I." The disturbing possibility is nevertheless present. The I [*le moi*] can content itself with being an I. Now, it is precisely liturgical (in)experience that provides the exemplary case of a decentering or marginalization of the ego. Powerless to bear apodeictic witness to the presence of God, and capable of proving only its own presence, consciousness cannot bear the meaning of liturgy (it can only know the reasons for it). This implies that if liturgy should be a reality distinct from possessing a knowledge of God and of man, this reality will reside in a transgression of every capacity for experience that consciousness can avail itself of, and will not be a function of the I [*Je*]. In the meantime of liturgy, man is deprived of the privileges of the I [*Je*], and cannot withdraw into the stronger conceptions of the self mentioned above ("transcendental I," "pure I," etc.) without them becoming weaker. Those for whom God is a you [*toi*] obviously do not cease to be an I [*moi*]. But before being self-same, man is in the first place, this other than God in whom God finds a you [*toi*]. The relation between the I and the You [*Tu*], of course, only reaches its completion in the reciprocity by which each is at once an I and a You, and even the night does not take away from man the right to address the Absolute as a you even though the Absolute keeps silent. But we would not understand what is played out in the night if we did not perceive the reversal that lets God be affirmed as the only I [*Je*], and by which, to repeat, man becomes nothing but the object of an aim he cannot take measure of in consciousness; and he must satisfy himself with knowing only this.

We will thus speak of a "liturgical disorientation of consciousness," or, to return to a distinction already put forward, of the "soul" putting consciousness into question. Inasmuch as he exists in the mode of consciousness, man cannot liturgically encounter God without finding himself bewildered. His consciousness is no longer the authority before which what is given to him presents itself and submits its credentials; it can only attest to the tension between knowledge and inexperience and can only negatively bear witness to an Absolute who refuses itself entry into its play. The soul would thus be the name of a passivity more essential than all intentional activity—it would be man's pure *exposition* to God. One should not, of course, understand by this an entity superimposed on or underlying consciousness. Consciousness and the soul are not two beings, but two modes of being of the same being—man. Liturgically "disoriented," it is not only in liturgy that consciousness can experience its own limits: liturgy is not alone in possessing the elements of a critique of consciousness; we know other ways of arriving at these limits and, if need be, of thinking them. On the other hand, it does experience its historiality in its purity; indeed, this experience can take place nowhere else. If man does have an eschatological vocation, one might think that the difference between soul and consciousness does not define us definitively. Liturgy proves, however, that it defines us on this side of death; and it warns against every glorification of consciousness—against every theorization of consciousness that does not undergo the critique conducted by the soul. Disoriented, and deprived of the object it would enjoy possession of, consciousness cannot accede to the heart of liturgy, or understand, if and when it is submitted to this critique, that inexperience is a negation that takes the form of a positive standpoint. This reveals what it would not be inappropriate to call a "conversion." Inexperience contradicts the worldly reasons that govern what we are; and should we consent to it, this contradiction takes its place along with all the subversions of our worldliness carried out in God's name. Critique and subversion certainly cannot cause us, in the nonplace of liturgy, to cease to exist in the mode of consciousness. The severity of consciousness and the soul's mutual contradiction can be somewhat pacified if we know what we are "doing" and what exactly we are not doing when we pray. But it cannot be annulled, and it reminds the man reconciled with the Absolute of the *pre*eschatological conditions under which he faces the Absolute. It is not therefore without importance that we have identified this contradiction, for it enables us to discern the crucial problem for the man who decides not to be satisfied with his knowledge, and to turn to face God. But the Absolute, when it undertakes the critique of consciousness, perhaps points out the need here to recognize a preeschatological feature of "experience" as well. The disoriented consciousness is perhaps nearer to the definitive reality of being-in-consciousness than is the self-affirmation of the ego.

§ 57 Being and Act: Elements of a Problematic

We must now pose the question of passivity from a more general perspective. Passivity is obviously a theme and an experience before man commits himself to liturgy and thinks the implications of this choice. It becomes evident to us in two particular ways.

a. In the first place, the being to which modern philosophy gave the name of the "subject" exists objectively in the world. The ego is inseparable from its flesh—it forms one body with it. Interiority is inextricable from exteriority. This is the reason for a certain availability as well as an indisputable vulnerability. Because the I [*le moi*] does not "have" a body, but "is" the body (and correlatively, the body *is* an I), it is absolutely correct to say that I can "see it," "touch it," without seeing or touching the "machine" in which, according to Ryle's formula, a "ghost" is concealed.[4] I do not simply take the hand of someone; I take someone by the hand. Another human being is certainly not available to me in the way a thing is available—*verfügbar*—to me. Things are only ready to hand, or are given over to my field of vision, whereas a human being, a man, say, faces me. Things are only thinkable as other than an I (as nonsubjects), whereas a man is an other self [*moi-même*]. I can control things, but he is the neighbor I must love as myself because, although he is not a copy of me, we both belong to the same humanity. From the fact that what is interior to him, the "spirit," is objectively present to me, it clearly follows that I cannot treat him as an object without violating the meaning of our shared presence in the world, and without in fact violating the meaning of my presence in the world. It follows, however, that he is also ready to hand, and thereby open to possible gestures of friendship or of tenderness, but also to possible acts of violence. No body is pure action and pure initiative. Because I am a carnal being, passivity determines me just as fundamentally as does activity.

b. It might be tempting, then, to withdraw back into the life of consciousness as into a pure sphere of activity, safe in the knowledge that this life is a life of intentionality and—what amounts to the same thing—of intentional activity. But this temptation must be resisted. That one can always describe consciousness in terms of acts (that intentionality always possesses what Husserl calls the "character of an act") is probably not open to doubt. On the other hand, one can doubt that such a description avoids the pitfall of being an abstract formalism and gets to the heart of experience. Although this doubt could be expressed in several ways, we will restrict ourselves to just one. The phenomenology of perception reminds us constantly that, within its domain, priority is given to "originary impressions" affecting consciousness, toward which it does, of course, comport itself in an intentional mode, but which evidently constitutes a passivity or an affect. Intentionality is thus preceded by a self-giving [*autodonation*] that gives rise to it and propels it; consciousness only "goes" to things to the extent that things are imposed on it. One can thus understand that a phenomenology is possible, as in *Being and Time*, where no mention is made of intentionality, and where the ego (or, as it happens, Dasein) is defined purely and simply as disclosure or as an opening, *Erschlossenheit*, onto a world that invests itself in it. This is not to deny that there is intentionality precisely to the extent that there is consciousness. But it forces us to recognize that the intentional life of consciousness is secondary, and that consciousness is itself secondary in relation to the primordial logic by which the world takes hold of the I [*le moi*]. Before consciousness has opened up its vantage point, the world has always already taken possession of man. Conscious activity is thus a responsive activity, an action that corresponds to a passivity.

These elementary and cursory remarks suffice to make passivity intelligible (but who has ever thought that man is pure action in itself?), though they do not, of course, suffice to account for man's liturgical relation to God. Should, however, liturgy also require us to dismantle this framework, they do at least provide us with a conceptual framework in which to distinguish "Being" and "act." Two principal points of interpretation come to our attention.

1. Paragraph b above has already indicated one of them: the most spectacular task of interpretation (and, more importantly, one of the most urgent) is to dissociate two destinies, that of the subject and that of the man confronted by the Absolute. We do not have to demonstrate here—the task falling to the historian of metaphysics—that the subject is mortal and perhaps (who knows?) already dead. But liturgy demonstrates its inability to face God in any case without disintegrating before the paradoxes of inexperience and the ambiguity of experiences incapable of bearing demonstrative witness to God. Faced with these paradoxes and ambiguities, we are moved, not to resign ourselves to failure, but to reorganize the questions, and such a reorganization is not entirely beyond us. It will come as no surprise that the Absolute cannot enter into the subject's field of experience without this leading to impenetrable perplexities: when man defines himself (or is defined) as a subject, the Absolute can only come to experience as a representation of itself, the consequences of which are easily recognizable. The Absolute's rejection of the reign of the subject in liturgy must, then, be carefully examined; and one should see in it, beyond the disorientation of consciousness, the rejection of every equation of Being and—in whatever way one might care to

think it—action. Not only is liturgy inoperative, it dismantles the constitution of subjectivity. And yet, in dismantling it, it forces us to think that the carnal dimension of existence may provide a better paradigm for understanding the relation between man and God than a hermeneutics of interiority ever could. Liturgy compels me to exist objectively before God, and it compels me to recognize in this objectivity a making available. Action is subordinate to passivity—or, more exactly, to its possibility. Man fundamentally exists only within the dimension of exteriority; according to an anthropomorphism that should not escape our notice, he is "in God's hands." It would be by no means aberrant to say that his objectivity is, then, yet more radical than that of the flesh, and is similar to the objectivity of the thing—to say, therefore, that he is in God's hands as clay (which is not conscious of this) is in the hands of the potter.

2. Such comments require us to emphasize the notion of the opening once again. It must be taken up again insofar as it attempts to name something prior to intentionality, something absolutely prior to the life of consciousness. But, from the foundation of conscious life, we progress in liturgy to its methodical bracketing. The world does not, in fact, invest Dasein without Dasein consciously responding to this investment; a primary passivity calls for and underpins the activity of consciousness, and more generally, all the acts by which Dasein makes the world its own. But such is not the case when man faces God, and the "soul" undertakes the critique of consciousness. Man's opening onto the world and the world's taking possession of man are necessarily proved or reflected in the life of consciousness. And yet, if it is undeniable that man's opening to God is also proved and reflected in the life of consciousness (the status of this "proof" and this "reflection" obviously finding themselves significantly modified), the circle that would otherwise unite passivity and action, the opening onto the other and transcendence toward the other, finds itself ruptured here. Passivity *can* assume the form of an affect (and, by implication, conscious activity), but does not *have* to assume it. (One can resolutely side with Hegel against Schleiermacher and note that knowledge here occupies a position of strength that no "feeling of absolute dependence"[5] could ever occupy.) There is good reason to recognize in patience, whose semantic links with suffering [*le pâtir*] are strong, the privileged mode, perhaps temporally insuperable, in which man enters into a relation with the Absolute. The hypothesis of a perpetual patience tells us thus that passivity [*passivité*], in the specific and undoubtedly unique case of liturgical (in)experience, is

not assimilated into the logic of affective life. Man is liturgically available to God, but God is unavailable to him (the greatest mystical experiences do not mean that the wait for God is definitively over). The patience that, in the sphere of conscious experience, undergoes only the time that passes is thus well qualified to manifest the meaning of a passivity that maintains no necessary relation with emotions and affects. This does not mean that the essential always occurs unbeknownst to us. But it does enable us to be more specific. We should reject the notion that action is coextensive with being, a rejection that gives rise to no major difficulty. We should also say, if liturgy manifests what is proper to man, that being-before-God is fundamentally defined in terms of an exteriority more profound than any interiority. It is evident, however, that the liturgical dismantling of the subject and the liturgical disorientation of consciousness are very much experienced in consciousness. How does consciousness experience its inexperience—how does it "live" it? By what logic can it circumvent the constitution of the I [moi] as subject? In order to respond to these questions, we must give an account of the mode of the self in which man relates to Being, which he will inevitably discover in liturgy. We will thus have to speak of the gift.

§ 58 The Primal Scene

Liturgy is a plural experience. Formally conceived, it is the tension between being-in-fact (the empirical I) and being-in-vocation (the eschatological I). Conceived of in terms of its concrete historical site, according to the rationality governing it after Easter, it is the verification of the reconciliation between man and God; the reconciled man knows that he has not simply turned to face the "Highest," the "Almighty" and the "Redoubtable," but to an Absolute that grants peace and alliance. He does not encounter a "frightening and fascinating mystery,"[6] but a benevolence. Moreover, reconciliation, which contains the preeschatological meaning of existence, refers to the promises that disclose its eschatological meaning: the absolute future already exerts a hold over the present, and it would not be unreasonable to say that the liturgical play, in a certain sense, already imitates the realization of the definitive. Finally, there is a final dimension that should not pass by unnoticed: the man reconciled with God, even though he exists within the horizon of his absolute future also recollects his absolute past; liturgy does not speak the language of the eschatological without also speaking that of the originary (though the distinction between the two, admittedly, is not always easy to discern). This is what is to be clarified, and we will do so by suggesting that liturgy symbolizes the perpetuation of the first passivity of all in the present, that which precedes every act of being, the "creation."

A paradox inscribed in the logic of the gift demands our attention here: because the gift (the thing given) is what the giver relinquishes, the giving (the act of giving) carries within itself the conditions of its forgetting. What was given can, of course, retain a trace of the giving, and thus bear witness to the giver. Indeed, it will doubtless be said that it "should" be so. One would probably be right in saying that it is often thus, and that man more or less recognizes and respects the fragile link between the gift and the giving. The fragility of this link must nevertheless be understood. That it can eventually be exposed to ingratitude is not an accidental feature of the gift; it derives from its essence. Although it radically combines the gift and the giver, giving is punctual [*ponctuelle*]. When the gift alone remains, the signification of the gift—being above all the memorial to a giving—always runs the risk of being effaced because the gift is no longer perceived as such, but as a possession. Ingratitude, in this regard, is at once an error of interpretation (it fails to perceive that the gift refers to the giving) and a consequence of the effacement of the giver behind what he has given. One can certainly conceive of gifts that ensure that the giving is unforgettable, and which bear the signature of the giver: such as when I offer a book dedicated to a person or a work of art of which I am the artist. The signification of the gift, in such cases, is imposed objectively and permanently on whoever receives it: and he would be entirely responsible for his own ingratitude. But even in such cases, the disturbing possibility remains: the giver has no right over what he has given; the destiny of the gift lies in the hands of whoever has received it.

It will not come as too great a surprise, then, that the gift par excellence, that of Being, can completely escape our notice, and that man can live and think his relation to Being without recognizing that he exists by virtue of a giving. This forgetting is inscribed in a certain global structure of experience: the world. A reality entirely different from creation,[7] the world must—here—be defined as the denial that Being is a gift; and insofar as being-in-the-world defines the initial logic [*logique initiale*] of existence, this denial is a judgment man has always already made, an a priori. No more than the gift ceases to be a gift when it no longer evokes in me the memory of a giving does man cease to owe what he is to the fact that he is born into the world. Atheism or paganism, whether existential or thematized, can neither kill God nor give underived existence [*aséité*] to the world. But in their transcendental or existential forms, they clearly and distinctly manifest that one can only know [*connaître*] Being as a gift (experientially and theoretically) by undertaking the critique of the world. Must I be what I am? The most clear-cut form that this denial of the gift can assume consists in attributing to man in part the ancient privilege of the *causa sui*. By working or producing, it will be said, it is also myself that I produce. It is no longer in a derived or metaphorical sense that man is said to be a creator. On the contrary, he is the creator par excellence. He is responsible for his own becoming. He does not, of course, provide himself with existence. But he contributes to his own genesis: he no doubt provides himself with the modes of being by which he concretely exists and, perhaps, also with those by which he will exist definitively. The argument is too well known for it to be necessary to develop it here. But it is here that liturgy provides an experiential refutation because it presents itself as the experience in which the laws governing the constitution of the world are transgressed, in which world and earth do not interpose themselves between man and God, in which action (the self taking a stance [*la position de soi*]) finds itself absolutely subordinated to passivity (being given a self [*la reception de soi*]), and in which the creation ceases to be erased. One is thus tempted to say of liturgy that, within its order, it simultaneously verifies the gift (the thing given) and the giving, or, if you prefer, that it links the gift inextricably to the giving.

Can one be present at one's own creation? Common sense compels us to respond in the negative. For me to be present at anything at all, it is necessary for me to be. I cannot be if Being has not been given to me beforehand: I can or should know [*savoir*] that I exist by virtue of a gift, and I can and should know [*connaître*] the giver and keep in mind the giving, though I cannot be witness to it. It does not seem necessary, for the gift to refer clearly to this giving, that the experience of the giving be granted to us. Whoever prays does not come into being in the "act" of praying. On the other hand, these apparent truisms, ontic and logical, cannot conceal the fact that the gift, in this case, is not something that we can possess in the way that we possess some thing (it is only metaphorically that we can "have being"), and that the absolute past in question here is not that of a bygone origin, but actually reigns over the present. The lexicon of the gift and the corollary lexicon of appropriation can be deceptive inasmuch as they suggest the idea of a foreclosed giving, and a gift that continues to exist after a giving, which can only be preserved as a memory. Forgetting the giving is possible in the case of the gift of Being just as it is possible in the case of every gift. But what exactly does one forget in this case? Nothing other than this, which sets this gift apart from all others: that the border between Being and non-Being *actually passes through our present,* and that we cannot face God *without admitting that he continues his benevolent giving.*[8]

We will also speak of "the primal scene" [*"la scène initiale"*][9] to describe the experiential contents proper to liturgy and the recourse to the originary that this implies. Whoever prays keeps in mind not only the divine generosity that has created Being, but also that it has been made available to him and his freedom: the passivity of liturgical (in)experience actually renders him present at his origin. We cannot, of course, think the giving without thinking the reality of the gift — without recognizing, in this case, that the gift that creates Being actually enables us to be, endows us with a "nature," and gives us a temporal future. Liturgy compels us to recognize the reality of the gift to be inextricable from the actuality of the giving. The gift, for whoever prays, is not the trace of the giving, given over as such to our interpretations and our possible misinterpretations, capable of eventually compelling us to recognize the giving. The giving is not signified by it but is re-presented in it. It thus reveals to us somewhat more precisely what we were trying to say before: that at the origin the self is not self-positing but is given to itself, and that the reception of the self never ceases to put our self-positing in question. The "primal scene" thus understood does not haunt liturgy as a past that we have not succeeded in ridding ourselves of and that would obsess us to the point of unhappiness. On the contrary: faced with the restlessness resulting from the threat that nothingness poses Being, it reminds us that the all-powerful divinity does not put man in danger, but keeps him alive. And thus it is a permanent source of gratitude and joy. Once again, however, we must consent to exist by the grace of a giving. We will see that we cannot do this without giving rise to important problems.

§ 59 Abnegation

One question underpins all others here: that of the status of negation. By disorienting consciousness, or by removing the subject from the position he occupies in the modern organization of knowledge, liturgy not only casts doubt over certain theories; it does real violence to the being represented by "consciousness" or the "subject" that now appears incapable of bearing its fate. If it gives us access to what is most proper to man, we take it to be a given that this violence is beneficial. Nevertheless, it does not cease to be a violence, and to collide head-on, in the name of being-in-vocation or of being-of-the-gift, with the resistant reality of being-in-fact. Obviously, this collision has been inevitable from the moment liturgy was thematized as an overdetermination of being-in-the-world. The collision nevertheless assumes a somewhat more disturbing air here. The overdetermination or subversion of facticity actually presented itself to interpretation as a work of man, and paradigmatically as an asceticism, as a deliberate rupturing of the native order of experience. Whoever negates the laws imposed by world and earth by opening up the nonplace of liturgy affirms a knowledge as well as a project. And yet we are confronted here with an entirely other questioning, a questioning that may seem rather odd. In the night of liturgical inexperience, in the disorientation of consciousness, or in the "primal scene" that represents the giving that creates Being, man ceases, in effect, to be answerable for himself and, to all appearances, embodies only an impoverished figure of existence. The inoperativity is radicalized in the passivity of whoever exists in the first place as the object of care of another. The constitution of the nonplace is radicalized by the twofold distance that deprives us of the historical measure of experience without offering the fruition of the eschatological. The joy to which the gift gives rise is only possible for whoever accepts its elementary grammar and lives on a giving that prohibits him from being in possession of himself. Man does not have his own ground within himself. He cannot exist primordially in the mode of substance and confirm the definition that Boethius gave of the "person."[10] But one would hesitate to say that it is easy to base it on the Absolute alone.

To designate the forms in which man consents to such violence, we will speak of "abnegation," and will distinguish several moments within it.

a. Abnegation represents for consciousness in the first place the confirmation of its inexperience. Liturgical inexperience, we have said, is doubly frustrating because it rejects the blurred—but incontestable—pleasures that the "earthly" familiarity of the sacred has to offer, and because it refuses the joy it anticipates in definitive proximity to God. The rationality and coherence of these refusals should not escape us, and liturgical theory has no difficulty in recognizing, when inexperience bluntly contradicts our knowledge [*connaissance*] of the manifest God, the rationality and the coherence proper to preeschatological experience conceived as the interim between the provisional and the definitive. Abnegation knows no more than this (and it is certainly not necessary for it to be able to articulate what it knows in this way). But it does know, on the other hand, how the double frustration can be lived, not in the mode of a rupture, but also, and perhaps first, in the mode of conciliation. Refusing, definitively, to dwell on the earth and renouncing, provisionally, the vision of God, abnegation can thus endure inexperience without fear. It knows [*connaît*] the weight and importance of this negation. It nevertheless accepts that negation reigns over man's confrontation with God today, and that man can survive this negation because it does not negate the proximity and the condescension of God. Thus, and to the same extent, it accepts that the limits of consciousness are not those of the preeschatological relation between man and the Absolute.

b. Abnegation must be understood, then, as a radical form of making oneself available, and as a sanction for the liturgical dismantling of the "subject." Whatever the history of the subject and the chapter it represents in the history of metaphysics, one point is incontestable: this chapter bears witness to a permanent possibility that should perhaps be understood as a permanent temptation; the identification of man with the subject is not a risk that can be imputed to theories alone, but is inscribed in the logic of man's relation to himself. Because doctors of philosophy have no monopoly over abnegation, those who decide not to exist in the mode of the subject are obviously not required to know the theoretical stakes of their act. But because this gesture is thinkable, doctors of philosophy should not fail to recognize its importance. Abnegation therefore accepts that the Absolute, once man is liturgically turned toward it, takes away its right to embody the figures of humanity afforded him in modernity. (Our intention is not, of course, to represent a "postmodern" position, the concept of which, if it exists, remains enigmatic to us.) By thus accepting the violence the Absolute does to man, abnegation constitutes a violence that man inflicts on himself. The negation is compelled to take a stance; abnegation includes within itself the taking of a stance, and adopts a way of being in which the man who makes himself available to God situates himself nearer to what is most proper to him than the subject ever could: that is why liturgy does not condemn man to nonsense. The negation must also nevertheless be accepted for what it is—a negation: that is what abnegation shows itself capable of when it compels the I [*le moi*] to exist solely as the object of the divine condescension over which consciousness has no control or—what amounts to the same thing—compels the I to be nothing but its opening to God.

c. We must now speak of the will [*le vouloir*]. There can be no doubt that whoever prays wants [*veuille*] to pray, that liturgy is born of a knowledge [*un savoir*] that solicits our freedom, and that it is also of the order of a project. The paradox, however, is that the will [*la volonté*] grants access to liturgy, that it is itself omnipresent there (in the form of an intention that directs our attention to the Absolute, or to its future coming), but that this will is itself deprived of any hold over the Absolute. Abnegation does not wish to put an end to the will because it would thereby lose itself in [*s'abîmerait... dans*] incoherence. But it is an absolutely exemplary case of a will totally submitted to the will of another, and which opens up the space of liturgy as nothing but an empty space. The will brings into being [*fait être*] (and this holds true if my will is my own just as it does if I submit my will to the will of another, or, if I so choose, to the will of God): it is not in the first place the will to will, but the will to do. Abnegation, on the other hand, brings nothing into being. It produces nothing. It maintains man at the disposal of the God it knows to be benevolent, without requiring this benevolence to have been proved within the element of experience, while accepting the play of negation that affects experience in the present. It lets be. And over what it lets be, it refuses to exercise any power.

§ 60 The Will to Powerlessness

A brief debate on the nature of the will is unavoidable here, a debate with the philosopher for whom man is, above all, a willing animal, and in whom this thought on man culminates with blinding clarity—Nietzsche. In the concept of the "will to power," Nietzsche wants nothing other than to bring all will to light. The will to power is not one will among others, coexisting with the will to do good or the will to truth, for example. Rather, it is the will as such, independent of the objectives that might be assigned it, the will such that we cannot ignore its secret without ignoring who we are (what life is) and what the meaning of Being is. The will wills for this or that. It provides itself with objects. It is a relation to the world in which it assigns itself goals. But beyond this, it is the essence of this relation, and the very essence of the self. The will is ipseity. It is the substance, the foundation that governs the grammar of existence. What, in truth, it wills for, above and beyond the diversity of its intentions, is nothing other than "power," the always more vibrant positing of itself, the self's always-being-more. Power, such as Nietzsche understands it, and despite the unfortunate expressions to which the theory can give rise, is neither spectacular violence nor the execution of a force or a power. Although it does, of course, have its masterwork, the creation of values, it has no privileged domain (therefore it exists in no domain it would abandon in favor of another). It is "simply" the first and last word on life—"the grounding character of beings," as Heidegger's commentary puts it.[11] The will to power is thus the constant for which every other faculty, reason being chief among them, is nothing but the variable. The will to power is the power of the will, in the service of a boundless affirmation of the self.

A corollary follows from this, however. Although the will to power is what is essential, the essential is what man can deny. Against the empire of the will to power, the "will to powerlessness" can rise up, which constitutes, if one must take the coherence of the Nietzschean text seriously, a metaphysical suicide in due form, for which Christian experience provides (for the "people") the complete example. The will to powerlessness—submission to values such as they are and the incapacity to will new values, the *ressentiment*[12] that negates the possibilities open to man, the refusal to be the author of oneself—denies the originary rhythm of life, and its negation is devoid of any real affirmation. It is not a nonwill—but it is very much the nothing [*le rien*] that it wills. It wills the death of man, the death of life, and will not resuscitate them. It promises another world, and provides but a semblance of one. Its work [*œuvre*] is, therefore, indistinguishable from nihilism.

This provocative theory cannot go unanswered, and the answer comes in the form of a question. Are we forced to choose between the alternatives of the will to power and the *ressentiment* that leads to nihilist negation? Nietzsche knows no beyond to the will to power (which would be a beyond to Being). It and it alone is constant. Every value that claims to elude its logic of life would succeed only in consigning itself to a logic of death. Having sunk its roots into the entire intellectual and religious past of the West, it alone can survive the "most disturbing of all guests" who "knock at the door"[13] in the last years of Nietzsche's philosophical activity. The contradiction between the axiomatics governing the Nietzschean text and those governing the interpretation of liturgy is too fundamental for the latter to refute the former without running the risk of being a platitude or naive. The will to power cannot be thought through to the end without also thinking through the "death of God," the "eternal recurrence of the same," the "overman" and "justice." In view of the most consistently contradictory view that Christian discourse and experience has ever faced, one can obviously take none of the knowledge on which liturgy is grounded for granted: this knowledge must be left to display all its claims to truth, which is not the intention of the present analysis. Let us, however, make one point to contest the notion that the will to power maintains a relation of absolute antagonism with nihilism. What, in effect, does the will to power will? It wills the triumph of life, it is life taking a stance and willing itself—and this triumph is guaranteed, against the obvious objection of death, by the theory of the eternal recurrence of the same. One cannot, however, help noticing that this triumph is theoretically costly because the will to power in fact annihilates all that does not fall within its control. God, values, the truth—all this can perish at the hand of nihilism because none of it is essential. But, in positing that none of this is essential, and that the will to power is alone fundamental, it is also at the hand of the will to power that all of this is allowed to perish. Nietzsche had foretold two centuries of darkness or of the "desert."[14] It remains for us to patiently await another one of these centuries, and only the will to power can enable this patience to be fruitful. But is the reduction of the human to the will to power itself entirely free of complicity with nihilism? The will to power is, of course, defined as pure affirmation and pure self-positing; and it is for this reason, because it is the power of "life," that it is the ultimate secret of Being and of becoming, and must not be held to account before any other authority, in such a way that all but it can collapse. Because it has taken away man's right to truly be whatever the will to power is not, one fact remains, however. The will to power alone can establish itself as the only recourse in the face of nihilism because it has annihilated every other form of recourse and, notably, every other form of willing.

We should not fail to notice the true—theoretical and experiential—position of strength that the will to power manages to occupy. The mere mention of power should not alarm us. The will to power is not a will to war and brutality. It is to assent to life and to the self and is man's consent to his nature. This should tell us that it is a question here of a will all of whose projects, from the lowliest to the most grandiose, are in the last resort projects of the self. The objective aims the will to power sets itself are secondary; its true task is man's perpetual engendering of himself, and when the time comes (because man attests only imperfectly to the reign of the will to power), of the overman. The will to power is a will-to-be and an ability-to-be; the two overlap because it wills (only) what life itself "wills": to persevere, to affirm itself, and to grow. It is at this point, in light of Nietzsche, that the reasons behind abnegation become clear. It is thus a question, for Nietzsche as for us, of the future of man. The terms of the question are, however, entirely different. In liturgy, it is a question of an absolute future and of the modes in which we wait for it, and of the *eschaton*, whereas Nietzsche's doctrine of eternal recurrence precludes every eschatology. But, for us as for Nietzsche, in linear and historical time as in cyclical time, man is defined by what he is not yet; he is what must be "overcome," as Nietzsche says, or what still awaits its accomplishment. Can man then be the master of his own becoming? Or must this future be thought within the order of the gift? Inscribed within the will to power, the humanity of man is for Nietzsche nothing other than the faculty of self-transcendence, the being-more that man confers on himself. (It will not be doubted, moreover, that Nietzsche is thinking of a genuine dimension of the will—his own *worldly* destiny.) Abnegation can only appear, then, as the misinterpretation committed by he who refuses to provide himself with his own future, and who chooses death over life. Appearances can be deceptive, however, and they deceived Nietzsche himself. The reconciled man has, of course, not only refused to preside over his own future (which does not exempt him of responsibility for his own actions), but also over his present. However, the liturgical context in which this refusal unfolds in exemplary fashion reveals the affirmations that underpin it. Thus abnegation wills more than the will to power wills. It does not bring into being; it lets be. But in letting be, it puts itself at the mercy of a God to whom it relates through promises, and who promises more than the immanent reality of "life." It is the witness to and the index of an incontestable powerlessness: man can neither reconcile himself with God nor provide himself with his own absolute future. This powerlessness is nevertheless a forceful critique of the will to power. Capable of verifying that the gift of reconciliation has already been made, abnegation can verify that, even on this side of death, man can do more than "live." It is thus entitled to ground itself in the commitments that have bound it to the Absolute since Easter, and to make intelligible a future that the will to power cannot simply think and control. Abnegation is eschatological expectation; it knows that the question of man's future is a real question; and it knows the logic of the *eschaton*; and that enables it not simply to contradict Nietzsche, but to respond to him genuinely. All that remains is to let the implications of this response unfold. We will do so by introducing a concept into the discussion: we will speak of "dispossession" or "disappropriation," or indeed of "*kenosis*." Does man accede to what is most proper to him (preeschatologically) by ridding himself of what is (natively) most proper to him? This is what we must now attempt to determine.

Toward a Kenotic Treatment
of the Question of Man

Before turning once again to the elucidation of the next to last realities, let us first reexamine the initial conditions of experience.

§ 61 Being-in-the-World and Appropriation

Since a negation [*disappropriation*] remains unintelligible insofar as what it negates is not understood, we cannot economize here with a brief interpretation of appropriation if we are to discern in it an elementary trait of being-in-the-world, understood in its broadest sense. The world, as we have said, is presented to experience in the form of two antagonistic but correlative perspectives. If we follow *Being and Time*, I am not born into the world as into a homeland; I am not originarily at home there; and even if I do not come from elsewhere, my residence is assigned to me there as though it were a foreign land. If we follow the philosopher's later texts, it can present itself to me as an ancestral land, a soil, the dwelling place in which my place has been immemorially prepared for me. The dialectic of "world" and "earth" cannot conceal that in the one case as in the other, whether my existential condition is that of the not-at-home or of an autochthon, the I [*le moi*] cannot be present in the world without existing in the mode of appropriation, on two principal levels. (a) The world does not first present itself only as appearance and as spectacle, as the not-I simply manifested to the I. It can delight us, give rise to contemplation and to theoretical interest in it. But it also gives itself to us in the form of things that solicit not only the gaze that contemplates them, but also the hand that caresses them and can take hold of them, use them, transform them—make them its own. Having and property, in the most common sense of the term, derive from taking possession, and constitute a native way of being, a way we neglect to think at our peril. This is said simply for the record. (b) But there is more. In man's relation to the beings who populate his world, a wholly other appropriation to that of having this or that thing within one's grasp is in fact played out, and which must be conceived as the constitution of an "own world" ["*monde propre*"] or as dwelling [*habitation*]. Since man is not defined by his being present in one place rather than another (because it is essential that we are in the world but accidental that we find ourselves in Cambridge or in Paris), it is in fact the world itself that man takes possession of, it is the world he inhabits [*habite*] when he takes possession of a place to make of it his dwelling place [*demeure*]. The world, need it be said once more, is not a being, and cannot be something we possess in the way we possess a thing. It becomes, then, "my" world in a sense that is not simply approximate, through the mediation of the relation we maintain with things. An animal does not inhabit [*habite*] the world: it inhabits [*habite*] its territory. Man's privilege, by contrast, is to have no real territory. It is, of course, in a particular location that he makes the world his own by building houses or by surveying the land for them. But we would scarcely understand what he is doing if we failed to perceive that the particularity—this house, this land—refers to a universality, and that it is always the world itself, the world common to us all, that we appropriate for ourselves when we inhabit [*habitons*] the places given to us or that we provide for ourselves. Once again, this is said simply for the record.

§ 62 Death and Disappropriation

The important objection that derives from the unquestionable link between being-in-the-world and being-toward-death is unavoidable. We have no reason to doubt that appropriation is an essential characteristic of our presence in the world. Long before becoming a problem of political economy, property is an existential reality greater than any right of possession guaranteed by a code of law will ever be. We nevertheless meet with the absolute limit to all appropriation once we introduce death into the debate. We meet, of course, with the proof that we make the world and the things available in it our own only through our existence conceived as a reprieve—which is utterly trivial (and, therefore, does not require the services of a philosopher for it to be brought to light); but we also meet, in particular, with the proof that nonpossession affects man's relation to himself—which is less trivial. Man can face death as the only eschatology, or he can face it by trusting in the promises made at Easter (or in yet other ways, by grounding it in other reasons for hope), but the difference between them is great. But, in either case, death is given to interpretation as what cannot be called "mine" without extreme stipulations. The dignity of the *ars moriendi* is not open to question; and if one could learn to die, one could speak of "my" death, and one could say, "I will live it, and perhaps it will provide me with the final opportunity to be and act as man, with perhaps the opportunity to be and act as supremely human."[1] On the other hand, the ancient charm of the art of dying, and its recent reappearance, cannot conceal the precariousness of the strategies of appropriation they set to work. Man must confront his death, not as a final judgment nothingness makes on Being, but as the final judgment on every self-positing and on the self's every appropriation. We wish to live our death, and can perhaps recognize in it, beyond it being the final empirical fact, our ultimate possibility. But, if it is obvious that I can give meaning to my death, or decide to die (even though, just as obviously, I am not obliged to give a meaning to my death, and even though the circumstances of my death can very much prevent it since not everyone is given the time in which to live his death), then it certainly does not follow that self-positing makes the negation secondary, or that death is finally "mine" because I would still exercise some ultimate power of appropriation over it. The art of dying, then, comes up against a dispossession that exceeds every strategy of mastery; and it cannot therefore assert its rights while simultaneously acknowledging that death remains the clearest figure of what cannot be mastered in the world: it cannot be promised to anyone that he will live *his* death[2]—and whoever wishes to live *his* death actually deludes himself if he does not know the a priori restrictions governing this desire.

§ 63 Nonappropriation Prior to Death

A question arises, then. Do the logics of appropriation conceal a more primitive fact? Man's grip over beings and the constitution of an "own world" are primary on account of being fundamental structures of experience. We may have chosen to take up residence somewhere in the world, but we have not chosen to be the sorts of beings who dwell in the world. We do not appropriate everything, but we cannot exist without participating in the play of taking possession: our participation in this play is not a right we may or may not avail ourselves of, but a transcendental necessity [*contrainte*] to which we are subject. The unquestionable link uniting being-in-the-world and being-toward-death nevertheless suggests that this play is open to misinterpretation if we do not recognize precisely what is involved here; it suggests that man's condition is that of *poverty*. My death is not thus what will dispossess me, but what already dispossesses me today. It is not only the absolute limit of all presence in the world; it imposes a fundamental condition on this presence. In the conceptual figure of poverty, we are thus required to think the threat it poses to all that we "have" or attempt to have and, finally, how every attempt to set this threat aside is doomed. A properly ontological sense is thus substituted for the economic meanings normally attributed to poverty. Ordinarily defined in terms of a shortage that does not alter the humanity of man, which leaves what he is intact, poverty appears to us here as radical destitution. Hitherto unthought, or almost unthought throughout the entire history of philosophy, it takes its place here among the primordial facts. It is only at the hour of his death or at that of his birth that man appears *entirely* in the guise of the destitute, as one to whom every right of possession is denied or as one who has yet to appropriate anything. This poverty must be deciphered, as a watermark, in every experience the I has of itself and in its relation to the world: we would misunderstand the spontaneity presiding over every appropriation if we did not allow it to manifest the nonpossession to which it responds, and without which we would be unable to ascertain its true meaning and to grasp the real problem.

Here again, it is clearly a question of an ambiguity in the very fabric of being-in-fact. Whether we speak of man's place in terms of "world" or "earth," death always stalks the present in which man dwells in the world or on the earth and reminds him of the fragility (the ultimate "vanity") of all appropriation. Nonpossession has the first and last word here. One can always recognize the face of divertissement, then, in the control we exercise over things, in the constitution of the "own world," in every dwelling place and in all property. It should come as no surprise that what gives rise to divertissement, or at least to its risk, is nothing other than the native and inescapable characteristic of our presence before things and ourselves. The inextricability of being-in-the-world and being-toward-death grants the final victory to disappropriation over appropriation, but the mortal's destiny, which is to exist in the world only by dwelling in it and making it his own, is not called into question as a result. Although destitution's final victory denies neither the present reality of possession nor the native character of taking possession, those who participate in the play of appropriation should still recognize the irony of knowing the fate of all appropriation, even if they cannot not partake in it. The transcendental is thus shrouded in ambiguity. But this is not to suggest that this ambiguity cannot be dissipated: the critique of appropriation, though theoretical, is not without concrete implications.

§ 64 Asceticism and Dispossession

Thus we will speak of "voluntary poverty" and of what it gives us to think. Just as man is the only animal capable of keeping vigil, as we have said, he is undoubtedly the only animal capable of challenging his participation in the play of appropriation. He is certainly not the only animal capable of participating in this play, however: dogs and cats participate, as do all other animals who know how to take possession of their territory (in the absence of having a world, in the strict sense), to make things and places their own. One does not, however, expect the cat or dog to refuse possession, even if one can expect their behavior to include giving [*des conduites de don*], noticeably to their offspring. Cats and dogs will never deprive themselves of anything, and will never impose a lack on themselves out of instinct (even though the absence of its master can deprive a dog or, more rarely, a cat of its appetite); nothing can drive them to do so; and because they do not live within the horizon of their death, it must be said that they perhaps know how to possess better and more surely than does man: there is nothing that can challenge their capacity for appropriation in the here and now, on the one hand, but they are utterly incapable of subverting the native conditions of their relation to things, on the other. But man is capable of such subversion; although it is paradoxical, it is not entirely untrue to say that he describes who he is more precisely when he thinks of himself as poor than when he avails himself of his right to property. Property rights do, of course, exist, and the benign practice of economic philosophy that consists in founding them — or, if you prefer, in devoting itself to grounding them in the very being of man — will not have been entirely in vain. They nevertheless efface themselves before the peculiar right represented by those who are not content to simply see the irony in the links between "being" and "having," and who attempt to disqualify such links, or at least to marginalize them. No authority, it is true, will ever compel us to desire poverty, understood according to its economic reality. The work of dispossession already accomplished by our death gives rise to a suspicion concerning all appropriation (does not the desire to possess betray a refusal to die or a forgetting of death?), but it does not simply compel us to take leave, insofar as is possible, of the logics of appropriation. The speculative coherence of voluntary poverty and the powerful demonstration it is capable of should not be lost on us, however. Alone in having a world, man can also subvert the situation he natively occupies in the world. This subversion is a violence, and this violence an ascesis, the implementation of a project rather than a spontaneous action. What is at stake in it is, in any case, primordial. Whoever desires poverty (and one imagines that his relation to appropriation may be reduced but never annulled) wants nothing other than to accede to the truth of his being. We may all know that we are, in fundamentally ontological terms, poor: we need only make a small effort to reflect on this to know it. We all live this knowledge if we accept that our death challenges our every relation to possession. The freely made choice not to possess, or at least to possess less, is more revealing still. It proves that there is no equivocation between the ontological and the economic senses of poverty, that fundamental ontology can be translated into ways of being, into an ethos, and into concrete gestures that break with every kind of divertissement. It thus proves that nonpossession defines man more primitively than does his participation in the play of appropriation. And it proves—in particular—that this more primitive determination can govern the experience we have of ourselves and of the world.

§ 65 Liturgy and Dispossession

To allow the reasons underlying dispossession to unfold more fully, we must put these cursory remarks within the liturgical context. It is not necessary to thematize man's relation to the Absolute for voluntary poverty to present itself to our freedom as a rational choice— and, even without making this choice, for us to be able to recognize in it, to a greater or lesser extent, a path we can follow that is faithful to what we are. Because it lays man bare, because it annuls all that can blur the links between being-in-the-world and being-toward-death, and because it manifests our rejection of logics that we sense, whether dimly or clearly, can alienate us, voluntary poverty gives itself to be thought and can seduce us, despite the violence that constitutes it. Poverty is the way one ought to live [*la plus juste manière d'habiter*] in the world and to be oneself. We do not lack the conceptual means to state that this choice is, at bottom, the choice of the philosophic life, of life lived in truth. But the Absolute may need to enter into the discussion (and into the topic of experience) for its theoretical elegance to cease to fascinate us from afar and somewhat abstractly as a proposition, whose correctness is easily recognized, but to which one may be wary of consenting in practice. What is the liturgical meaning of poverty? The question concerns an eschatological symbolism, and consequently, the preeschatological hold that this symbolism exerts on man's everyday relation to the world and to things.

a. We will speak first of a reduction. From within the topo-logic without which we cannot think who we are, liturgy appears as a certain bracketing of world and earth. Whoever prays obviously does not absolve himself of all the laws that transcendentally govern the play of being-in-the-world: we pray here or there and build churches and chapels; and even if it simultaneously denies the atheism of the world and the paganism of the earth, liturgy is nevertheless a way of being there and of dwelling in places. There is no need to return to the paradoxical order that presides over this way of being (to the constitution of the liturgical "nonplace"). It is important for our purposes, however, to emphasize that he who prays leaves many things behind him, starting with the profanity of the world and the numinous secrets of the earth, as well as the dialectics that constitute history; he also takes leave of every relation with the real in which appropriation is an essential moment. Strictly speaking, those who liturgically face the Absolute neither have anything nor can take possession of anything. Nothing they could have in their possession contributes to the expression of their identity, and they are offered nothing they could take possession of. There is no question of lording over things; man is laid bare, and because his act of presence does nothing but put him at the mercy of gifts he can only patiently wait for, it must be said that he is—definitively—poor. Because it is an entr'acte, liturgy does not annul what it brackets: the world is all that is available to us within it. It must nevertheless be seen that the figure of the disappropriated man gives itself to be thought as an eschatological destiny, and represents what is fundamental and constant.

The "liturgical reduction" does not kill man (even if it is clear enough that more than one certainty on the humanity of man we believed ourselves to possess is no longer tenable). On the contrary, it proves that man can survive even though the ties uniting him to the world have come undone, when nothing is really at his disposal anymore and every appropriation becomes unimaginable. If it is true that liturgical experience enables man to accede to what is most proper to him, then it would be true to say that the liturgical reduction brackets what is inessential—and it would be natural to desire that this bracketing exceed the limits of the liturgical entr'acte, and that a way of life be established from which appropriation would be, insofar as it is possible a priori, disbarred. The liturgical reduction opens up a space in the world where appropriation loses its importance. But it also provides the question of voluntary poverty with a basis, and enables it to be posed with increasing urgency and in different terms.

b. To the (possibly atheistic) asceticism that recognizes in poverty, as a choice entered into freely, the possibility of arriving at a more genuine experience of the world and of oneself, we cannot oppose the asceticism underlying liturgy term for term. But, in the one as in the other, the desire for asceticism suspects the logic of appropriation of being a logic of divertissement, and wishes to establish a more primitive—more primordial, more genuine—commerce with the real. And, in the one as in the other, this commerce can only be acquired ascetically in the violent but fragile stance taken by those who set themselves up against the order of the world, or in any case against its everyday order, though they cannot institute or reinstitute ways of being that put an end to the ambiguities of possession. What separates them is nevertheless more important than the shared interests that unite all those for whom the humanity of man is a question of rupture, of contesting the native grammar of experience, for two reasons as important as they are obvious: because voluntary poverty, when undertaken for liturgical reasons, has no status other than anticipatory, and because, once again, it has no other aim than that of subordinating being-in-the-world to being-before-God. Two points in need of interpretation arise. (1) Wherever it is practiced (within the monastic community, in eremitism, in secular life, etc.), voluntary poverty is not content to be a derivative of liturgy—of worship—that furnishes it with the pure example of disappropriated existence: it is, itself, liturgical. Every decision to live in poverty harbors a critique of divertissement: but this critique, which introduces poverty into everyday existence, is a critique of the greatest divertissement, that which forgets God. It is also clearly a question of knowing that death judges everything man possesses. But it is first a question of making liturgy coextensive with life by negating the structures of experience that prevent being-in-the-world from sheltering liturgy. The poor man thus marginalizes himself in a world where the spontaneity of appropriation founds the right to property, and this marginalization enables him to attend to what is essential. In rejecting the solicitations made to him by a reality given over to appropriation, he gains freedom: the Absolute can become his sole concern, and his presence before the Absolute can subordinate every other presence. (2) One should not conclude from this however that voluntary poverty is an act of eschatological transfiguration, although it clearly imitates the *eschaton* by letting the meaning with which all ceremonial worship is imbued reflect back upon it. By taking hold of a primitive sense of the humanity of man once again, poverty also manifests how being-in-vocation breaks with being-in-fact: it bespeaks the accomplishment of humanity, though only in an anticipatory mode. Indeed, in all likelihood, the force of an affirmation made in this anticipatory mode would not be understood if we failed to recognize that voluntary poverty, whatever the "theoretical splendor"[3] of the experiences in which it is inscribed, does violence to the provisional reality of our humanity without bringing about its definitive reality. Desired in itself and for ontological reasons alone, poverty can truly claim to embody the definitive: the poor man lives life itself; he is someone bereft of all masks, who can neither deceive himself nor anyone else on the meaning of his presence in the world in the time that leads him to death. And yet the poverty that has its roots in liturgical experience makes no such claim. It can take disappropriation a little further by inventing language games from which every possessive pronoun in the first person singular is excluded, by refusing to exercise the right to private property, and by practically refusing to dwell in the world (as we saw in the case of the *xeniteia*). But however great the distance it establishes from it, voluntary poverty is always a preeschatological disruption of the world's order that is played out in it (and not the apodeictic emergence of the definitive Kingdom); being-in-fact will never cease to bear on being-in-vocation. We should take note of what is initially evident straight away: that it is not enough to solemnly wish for poverty in order to escape the logics of appropriation once and for all and to build a heavenly city this side of death. It should be noted, however, that he who desires poverty for liturgical reasons knows that he does not thereby come to possess his absolute future, and that his marginalization does not remove him from the world. The a priori rules governing the constitution of the "own world" are not abolished by even the most severe poverty, and man's conflict with appropriation is an infinite conflict. It must also be acknowledged that whoever desires poverty takes up a position—he clearly states that God alone "suffices" for him—but also that this position is inextricable from a negation for which no coming to fruition of the definitive proximity of God can truly compensate. One can choose to be poor for numerous reasons—but in choosing to cut his ties to the world, whoever makes this choice takes up a strong position only in theoretical terms. Whoever refuses to take advantage of the availability of things is not alone in knowing, though he does know it a little better than others, that the Absolute is not available to him, and that his absolute future is intelligible only within the order of the promise. But insofar as the promise has yet to be delivered on, he can appear only as someone in a state of deficiency; the man reconciled with the Absolute can only appear to us in the scandalous guise of the belittled man.

§ 66 Mad about God/God and Madness

Madness must also be taken into consideration, not so as to claim that ascetic poverty and the pathways associated with it[4] are irrational (we have seen that these are not lacking in reason), but so as to speak of their extravagant rationality. There is certainly an ascetic moment in all liturgical gestures. Because liturgy is not a dimension of being-in-the-world, and because man cannot face God without thwarting the a priori domination the world exercises over him, no one is born in possession of what is most proper to him. We do not gain access to ourselves without doing violence to the initial conditions of experience or, at best, without dissipating the chiaroscuro in which they maintain the eschatological meaning of ipseity. (And, as we have said, there is no need to question liturgy in order to make asceticism intelligible.) But if whoever refuses to concede to the logic of inherence the right to define him exhaustively is required to break with it, asceticism justifiably makes us anxious when it confronts us with gestures that derive from no universal requirement. The ascetic will doubtless account for his supererogatory acts by reminding us that they belong to the logic of being-in-vocation, and that one cannot speak the language of vocation in any meaningful way without also speaking that of the indivisible singularity of destinies. One can also expect the humility of an admission from him: the most profound break with the order of the world is not the privilege of whoever sets himself up most conspicuously against that order, but of whoever can do so in the strictest incognito, in the Kierkegaardian experience of the "Knight of Faith." On the other hand, neither this reminder nor this admission can make the challenge of ascetic extravagation [*outrance*] meaningless, and, in truth, neither can prevent us from perceiving what is at stake beyond the fate of the "individual" or the "unique" and which are important for the entire *disputatio de homine*. The problem of asceticism is one of literalism, and the problem of its interpretation lies in the suspicions surrounding every literalism. From the fact that nonpossession defines man (and, a fortiori, whoever encounters the Absolute) more profoundly than any relation of appropriation and possession, the ascetic infers that he cannot live a life faithful to its essence without a literal rejection of property. From the fact that world is not man's definitive homeland, he may infer that life faithful to its essence cannot be lived without a literal rejection of all worldly dwelling. Everything is amenable to his negations. It is easy to see how, with the hope for a new "land" where divine generosity will restore a "creation" that is today destroyed, the ascetic may attempt what we know he cannot completely accomplish—the renunciation of all participation in the play of the world, or at the least, the reduction of his participation in this play to the bare minimum. The objection will be raised—and quite justifiably so—that such a renunciation or attenuation does not really represent a set of facts the objectivity of conduct could serve to guarantee. But, beyond the somewhat banal validity of this objection, one point should not escape our attention: ascetic extravagation makes a transgression visible that, though certainly not existing in virtue of this visibility, does not exist in its entirety unless it is capable of manifesting it. Despite the strangeness of these gestures, and even though they are not universally required of everyone who wishes to encounter God, the ascetic does, in fact, act on behalf of everyone and as everyone's proxy. The spectacular marginality of whoever wishes to refuse possessions, a place to live, and so on does no more than express in particularly concrete form the marginality that would, in any case, affect anyone subordinating his being-in-the-world to his being-before-God. It may be that the literalism of the ascetic provides a naive interpretation of this subordination. But naïveté can be right. And without it, we might remain unaware of precisely what we are doing when we decide to exist face-to-face with God. Ascetic extravagation is not significant because it exceeds what everyone is strictly bound to do if they wish to lead a life that pleases God: it is significant because it pushes to the limit a logic that is already present, even if no more than discreetly implicit, as soon as man is willing to encounter the Absolute and the Absolute alone "suffices" for him. We do not need the ascetics' extravagation for liturgical disappropriation to be thinkable; nor do we need them for it to be part of our experience. They do, however, provide us with the best mirror in which to perceive what is ultimately at stake in this experience—that, in order to exist face-to-face with God, man may dress in clothing closely resembling the lunatic's.

We are not, of course, suggesting, by using the vocabulary of madness, that the Absolute alienates whoever consents to radical disappropriation, or that the experience of disappropriation equates to that of the collapse of the I (but see § 71 below). Because the French language affords us the distinction, we should perhaps speak of the "fool" [∂u "fol"] rather than of the "lunatic" [∂u "fou"]. The lunatic's madness is fated whereas the fool's is an act of freedom. To a figure of pure passivity is opposed a choice, or at least the possibility of consent. These basic truths, which it would serve no purpose to elaborate on here, obscure a profound symbolic solidarity, however. Within the symbolic order, both the lunatic and the fool bear witness to their wounds. The fool negates his belonging to the world, while the lunatic's insanity prevents him from happily participating in human society, but one should not equate this negation and this prevention. (The fool, for example, may with others decide to live a life that is not of this world, but the lunatic is always alone.) On the other hand, one can, and indeed should, recognize a real proximity between them. The fool's extravagation and his uncalled-for conduct demonstrate a project of transgression, but the transgressor assumes the characteristics of the mutilated human, poorer than any other, who renounces his claim over the world without enjoying the rights afforded by the definitive and the transfigured reality of the Kingdom. The fool's experience has its own eschatological horizon, which alone enables us to account for it, while the lunatic's experience is obviously devoid of any such horizon. But, before providing an account of it, and in order to provide a better one, we should leave ourselves prey to its disturbing effect: toward this end, we should recognize that the fool's madness is just as much a symbolic representation of death as is the lunatic's. If we leave aside the liturgical justifications he puts forward, the fool is the neighbor of the lunatic —

they are perhaps even indistinguishable, the fool being nothing but a lunatic for any way of thinking that does not recognize the eschatological and what is at stake in it, and (which is more important for our purposes here) for any way of thinking in which the *eschaton* is conceivable only as men dwelling peaceably in the world. From the vantage point provided (or perhaps epitomized) by absolute knowledge and the reconciled existence possessing this knowledge, what reasons for the fool's extravagation could be said to be opposed to Hegelianism? To questions it would be scarcely worth developing here, we will respond by discerning in the conduct of the fool a certain touch of humor.

§ 67 The Humor of the Fool

Who, indeed, is better placed than the humorist to undertake the critique of experiences said to fully encompass the definitive truth of the I? There are, of course, others who could do so. We did not need the fool's experiences to recognize the aporias in Hegelian eschatology, and it only intervenes at the conclusion of the interpretation of the penultimate realities (or rather at the conclusion of an initial sketch). But this intervention is not simply redundant. We do not need the fool to know that, although man can live in peace with God on this side of death, it does not simply follow that, after Good Friday, the world appears to us as a homeland we have finally been granted. Even though he has no new theory to offer us, the fool reminds us (or, perhaps, teaches us) that theories are not simply refuted at the theoretical level: they have practical implications it may also be important to refute. It is here that humor appears in the strange face-to-face encounter in which the "fool," who, from the perspective of the "sage" (to use the name Kojève gave to one possessing absolute knowledge) formally embodies a bygone figure of consciousness, suspects the sage himself of embodying only a provisional moment in the history of spirit, a moment, moreover, that would not bear reliable witness to the definitive. The fool certainly does not deny the wisdom of the sage or what constitutes it. He does not deny that the appropriation of the "saving grace of the Cross" no longer permits us to live in the atheistic "world" or the pagan "earth" of the beginning, and enables us to enjoy proximity to the divine. He does not invalidate the theological kinds of knowledge [*connaissances théologiques*] that constitute the sage's joy. He does not, finally, deny that morality, when truly understood, has real eschatological implications. But to

wisdom thus delimited, whose true grandeur we could not fail to recognize [*méconnaître*], is there really no beyond? That is what the fool's
extravagation absolutely refuses to concede, for it is such a beyond
that it claims to symbolize and anticipate. The fool does not—nor
should he—attempt to pass himself off as the representative of
humanity definitively at one with itself; nor does he propose another
paradigm to "wisdom" by which we could think a transubstantiation
of our present into an absolute future. Disappropriation, and everything related to it in the ascetic project, confers no right to claim the
eschaton to be realized. The fool attenuates his relation to the world
but he does not cease to dwell in it; he wishes to exist solely in the
mode of liturgy but does not, for all that, free himself from the control of being-in-fact. This does not, however, rob humor of its rights,
and may even strengthen them. The "sage" thinks himself to have the
last word, believes his experience insuperable, and predictably thinks
that the fool's experience belongs to an obsolete experiential sphere
that continues on today anachronistically, unaware of the true logic
of existence lived in the light of the reconciling Cross. And yet,
because he is himself moved only by the desire for definitive proximity to God, and because he knows that man can live in peace with
God today even without this desire being fulfilled, the fool can in turn
object that the sage at bottom satisfies himself with very little. He
does so for two reasons: in the first place, because he is satisfied with
a happiness that bears all the traits of the provisional (since speculative knowledge [*connaissance spéculative*] emphasizes God's presence as
other than parousiacal, since the promises made at Easter—which the
sage is unaware of or which he has failed to recognize [*méconnaît*]—
remain unfulfilled), and, in the second place, because he does not
really try to anchor in the present all the eschatological significance
it can take on. Because he wishes for the definitive (the "angelic" life)
more than anyone, but can only accede to the fragile domain of anticipation (which obliges him to see the humor in his own experience,
too), the fool thus smiles at those who claim that the *eschaton* has
already been realized. Because he knows that man cannot desire that
God alone be sufficient for him without translating this desire into
extravagant conduct, he can recognize in the sage's experience a
certain, paradoxical impotence to let the definitive shine through in
the provisional ahead of its time. The sage can always pretend to be
deaf to the fool's humor, and to the real threats to his wisdom it
expresses. On the other hand, humor does not need those against
whom it directs its protest to recognize it in order to complete its

task. It is enough here that *we* recognize it and let ourselves be instructed by it.

§ 68 Toward a Liturgical Critique of the Concept

The time has come to determine, and not only by means of excursus, the liturgical status of knowledge [*du savoir*], and more precisely of knowledge [*de la connaissance*] through concepts. In Hegel, access to the concept marks the end of the journey of consciousness. Conceptual knowledge [*savoir conceptuel*] not only judges (and condemns) any appeal to the ambiguous immediacy of *Gefühl*, but also clearly and distinctly arrives at a meaning that religious "representations" actually leave unthought, thus presenting itself as the last word on the matter, as intranscendable. Hegel knows, of course, that the concept is not the only element in the relation between man and the Absolute and that the experience of thought is not the only experience proper to reconciled existence. But when man has—legitimately— paid the homage of his liturgies to the Absolute, it is to the concept that he is returned, as though to a norm that sets the standard for all experience, with no possibility of another authority creating such a norm. It is in an insuperable mode that the concepts laying claim to God become manifest to man. Possessing them, therefore, must engender beatitude.

There are arguments afforded by liturgy that nevertheless permit, or rather oblige, us to reject the theory.

a. There is no doubt that God gives us much to think and that he gives himself to be thought. If liturgy comes after the "cognitive delay" without which we would not know what the name of God means, we will readily concede to Hegel that knowledge has a certain privilege. Even when the fundamental theses of Hegelian eschatology find themselves denied in favor of a logic of "next to last," which includes within it a logic of "inexperience," it is still a question of knowledge enabling man to calmly live this inexperience by allowing him to decipher it as a specific mode of experience. This is not to say, however, that when the question of a "delay" arises in this way, one has to work one's way through the entire domain of thought and to think everything thinkable before theological prose can be succeeded by the hymn, doxology, or the pure and simple act of presence before God. On the contrary, liturgy impresses itself on us first of all as a matter of urgency. In its first premises, thought recognized in the

Summum Cogitabile the Person par excellence, who it is not enough to speak of, but to whom one must speak, or before whom one must remain silent to hear his silence or his word. What is to be thought is given by God, but he first gives us to think that the work of the logos will lead to misunderstandings if it does not enable us to encounter God. Liturgy requires knowledge. But knowledge calls for liturgy. (We must perhaps dare to say that it would participate in an insidious logic of divertissement if this were not the case—this issue not being absent from the polemic Kierkegaard directs against Hegel.)

b. The hierarchical relation between the "concept" and "representation" and their sharp contradistinction thus become singularly problematical. Would "representation" be sufficient for man to take possession of what is most proper to him? For Hegel, this is a scandalous hypothesis. Yet it arises emphatically as soon as we wish to justify the (pre-)eschatological meanings inherent in liturgy, which attests to the peace that reigns between man and God and reveals ways of being in the shadow of death and in the element of the provisional that bracket death's claim over man. This is not the whole of reconciled existence. Divine forgiveness and the manifestation of the forgiving God must be thought. Divine forgiveness should, however, make possible the reconciliation of mankind. But it is, first of all, when he receives forgiveness, and gives thanks for it, that man shows us a countenance that is to be his forever—but to receive forgiveness, it is certainly not required that he have acceded to what Hegel calls the "concept," nor even that he can give arguments in conceptual form (in the ordinary sense of the term) for his joy and his hope. The "kerygma" that authorizes liturgy, the gospel to which the act of grace responds, does not render conceptual elaboration (in the common sense of the term) futile. The narrative that bears witness to God's acts among us does not constitute the only possible theology. But to the idea of a vesperal, all-enveloping knowledge that reduces them to the level of mere preliminaries to the fully rational apprehension of the truth, they oppose a morning of knowledge, where the essential has been communicated and comprehended, and where not everything thinkable has not been thought. Hegel's contemporaries do, of course, still think and pray, after eighteen centuries of Christian thought that are as much centuries of intellectual history, and which, it will be agreed, are responsible for an authentic deepening of speculative thought. One right must, however, be granted them at all costs, that of being able to encounter God without possessing speculative mastery over what they believe and, a fortiori, without them being required to achieve an insuperable and "absolute" organization of their knowledge. God gives rise to the work of thought and to the indissoluble gratitude of the reconciled man. The words that man makes use of to speak of him are incapable of entertaining all God gives us to think. The image gets mixed up with the concept, and the narrative with argument. They nevertheless accomplish the work that can be expected of them if they provide, in the absence of an intranscendable science, the means of a praise that knows exactly to whom it is offered. There is nothing to prevent whosoever wishes, even after the necessary critique of Hegel's eschatology, from maintaining the distinction between the "concept" and "representation." On one condition, however: before the God who makes himself his ally, he must know that enjoying possession of the "concept" is not really necessary for man to lead the existence most worthy of him.

c. One should thus clearly recognize an aporia that culminates in Hegel, but which has haunted every philosophy of history, and which unbalances the Hegelian edifice—all the more so to the extent one perceives it as a theological structure powerless to let us think the experience of the child, or of the experience that resembles it, otherwise than as embryonic. Childhood could not have been defined otherwise than as a lack from within the terms that Hegel shares with the entire metaphysical tradition of the West. The full exercise of reason is refused the child. The wisdom (in the ordinary sense of the term) that the philosopher seeks is unattainable for the child—inasmuch as man is only truly human when he displays his "wisdom" and "reason," the child is thus nothing but the beginning of man: he is of no interest in himself but only in relation to what he will (perhaps) become. It takes no great capacity for inference to recognize that where (in Hegel) the possession of conceptually insuperable knowledge governs the advent of finally self-identical man, neither the experience of the child nor any experience resembling it can have any eschatological significance whatsoever. The prayers of the child and of those resembling him—"simple" people—falsify this theory however. For those who do not, nor could ever, possess "absolute knowledge," or more broadly, strictly conceptual knowledge, the practice of praise and the act of grace are nevertheless possible. The child and the "simple" person do not, of course, know everything they do when they pray. They are unaware that they thereby question their belonging to the world. They do not realize the subversive power of their acts. But because they know enough to encounter a God whose benevolence they know [*connaissent*], it must be said that they have it within their power to make gestures of definitive value, and to implicate (doubtless without their knowledge) properly eschatological modes of being in the provisional. The child and the "simple" person ("the collier" ["*le charbonnier*"])[5] do not deny what God gives them and us to think. They will probably have the humility to believe the "sages" to be more learned than they in things divine. We cannot, however, propose a liturgical organization of the *disputatio de homine* without demanding from the sage a more far-reaching humility: he must in fact admit that his wisdom does not possess the necessary conditions for fully human existence (inasmuch as it can be lived in the time that leads us to death) and that it is, therefore, superfluous.

§ 69 The Minimal Man

Thus we can grasp the extent of a disparity. The arguments that defend the fool's extravagation and that justify his irony are strong. However, they can neither prevent the disconcerting effect the fool has on us nor nullify the theoretical importance of the resultant embarrassment. What names are we to give to man and with what concepts are we to think his humanity? There is no lack of possible responses to this question, and they can be made in the specialized lexicons of diverse philosophical traditions without contradicting each other. Man is an animal whose lot it is to have a world. He is a rational animal charged with a twofold task: the hermeneutic (to discern meaning) and the apophantic (to spell out meaning). He is a political animal capable of providing the "co-being-there" that, a priori, defines within the setting of a city where the greatest possible freedom and justice could reign. He is the technician who takes in hand the destiny of things. He is the artist—the "poet"—whose works offer us, if we are to believe the philosopher, the greatest presence of Being. He is the liturgist in the world with the power to face God. We could go on, and go into detail, without the fool raising serious objections to the concepts—in the plural—that record the plurality of experiences in which man articulates his identity. But in the absence of theoretical objections (we cannot represent someone whose participation in the liturgical play would in itself be sufficient to define him), there is nevertheless one objection that is acutely evident in the very practice of the fool. It belongs to the concept of liturgy to subordinate being-in-the-world to being-before-God, but there is no need for the fool's testimony to defend or illustrate this concept: the liturgical act of subversion is after all accomplished in the most perfectly discreet fashion every time someone attempts to pray, and thus demonstrates a characteristic of his humanity, the ultimate characteristic no doubt, the characteristic that enables us to question the a priori conditions of experience and the relation they maintain with divertissement, but which nevertheless abrogates nothing of what we do as humans when we are not praying. And yet, if it is not such an abrogation that the fool undertakes, he certainly does bear the responsibility for the critical stance that he adopts or, if you prefer, for the multiple ways in which he distances himself. The fool does not seek the abolition of the logos, the notion of which would be absurd—but he does affirm for us that giving praise is more worthy of man than is the highest exercise of reason. He does not deny that ethical exigencies are related to political duties—but it is by assuming the guise of the servant that he fulfills these duties, from the margins of the city rather than by taking a seat in its assemblies. He does not deny that "poetry" is one of our essential possibilities and that it enables us to leave a trace of our passage in the world—but his masterwork is liturgy, which is no more a *poïësis* than it is a *praxis*, and the essential function of which has nothing to do with leaving a trace in the world. As regards the categories under which the humanity of man is ordinarily thought, he denies the pertinence neither of those which do not name the liturgical dimension of his being explicitly nor of those which do not name it at all—it is nevertheless in the most tenuous way possible that his experience falls within these categories.

It is thus in the form of the *minimal man* that the fool confronts us, in the form of a "neighbor" in whom we perhaps hesitate to recognize, in the proper sense of the words, a "fellow being." The disparity certainly does not detract from what is fundamental or "essential." Beneath the divergence in conduct, the humanity of the fool is for us—obviously—indubitable. No formal ontological question of the person arises here, although questions nevertheless arise thick and fast if one keeps in mind that the fool provides us with a basis, not for conceiving the possible standpoint of *homo religiosus* faced with transcendence (he could do so, but that is another matter), but for interpreting reconciled existence. The paradox is thus that between the completed and the incomplete, during the time in which the words of reconciliation pronounced on Good Friday and the words of the promises given at Easter still resonate, the remarkable fate of those who hold to these words, should they be radically concerned with the Absolute, is to be reduced to the essential (and in which the essential, itself, can appear to us as mutilated). This reduction is obviously not necessary. Because ethics has a liturgical status, and ethical exigencies are inextricable from political duties, the logic of the penultimate cannot unfold exclusively as a logic indifferent to the life of the city. Because history was perhaps completed when God said his final words, but has undoubtedly continued on, no one can judge conjugality to be anachronistic. And because the reconciliation of God and man is also the reconciliatio of God and the cosmos, the liturgical relation between man and God cannot annul the relations of knowledge [*connaissance*], mastery or transfiguration that man maintains with the cosmos. For the reconciled man, nevertheless, it is only justifiable to find joy in the peace granted to him and in the peace that should reign between fellow men—*and nowhere else*. And yet the fool who finds such joy is disconcerting to us because his behavior is iconoclastic. The concepts with which we think the humanity of man engender paradigms and images of man, but these images disintegrate here. The fool is inferior to the philosopher, inferior to the scholar, inferior to the politician. He effaces himself behind them, and it comes as no surprise that he receives no mention when we try to think the insuperably human person. But he does not efface himself without burdening us with a problem: what if, liturgically reduced to the essential or even to almost less than the essential, the minimal man's experience of himself and of the Absolute is an experience richer than the philosopher's or the scholar's? What if he has arrived at the truth of his being and has taken his (preeschatological) capacity for experience to the limit? To respond to these questions, we must first, by way of reiteration, set out the perplexities that disappropriation introduces into the *disputatio de homine* (in § 70). The preeschatological destitution to which the fool's experience attests will be assigned its hermeneutic site (in § 71), which will enable us to conclude the debate we have engaged in with all the theories of religious emotion (in § 72). It will then be possible to link dispossession and beatitude in the hermeneutics of an experience we consider to be fundamental (in § 73).

§ 70 Man in His Place: Reprise

The elegance of an option may fascinate us, but it cannot compel us to opt for it: poverty and "holy madness" manifest a real secret of the humanity of man, but this secret remains an enigmatic interim where we seem to lose all measure of what we are. We cannot provide an account of liturgy without referring to the eschatological; the transgression and subversion of the initial must first be mentioned because the a priori conditions of experience maintain the initial in a state of ambiguity. On the other hand, we cannot appeal to the ultimate without acknowledging that (for once) the trivial evidence is truthful, and that the *eschaton* is not available to us in any modality whatsoever. We can, of course, fall back on the a priori, but that would be to bracket the history in which we have made it possible to pronounce the name of God (or in which God has enabled us to pronounce his name) and to exist face-to-face with him. We can also suppose that the definitive exercises such a hold over us today that our present no longer depends on any future, but that would be to forget that man reconciled to the Absolute has received promises and exists in the element of the unfulfilled. It is too late for the transcendental to suffice for our definition, and too soon to suggest an equation of the real and the eschatological: the present (our present, the present lived within the horizon of divine manifestation) gives itself to be thought under the category of the next to last. But if it is reasonably simple to form the concept of the penultimate, an aporia seems to arise when we notice that the logic of reconciled existence is in fact a logic of negation. The next to last is neither the provisional nor the definitive. It does not, of course, entirely break with the provisional (only death can annul the laws of being-in-fact) but the logic of the definitive is already at work (the Absolute has irrevocably offered its peace and it can "reign" this side of death). From the interpretation of the "night" to that of the fool's extravagation, however, the path traversed has taught us to first discern in the preeschatological interim the combined conditions for a certain extenuation of being-in-the-world and an incontestable critique of eschatological anticipation. The refusal to exist in the mode of appropriation gives us no leverage over the goods [*biens*] to be possessed for eternity. The *eschaton* does not come to be realized simply because we wish to attenuate our participation in the play of the world as much as is possible. The fool's extravagation shows him to be a minimal rather than a transfigured man. If his experience is not to be disqualified, if one must admit that it in fact houses the greatest proximity there is between (mortal) man and God, it must then be said that it is beyond all measure: this is not to say that it is measured (and found wanting) against a limitless presence in the world, or measured against the entirely realized *eschaton*, but that it rejects these as measures. On the other hand, do we not avail ourselves of other measures of the humanity of man or, if you prefer, of other hermeneutic sites? There can be one and only one response to this question: we will say of the fool that he "symbolically dwells in Good Friday."

§ 71 *Anthropologia Crucis*

A shift in focus is required, then. We can ask the fool to justify his excessive behavior—and, to a certain extent, this is precisely what we have done. If the fool's madness weighs on him as a destiny, one readily discerns in this madness the features of a project—man's decree as to the meaning and the truth of his humanity. The lunatic's experience is a passivity, whereas the fool's experience gave itself to be understood primarily as a decision: the fool showed himself to us as one who removes the mask each of us wears to leave visible the true face of man. And yet no mention of the Cross can be made without doubting that the fool's experience gives itself to be understood entirely in this way, and without discerning in it—these words being introduced of necessity—the blinding reality of a passion. The fool shatters the images we have of man, and this is, at first glance, the fool's very function and his triumph over ways of being that are inessential, bound up with divertissement, or both. This reading does, however, meet with experiences in which we cannot recognize the implementation of a project, and in which the Absolute alone can account for, if such an account is required, man's deviations. We can choose poverty, or the dispossession of will or desire. We can, in order to express a desire with hyperbole, commit the conceptual solecism of positing that God alone is sufficient so as to infer that he alone is necessary. But how can we use the language of choice, when the fool is presented to us in the guise of Bernadette Soubirous browsing on the grass in front of the grotto where she had her visions, or in that of Jean-Joseph Surin sharing all the sufferings of the lunatic, or again in the Byzantine *salos* or the Russian *yurodivi*, where we feel that they do not play the role of the lunatic among us without also being associated with his pathology? The possibility of this madness being feigned and of irony lying hidden within it cannot, of course, be ruled out. Philippe Neri dons the buffoon's clothing by day, but spends his nights in contemplation and praise. The *salos* and the *yurodivi* feign immorality (this probably being the most recurrent feature of their experience), but criticize every moralism all the better for it.[6] We may nonetheless refuse to let ourselves feel reassured. Even if he is imitating (but can one do so without risking madness?), the fool represents a frightening alterity in the world. Humility is not sufficient to explain the reasons for his humiliation. That is why, if we wish to reject the notion that the fool appears solely as witness to an incoherence and the collapse of meaning, we cannot avoid assigning to the historical Good Friday the task of interpreting his experience under the conceptual figure of the Passion.

The entire architecture of the question of man is necessarily involved here. The question is ordinarily posed—in an apparently obligatory form—in a specular way. In "the question of man," the subjective genitive is also the objective genitive: to pose the question is to put oneself in question, and to answer solely for oneself. Knowledge [*le savoir*] thus completes itself in reflection. Even if one cannot question the humanity of man without combining prescription and description, and although whoever is questioning has no need to claim to embody the fully human man in order to validate his questioning and his responses, this specularity is not thereby contested— it is merely a question of pointing out that the mirror reflects not only, nor primarily, my indivisible particularity, but that the image in fact reveals the face of everyone. And yet the play of the mirror finds itself annulled as soon as the image no longer provides the measure and the key for its interpretation and confronts us with a pure and simple enigma. We can, of course, recognize the humanity of the fool, just as we can recognize the humanity of the lunatic and of everyone, without requiring that the Cross be the hermeneutic site of his poverty. Our capacity for experience includes the possibility of a confrontation with the nonsensical, of a pure experience of the negative. Insanity [*dé-raison*], or whatever manifests itself as such, does not result in man's death (even if we must recognize in it a symbol of impending death), and perhaps requires that we affirm all the more categorically the fundamental solidarity that binds us to the *extra-vagrant*, to those who seem to exclude themselves from human society. This being duly conceded, the categorical character of the affirmation will, however, never permit the alchemy that might transmute nonsense into meaning. It is for this reason that we are entitled to say that the only possible imputation of meaning in this case comes from beyond, and that in the fool's humiliated humanity, if it must have a place in the logic (though not in the teratology) of experience, we actually recognize the image of the humiliated humanity of God himself. Thus can we specify the fool's name: it is the "fool-in-Christ," he whose destiny becomes intelligible only in light of another destiny, that of the

Crucified in whom and by whom God restores peace between man and himself.

§ 72 Religious Experience: A Final Critique

Thus we can agree: the refusal to let the relation between man and God take shape in an experiential mode, or more precisely to let the "experience" unfold in the privileged element of feeling, finds here a strong a posteriori justification. A Christological theory of experience—and thus a theory for which the secrets of liturgy ultimately reveal themselves beyond every phenomenological given that claims to be of eternal value for everyone everywhere, or in any case to be of value everywhere the Absolute is known as the subject and promise of a relation, in the singular meeting of God and man in Jesus of Nazareth—would not have as its sole task the interpretation of the darkness of Good Friday and the dereliction of the crucified Christ. Man can enjoy proximity to the divine in the time that leads him to death, and we do not lack texts that can be invoked here as Christological confirmation. But is that proximity attested to and demonstrated only in joy? This has already been denied and we can deny it more forcefully still here. The Cross is, in fact and in the mode of a paroxysm, the place of inexperience. The existence of God is affirmed there, for one does not speak ("My God, my God, why . . . ?") to one who does not exist.[7] God, however, is not absent: just as the humanity of Jesus of Nazareth is the humanity of *God*, so the death of Jesus is *his* death, *his* Passion, and not a human drama for which he might show a distant compassion. The Christological relation between man and God ceases, however, to be governed by consciousness—and we would advise against the pious but virtually senseless reading that attempts to safeguard we know not what devotional interpretation of the Cross by supposing that the crucified Christ, in the midst of his agonizing sufferings, still enjoys from the depths of his soul the beatifying vision of God.[8] God can be closest to us (and there is no greater proximity than that to which Christology bears witness) even though the senses know him only as an absence. Man can encounter God, exist in the presence of God [*coram Deo*], without requiring him to grant us the fruition of his presence. The affective experience of God therefore loses all right to verify or falsify the relation between man and God.

The hermeneutics of religious emotions thus comes up against what is for it unthinkable. Certainly it does not see itself as disqualified.

The emotions of the religious man do not only betray the hold the "earth" has over consciousness; if the divine can be contaminated (experientially) by consciousness, the reticence to which the a priori risk of this contamination can give rise cannot render the affect so suspect that it must be hopelessly enshrouded in ambiguity. But since we cannot conceal that the relation between man and God can also be accomplished in the form of *experimentum crucis*, we must always begin by referring to the excess of inexperience over experience, to the point of the pure and simple negation of experience. The desire for the *eschaton* ("restlessness") is inscribed in man, even if it has to be deciphered as a palimpsest, but this desire can be assuaged in advance within the limits of being-in-the-world. This frustration of the desire is of greater importance, however, because it redirects us from what seems totally arbitrary, from what we cannot really integrate into an organic and necessary development of experience (the sacred is immemorially accessible to us, but God only touches the experience of consciousness in and through grace), to the point where we can unpresumptuously speak the language of universality. It would doubtless be improper to interpret "spiritual life" to be so tragic that its most common experiences (aridity, the "night") appear to clearly and distinctly participate in the experience of the crucified Christ. But it is not in the least improper to suggest that the experience of the crucified Christ, of the minimal man par excellence, manifests precisely what separates the penultimate from the ultimate, and can thus in the final analysis interpret "spiritual life" as it is to be lived in everyday life. The crucified Christ is the bearer of reconciliation as well as the first to be reconciled. The fool, on the other hand, is important to us only insofar as he is a fool-in-Christ: not the (anachronistic) witness to a combat with the angels in which numinous forces reduce man to incoherence, but paradoxically, the witness to an alliance and a peace. His destiny is preeschatological and counts here only in this regard. Thus the notion of an *anthropologia crucis* tells us that, for the man reconciled with the Absolute, Good Friday is not the bygone past of a restitution of the origin, but remains the secret of the present at as great a distance from the absolute future as from the initial. One thus learns from the fool and from those who resemble him, as one learns from the crucified Christ, that it is the lot of the reconciled man to exist face-to-face with a God whose paternal countenance is not hidden from him, *coram Deo*, and that all affective confirmation is strictly speaking inessential here.

§ 73 Perfect Joy

There is more that can and should be said. A well-known apothegm, handed down by Francis of Assisi to Brother Leonard, expresses it well:

> I return from Perugia, and through the deep of night I have come here, and it is wintry, muddy and so cold that icicles of frozen water form on the edges of my tunic and scrape my legs 'til blood flows from their wounds. Muddy and frozen to the bone, I arrive at the gate, and after knocking and calling for a long time, a brother comes out and asks: Who is it? And I respond: Brother Francis. And he said: Go away, this is no decent hour to be out; you are not coming in. . . . But I return again, stand before the gate and I say: For the love of God, take me in this night. And he responded: I will not. . . . [And I replied:] I tell you that if I remain patient and am not shaken, there lies the true joy and the true virtue and the salvation of the soul [*Dico tibi quod si patientiam habuero et non fuero motus, quod in hoc est vera laetitia et vera virtus et salus animae*].[9]

It is a question here of humiliation, and a question of joy; patience permits the one to engender the other. Could the Cross and the experiences lived in its shadow therefore enable us to displace the terms in which the question of happiness, or of beatitude, are ordinarily posed? To the logic of multiple negation and disappropriation that we have let unfold, it would be easy to object that it is a logic of unhappiness: either a nihilistic logic (the Nietzschean objection) or an outmoded logic of unreconciled existence (the Hegelian objection). And yet this twofold objection fails in the face of affirmations stronger than any negation or tension. Because the *eschaton* cannot be realized this side of death, the humiliated man (the pauper, the fool, etc.) does not, obviously, possess the definitive reality of his being. The reasons why humiliation can be borne with patience, and why this patience is the source of real joy, nevertheless break through the closure of being-toward-death and are therefore eschatological reasons. We have said that the only concept with which to think a homeland befitting the measure of man is that of the Kingdom of God (in § 37), but God can, of course, reign over man this side of death. We have also said of those who liturgically encounter God that they exist from their own absolute future onward and, in a certain way, bracket their death (in § 24). For those whom only the Cross makes experience meaningful, but for whom joy originates in humiliation, we may then say that he knows to interpret Good Friday in the light of the event of Easter, and that his joy brings to a conclusion the fulfillment of the promises made at Easter in advance. Joy does not, of course, annul what gives rise to the work of patience; and it would always be irresponsible to appeal to a final transfiguration of all things while forgetting that he who is risen is the Crucified, that he bears the stigmata of his Passion in his glory, and that every intellection of our present must pass through the contemplation of Good Friday. An experience of Good Friday that has already lived through the exultation of Easter is nevertheless possible. One does not expect it to have the last word because this last word cannot be spoken as long as world and earth—and death—govern over us. We will, on the other hand, receive a penultimate word from it. It is too soon for the question of man to be organized purely and simply as an *anthropologia gloriae*, and too late for world and earth to possess all the conditions for happiness. Thus the paradoxical joy that is born of humiliation may be the *fundamental mood* of preeschatological experience. The reconciled man, despite what Hegel might say, is still at a distance from his absolute future. And, despite what Nietzsche might say, the disappropriated and humiliated man is not reduced to nothing, and does not reduce himself to nothing, but lives now in the fulfillment of God's promises to come. Man takes hold of what is most proper to him when he chooses to encounter God. This argument can now be made more specific: we can now assert that man says who he is most precisely when he accepts an existence in the image of a God who has taken humiliation upon himself—when he accepts a *kenotic* existence.

Notes

Introduction

1. TRANS.: Martin Heidegger, "Die Zeit des Weltbildes," in *Holzwege*, *Gesamtausgabe*, 5 (Frankfurt: Klostermann, 1972), 111; "The Age of the World Picture," in *The Question Concerning Technology and Other Essays*, trans. William Lovitt (New York: Harper and Row, 1977), 153. With foreign-language sources throughout, where possible and appropriate, I have cited first the original work, then a suitable English translation.

Chapter One

1. Consider the following remark of Heidegger's in a text to which we will again have occasion to refer: "When, as we say, we come to our senses and reflect on ourselves, we come back to ourselves from things *without ever abandoning* our stay among things. Indeed, the loss of rapport with things that occurs in states of depression would be wholly impossible if such a state were not still what it is as a human state: that is, a staying *with* things." Martin Heidegger, "Bauen Wohnen Denken," in *Vorträge und Aufsätze* (Pfullingen: Neske, 1954), 152; "Building Dwelling Thinking," in *Poetry, Language, Thought*, trans. Albert Hofstadter (New York: Harper and Row, 1975), 157.

2. See Martin Heidegger, *Die Grundbegriffe der Metaphysik: Welt, Endlichkeit, Einsamkeit, Gesamtausgabe*, 29/30 (Frankfurt: Klostermann, 1980); *The Fundamental Concepts of Metaphysics: World, Finitude, Solitude*, trans. William McNeill and Nicholas Walker (Bloomington: Indiana University Press, 1995), §§ 45–46.

3. Martin Heidegger, *Sein und Zeit* (Tübingen: Niemeyer, 1963), 189, 276; *Being and Time*, trans. by John Macquarrie and Edward Robinson (Oxford: Blackwell, 1962), 189, 233.

4. One question remains unanswered, but must not be overlooked: If we maintain, as Heidegger does, that time is the horizon of Being, the *Temporalität des Seins überhaupt*, and if we are to be consistent and follow this logic to its conclusion, will we not be led ineluctably to the conclusion that the world, according to its phenomenological concept, must itself possess a history? It may, indeed will, be necessary to provide a response to this question one day.

5. TRANS.: Although *"étrangeté"* is the French translation for Heideggerian *Unheimlichkeit* when taken in the sense translated as "uncanniness" by Macquarrie and Robinson in *Being and Time*, *étrangéité* is Lacoste's own coinage and is translated here as "foreignness." In coining *étrangéité*, Lacoste is attempting to reproduce Heidegger's play on the etymological derivation and the conceptual sense of *Unheimlichkeit* (see *Sein und Zeit*, 188–89; *Being and Time*, 232–34), that is, as *Un-heim-lichkeit* (not-being-at-home, *Nicht-zuhause-sein*), and as the uncanniness characteristic of Dasein's being-in-the-world. This is made possible in French by *étrangeté* (strangeness, uncanniness) being related to *étranger* (stranger, foreigner). English offers a glimpse of what is involved in the relation between *strange* and *estranged*, but it affords no single comprehensive translation of *Unheimlichkeit*. The reader should therefore bear in mind that *étrangéité* encompasses both senses.

6. The verb *to dwell* [*habiter*], *wohnen*, is, however, almost absent from the perfectly mastered lexical work that is *Sein und Zeit*: one encounters only four occurrences of *wohne*, *Wohnen*, and *wohnen*. Three (p. 54; *Being and Time*, 81) appear in a passage where "dwelling" is given as the equivalent of "to reside alongside" or "to be familiar with" and the fourth (p. 188; *Being and Time*, 233) recalls the passage in § 12 when the analysis is preparing to put into relief the "originary" character of *Unzuhause*. [TRANS.: The translation here of *wohnen* as *"habiter"* in French and as "to dwell" in English touches on a more general and important point concerning Lacoste's rendering of Heideggerian terminology, or rather, we might say, his adoption of the corresponding "field" of French terms. The standard English translations for Heidegger's notions of *Wohnen* and *wohnen* are, of course, "dwelling" or "dwelling place" and "to dwell." However apt Lacoste's translation might be—and I do not doubt that it is—it ought to be noted that *wohnen* and the French *habiter* are commonplace, everyday words used in everyday registers; in ordinary parlance, they would, by and large, both be translated "to live (in)." In consequence, whereas the French reader would not see a sharp distinction between *"habiter"* as a rendering of a specifically Heideggerian term and as a more mundane verb and noun, the English reader would, naturally read "dwell," "dwelling," and so on as renderings of Heideggerian terms. The English reader should, therefore, be aware that Lacoste avails

himself of the resources of the French language in this semantic field (*habiter, habitant, habitat, demeurer, demeure, chez-soi, abri*, etc.) "in their own right" rather than as one-to-one strict translations of the Heideggerian conceptuality. It might be said that he has granted to the French semantic field, however indisputably it "is the translation of" the Heideggerian employment and elaboration of the German conceptual field, its independence or its own interdependence. Nevertheless, I have, in the main, translated *habiter* (and *demeurer*, which is its synonym in this text) as "to dwell," rather than as "to live," so as to avoid confusion with "to live" in the sense "to live one's life." I say "in the main" because doing so throughout would on occasion have entailed forced translations.]

7. Heidegger, *Sein und Zeit*, 189, 192; *Being and Time*, 233, 236.

8. Martin Heidegger, "Der Ursprung des Kunstwerkes," in *Holzwege*, 51, 62; "The Origin of the Work of Art," in *Poetry, Language, Thought*, 63 (translation modified), 72.

9. Heidegger, "Ursprung," 35; "Origin," 46

10. Martin Heidegger, *Erläuterungen zu Hölderlins Dichtung, Gesamtausgabe*, 4 (Frankfurt: Klostermann, 1981), 22, 23; *Elucidations of Hölderlin's Poetry*, trans. Keith Hoeller (Evanston, Ill.: Northwestern University Press, 2000), 41, 42.

11. Heidegger, *Erläuterungen*, 36; *Elucidations*, 54.

12. Heidegger, "Bauen Wohnen Denken," 156; "Building Dwelling Thinking," in *Basic Writings from "Being and Time" (1927) to "The Task of Thinking" (1964)*, ed. and trans. David Farrell Krell (New York: Harper and Row, 1976), 339.

13. Trans.: See Friedrich Hölderin, "In lieblicher Bläue . . . ," in *Poems and Fragments*, trans. Michael Hamburger (Cambridge: Cambridge University Press, 1980), 600, 601, for the text of the entire poem in the original German and in English translation, resp.

14. Heidegger, *Erläuterungen*, 42; *Elucidations*, 60.

15. Heidegger, *Erläuterungen*, 161; *Elucidations*, 186.

16. Heidegger, *Erläuterungen*, 175; *Elucidations*, 200.

17. We are digressing here (see our introduction) from the current usage of a word, according to which *liturgy* is a synonym for *worship*. This is not without good reason. The relation of man to the Absolute ordinarily lets itself be thought under the category of "religion." The history of the concept of religion is long and there is nothing to prove that its end is in sight. One moment in this history, however, rendered usage of the concept awkward if not ambiguous: the association of "religion" with "feeling," in the sense one finds confirmed in Schleiermacher, and which has survived Hegel's critique of Schleiermacher in more recent theories of "religious experience." A total disqualification of feeling (of affects) as regards "religion" is doubtless impossible, even though one must concede to Hegel (and we will do so in due course) that the relation of man to the Absolute has knowledge as its

privileged element. We will nevertheless see this disqualification come to pass, not to deprive man's relation to God, but to provide this relation with the possibility of a paradoxical accomplishment (see §§ 53–54). On the other hand, one might already suspect that religious feeling proves more clearly man's relation to the "earth," the "sky," and the "deities," than it proves or calls into question his relation to God. We will, in a word, have to avoid the significant theoretical difficulties to which every contemporary appeal made to "religion" or, worse still, to the "religious," leads. We have decided therefore to speak of "liturgy," let us repeat, in order to indicate from the outset a lexical disparity, a disparity we would like to maintain between it and the rationality and the conceptual systems of the "philosophy of religion."

18. Eugen Fink, *Spiel als Weltsymbol* (Stuttgart: Kohlhammer, 1960).

19. Cf. Friedrich Wilhelm Joseph von Schelling, *Philosophie der Mythologie, Ausgewählte Werke* (Darmstadt: Wissenschaftliche Buchgesellschaft, 1976), 2:33.

20. This point calls for a stipulation, which will reappear throughout the course of this study. The circular return from world to earth and from earth to world, which unites an existential atheism to an existential paganism, reigns over the initial structures of experience in such a way that it can suffice for us to exist in the mode of Dasein or in the mode of the "mortal." The option to refuse to exist in these modes does, however, remain. And we avail of it when we decide to enter into liturgy. We can enter into liturgy as soon as we know [*savons*] enough about the Absolute: as soon as we know [*connaissons*] it as someone and as the promise of a relation. [TRANS.: The consistent allusion the author will make from here on to the distinction between *connaître / la connaissance* and *savoir / le savoir* is worth mentioning. To interpret a highly idiomatic distinction very briefly and broadly, *connaître / la connaissance* relates to existential, experiential knowing in the sense of "being familiar with," of "knowing or being acquainted with someone or something," of "knowing of or about something through everyday experience," whereas *savoir* is more theoretical in that one knows or deduces *that* such and such is the case, and *le savoir* is conceptual knowledge. The French term used will be indicated when the author's preference for one or the other has seemed of particular importance.] This knowledge cannot, however, compel us to do anything. Although the man who prays "thinks of God by loving him" (Charles de Foucauld), we are perfectly capable of thinking of a God who exists without loving him, and thus without offering him the homage of our liturgies. Where, then, does the free transition that transforms the possession of liturgical knowledge into its liturgical implementation come from? We will respond by making use of a concept—that of *restlessness*. Such as it receives its classical formulation in the incipit of Augustine's *Confessions*, restlessness is that mark of the humanity of man which removes man from every satisfaction to which world and earth hold the key, and grants to man the eschatological satisfaction that, by definition, the Absolute alone

promises. The restless man can thus become bored with world and earth. He can dream of a beyond to world and earth. It is important in any case to emphasize that restlessness does not as such possess any knowledge. It is immemorially present. But it is immemorially steeped in ambiguity, which makes every desire ignorant of what it desires; world and earth, whose offerings we do not ignore, always repress it easily, and all the more easily because the immanent sacred of the earth can also deceive *restlessness* and offer to make up the deficit. Although it would not be illogical to claim that restlessness assures liturgy of an existential foundation, liturgy cannot appear if knowledge does not inform restlessness as to the ultimate stakes at issue here. On the other hand, if knowledge were not to accomplish its task, it would have to be said that restlessness would have no other destiny than that of being repressed, or of being perverted in the enjoyment [*jouissance*] of the sacred.

21. Georg Wilhelm Friedrich Hegel, *Vorlesungen über die Philosophie der Religion*, ed. Walter Jaeschke, vol. 1, *Einleitung: Der Begriff der Religion* (Hamburg: Meiner, 1983), 237; *Lectures on the Philosophy of Religion, Together with a Work on the Proof of the Existence of God*, vol. 1, trans. E. B. Speirs and J. Burdon Sanderson (London: Routledge, 1968), 1.

22. Martin Heidegger, "Dichterisch wohnet der Mensch . . . ," in *Vorträge und Aufsätze*, 191; "Poetically Man Dwells . . . ," in *Poetry, Language, Thought*, 223.

Chapter Two

1. Saint Gregory the Great, *Dialogi*, book 2, *Vita Sancti Benedicta*, PL 66 200 AB; Dialogues, trans. Odo John Zimmerman (New York: Fathers of the Church, 1959), book 2.

2. Let us pause briefly to understand the link between the symbolic and the ontological. It does not have to be proved that there is no ontic weight to any experience similar to that which Gregory went through. On the contrary, the experiences we have attempted to interpret throughout our study have an evident ontic depth. This ontic reality can call for interpretation, however, only on account of the play of the symbolic within it; and if we must concern ourselves with the symbol because it "gives to think," what it gives to be thought here is a redistribution of the field of experience. This redistribution, we will say again and again, only comes about under the conditions of the world and of the worldly, historial "fact" of experience: the symbolic order, in this case, is other than that of Being. But this redistribution—we will also say again and again—implicates (albeit in anticipation and inchoately) the eschatological "fact" of experience in a very real way: the symbolic order is thus not foreign to the ontological order. The symbolic practices in question here already shelter, in a sense, the reality of "Being that is not yet," which would simply not be able to "be" within the limits of the world, but which can be realized there, insofar as they are symbolized there.

3. In order to draw from the lessons of our interpretation of the two dimensions Heidegger recognizes in place, we will henceforth understand by *world* and by *being-in-the-world* a structure less specific than that of *In-der-Welt-Sein* and its cortege of determinations (*Unzuhause, Unheimlichkeit,* anxiety, etc.), which will encompass "world" and "earth." This will be clear from the context, or we will indicate when necessary if it is the particular reality of "world" or "earth" in question.

4. We lack a good systematic study of the phenomenon of reclusion. See *DS* 13: 217–28 (bibl.); on *xeniteia,* see the classic article by Antoine Guillaumont, "Dépaysement as a Form of Asceticism in Monachism," in *Aux origines du monachisme chrétien: Pour une phénoménologie du monachisme* (The Origins of Christian Monachism: Toward a Phenomenology of Monachism; Bégrolles-en-Mauges: Abbaye de Bellefontaine, 1979), 89–116; see also the monograph by Arnold Angenendt, *Monachi Peregrini: Studien zu Pirmin und den monastischen Vorstellungen des frühen Mittelalters* (Monachi Peregrini: Studies on Pirmin and Monastic Concepts of the Early Middle Ages), Münstersche Mittelalter-Schriften, 6 (Munich: Fink, 1972).

5. See, for example, *Apophthegmatica Patrum: Collectio Alphabetica; The Sayings of the Desert Fathers: Alphabetical Collection,* trans. Benedicta Ward (London: Mowbrays, 1975), apothegms 49, 116, 281, 399, 415, 494, 500, 736.

6. Peter Robert Lamont Brown, "The Rise and Function of the Holy Man in Late Antiquity," in *Society and the Holy in Late Antiquity* (Berkeley: University of California Press, 1982), 103–53.

7. The philosopher's oracular pronouncement "Nur noch ein Gott kann uns retten" (which elsewhere constitutes, strictly speaking, a purely analytical proposition) appears, as we know, in an interview given in 1966 and published posthumously in *Der Spiegel,* May 31, 1976: 209. [TRANS.: For an English translation of the entire interview, see "Only a God Can Save Us: *Der Spiegel*'s Interview with Martin Heidegger," trans. Maria Alter and John D. Caputo, *Philosophy Today* 20 (1976): 267–85.]

8. See Heidegger, *Sein und Zeit,* 176; *Being and Time,* 220.

9. This precludes the possibility of a debate that would oppose us to the Germanic disciples of Joseph Maréchal and of Peter Scheuer, Johannes Baptist Lotz and Karl Rahner, according to whom there exists a transcendental dimension of experience to be interpreted as a prethematic confrontation with the Absolute. It is of course banal and obvious that, if liturgy is possible for us, it does in a way fall within the category of the a priori: its reality proves that man's existence is not restricted to the modality of Dasein or to that of the "mortal." But however laudable the efforts made by the Maréchalian Thomists to set down the roots of the relation of man to God in the basic givens of experience might be, they nevertheless come up against unforeseen ambivalences. We are told that "transcendental experience" has to do with God—but does it not rather have to do only with the sacred proper to the world? We are told (by Karl Rahner in *Hörer des Wortes,*

2nd ed. rev. [Munich: Kösel, 1963]; *Hearers of the Word,* trans. Michael Richards [New York: Herder and Herder, 1969]) that it has to do with God's silence — but is it not rather a question of the muteness of Being? The main error of interpretation may lie in the unacknowledged projection onto the a priori of knowledge that has only come about a posteriori or "categorially."

10. TRANS.: I have translated *jouir de* and *la jouissance* as "to enjoy (possession of)" and "joy." The reader should bear in mind that the array of interconnected senses simultaneously at play in French is only vaguely evident in English: on the one hand, it includes the juridical sense of "enjoying a right" or of "enjoying possession of one's faculties" and on the other, the supreme joy (*jouir* means "to have an orgasm" and *la jouissance* refers to the accompanying pleasure) that this can occasion as when, for example, Lacoste speaks of "enjoying possession" of Hegelian absolute knowledge or of the *eschaton.*

11. See my *Note sur le Temps: Essai sur la raison de la mémoire et de l'espérance* (Note on Time: An Essay on the Rationality of Memory and Hope; Paris: Presses Universitaires de France, 1990), §§ 4–5.

12. See Claude Bruaire, *Philosophie du corps* (The Philosophy of the Body; Paris: Seuil, 1968), esp. 231–68.

Chapter Three

1. See chapter 1, note 20; Lacoste, *Note,* § 44.

2. TRANS.: As used in this volume, *condescension* is to be understood in its patristic rather than everyday sense, that is, as benevolence shown by God toward the human race; divine grace bestowed on rational creatures for their eternal salvation.

3. TRANS.: See 1 Corinthians 12:10.

4. See, above all, Gaston Fessard, *De l'actualité historique,* vol. 1: *A la recherche d'une méthode* (Of Historical Actuality, vol. 1: In Search of a Method; Paris: Desclée de Brouwer, 1960). There is a good commentary by Nguyen Hong Giao (written under the supervision of Fessard himself) in Grao's *Le verbe dans l'histoire: La philosophie de l'historicité du P. Gaston Fessard* (The Verb in History: The Philosophy of Historicity in P. Gaston Fessard; Paris: Beauchesne, 1974).

5. Does not the project of *Totalité et infini* consist in nothing other than founding ethics as first philosophy and founding a method that unveils moral meaning and moral obligations present in places of all experience? [TRANS.: See Emmanuel Levinas, *Totalité et infini: Essai sur l'extériorité,* 3rd ed. (The Hague: Nijhoff, 1968); *Totality and Infinity: An Essay on Exteriority,* trans. Alphonso Lingis (Pittsburgh: Duquesne University Press, 1969).]

6. TRANS.: *Intérêt* and *interest* are cognates and have a similar range and array of meanings, the different senses of *interest* in *disinterested* and *uninterested* being significant here. *Désintéressement,* whose root literally means "without (vested) interest (in)," by extension also means "unselfishness" or "selflessness."

Chapter Four

1. See Odo Marquardt, *Schwierigkeiten mit der Geschichtsphilosophie* (Frankfurt: Suhrkamp, 1973) for a coherent renunciation of eschatological motifs (and of all motifs of theological provenance) in the interpretation of history.

2. Georg Wilhelm Friedrich Hegel, *Phänomenologie des Geistes*, ed. Johannes Hoffmeister, 163–64; *The Phenomenology of Spirit*, trans. A V. Miller (Oxford: Clarendon Press, 1977), 131.

3. See Hegel, *Vorlesungen*, 4, 32, 62; *Lectures*, 4.

4. This declaration smacks of a paradox, for we learned long ago from Israel's experience that ethics is true worship. Have we forgotten, or must we wait until we remember this for a standpoint on the question of man, in which he is "Hellenically" known, first of all, as an animal capable of *theōria*, to collapse? There is some truth to this question. The most extreme anthropologies have certainly never treated ethical *praxis* as a divertissement. It can hardly be doubted, however, that in a civilization—that of the Christian West—where the most solemn codes were decreed by the practitioners of the *vita contemplativa*, the latter was deemed to be the utmost priority, the *vita activa* and the care of the ethical thus finding themselves in a subordinate position, but certainly without the unity of liturgical *theōria* and ethical *praxis* ever having been lost from view. Thus modernity or its end is not to be understood solely as a rejection of every anthropology of contemplation in favor of an anthropology of action, but also as the time when, after centuries in which the harmonious complementarity of the liturgical and ethical orders was not in doubt, the old prophetic challenge to worship reappeared. The liturgical unhappiness of consciousness is in part a contemporary problem deriving, on the one hand, from the equation of being and doing [*de l'être et du faire*], and, on the other hand, from a stronger emphasis than ever being placed on the infinity and immediacy of the exigencies of the good. The problem is also, and in equally large measure, simply the return of a very old debate.

5. [TRANS.: The phrase "no 'ought' from an 'is'" appears in English in the original.] The best defense and contemporary illustration of this thesis is probably that by R. M. Hare, *The Language of Morals* (Oxford: Clarendon Press, 1952).

6. See the summary furnished in Emmanuel Levinas, "La trace de l'Autre," in *En découvrant l'existence avec Husserl et Heidegger*, 3rd ed. (Paris: Vrin, 1974), 192–93; "The Trace of the Other," in *Discovering Existence with Husserl and Heidegger*, Studies in Phenomenology and Existential Phenomenology, trans. Richard Cohen and Michael B. Smith (Evanston, Ill.: Northwestern University Press, 1998).

7. "Good" and "evil" appear in *Sein und Zeit* only in §§ 58 and 59 in the analysis of "fault" or "guilt," *Schuld*, and in the existential interpretation of "conscience," *Gewissen*. They make their appearance, not as having existential reality, but as that which being-guilty furnishes with its "existential

condition of possibility" (*Sein und Zeit*, 286; *Being and Time*, 332). Nothing explicitly prevents us from speaking of "good" and "evil" once this condition of possibility has been analyzed and once every "vulgar" conception of conscience has been rejected. But the words should not to be uttered within the limits of a hermeneutics of facticity. And the translation of *Gewissen* as "conscience" ["*conscience morale*"] reveals itself to be somewhat inappropriate: when it is a question of *Gewissen* and its "call," morality (*Moralität*) is still a long way off, and we remain separated from what we ordinarily call "good and evil."

Chapter Five

1. We are employing three concepts here—*labor, work, action* [in English]—around which Hannah Arendt articulates her interpretation of the "*vita activa*"; see Arendt, *The Human Condition* (Chicago: University of Chicago Press, 1958).

2. TRANS.: *Désœuvrement* would ordinarily be translated as "idleness" or "inertia," but its appearance and employment in recent French thought in the work of Maurice Blanchot and Jean-Luc Nancy have led to attempts to translate it as "worklessness" and "inoperativity," the latter notably in Jean-Luc Nancy, *La communauté désœuvrée*, 2nd ed. (Paris: Bourgeois, 1990); *The Inoperative Community*, ed. Peter Connor, trans. Peter Connor, Lisa Garbus, Michael Holland, and Simona Sawhney (Minneapolis: University of Minnesota Press, 1991).

3. On nonnecessity and divine beyond-the-necessary, which we no more than indicate thematically here, see the detailed treatment given by Eberhard Jüngel, *Gott als Geheimnis der Welt* (Tübingen: Mohr, 1976); *God as the Mystery of the World*, trans. Darrell Guder (Grand Rapids, Mich.: Eerdmans, 1983), § 2.

4. Elsewhere, we have elaborated the strictly theological, or theologal procedures of such a subversion; see Lacoste, *Note*, §§ 66–95. The lines that follow [in the main text] set to work a knowledge less rich than that availed of by theology, and less rich than that availed of by philosophies willing to think what faith lives on, by those same philosophies for which faith is not confined exclusively to a knowledge enclosed within the medieval ghetto to which an inappropriate notion of the "supernatural" lifts the barriers. They are thus to be considered as a short introduction to my earlier elaboration—but they are sufficient in themselves for the framework of the present inquiry.

5. See Lacoste, *Note*, §§ 45–46.

6. See Heidegger, *Sein und Zeit*, 176; *Being and Time*, 220.

7. TRANS.: See 1 Timothy 6:16 ["dwelling in the light which no man can approach unto . . ."].

8. Hegel's polemic against Schleiermacher appears, of course, in the *Lectures on the Philosophy of Religion* and gained in importance after 1821

(the year when the first volume of Schleiermacher's *Die christliche Glaube: Nach den Grundsätzen der evangelischen Kirche im Zusammenhange dargestellt* [reprint, Berlin: de Gruyter, 1980]; *The Christian Faith*, trans. H. R. Mackintosh [Edinburgh: T & T Clark, 1928] appeared and when Hegel taught the philosophy of religion for the first time in Berlin). See Hegel, *Vorlesungen*, 23–24 (Hegel's manuscript), 175–76 (notes from the lectures of 1824), 285–86. (notes from the course of 1827); *Lectures*.

9. *Didachē*; "Didachē: The Teaching of the Twelve Apostles," in *Apostolic Fathers*, trans. Kirsopp Lake, Loeb classical Library (London: Heinemann, 1912), chapter 10, verse 6.

10. See Lacoste, *Note*, § 41.

Chapter Six

1. Edmund Husserl, *Erfahrung und Urteil: Untersuchungen zur Genealogie der Logik*, ed. Ludwig Landgrebe, Philosophische Bibliothek (Hamburg: Classen, 1938); *Experience and Judgement: Investigation into the Genealogy of Logic*, trans. James S. Churchill and Karl Ameriks (London: Routledge and Kegan Paul, 1973), §§ 15–46.

2. Ephesians 2:12.

3. J. N. Findlay attempted, not so long ago, to prove the nonexistence of God by arguing for the inevitable, "unescapable" [in English] character that his existence ought to assume. If God existed, "Anselm's proof" should be compelling: we would not be able to think a God who did not exist. And yet the hapless Anselm's proof is not compelling—it "proves" that God does not impose himself on us, and thus proves that he does not exist (Findlay, "Can the Existence of God Be Disproved?" in Antony Flew and Alasdair C. MacIntyre, eds., *New Essays in Philosophical Theology* [London: SCM Press, 1955], 47–56). The concept of a God who would ineluctably impose himself may not be a speculative monster. But the "God" of whom Findlay speaks is not the God of whom we are speaking, who solicits free consent while performing his own unveiling.

Chapter Seven

1. The problem of the Hegelian "end" of history is highly controversial. We still lack a monographic study of Hegelian eschatology (which, moreover, would have to interpret more silences than explicit declarations, and the general architecture of Hegelianism more than specific texts). In the [main text] that follow[s], we will confine ourselves to a thesis that, all things considered, is hardly provocative: if it makes sense to speak of an Hegelian eschatology (i.e., if the *novissima* are not something on which Hegel keeps a respectful silence, and which he would dispatch to a beyond—and to the beyond of his philosophy), one can only speak of it as an eschatology that has been realized. The "beyond," according to Hegel, is a "representation" and is thus, by definition, inadequate. Under the category

of a "finite" history, we should obviously not understand the end of time or an interdiction that time, after Hegel, places on what we ordinarily call "history": we will understand the possibility that this side of death shelters the definitive, that is, insuperably self-identical existence. We will make use of discussions by Reinhart Klemens Maurer, *Hegel und das Ende der Geschichte: Interpretationen zur "Phänomenologie des Geistes"* (Hegel and the End of History: Interpretations of *Phenomenology of Spirit*; Stuttgart: Kohlhammer, 1965); Hans Friedrich Fulda, *Das Problem einer Einleitung in Hegels Wissenschaft der Logik* (The Problem of an Introduction in Hegel's Science of Logic), 2nd ed. (Frankfurt: Klostermann, 1975); and Gaston Fessard, "Le problème de la fin de l'histoire" (The Problem of the End of History), in *Hegel, le christianisme et l'histoire* (Hegel, Christianity, and History; Paris: Presses Universitaires de France, 1990), 137–54. (These references are cited to provide a dossier of available writings rather than to lend credence to the authority of the authors.)

2. We are referring to some studies it would be hard to ignore: Claude Bruaire, *Logique et religion chrétienne dans la philosophie de Hegel* (Logic and Christian Religion in Hegel's Philosophy; Paris: Seuil, 1964); Albert Chapelle, *Hegel et la religion* (Hegel and Religion; Paris: Éditions Universitaires, 1964–71), 4 vols.; Jörg Splett, *Die Trinitätslehre G. W. F. Hegels* (G. W. F. Hegel's Doctrine of the Trinity; Freiburg: Alber, 1965); André-Mutien Léonard, *La foi chez Hegel* (Faith in Hegel; Paris: Desclée de Brouwer, 1970); Emilio Brito, *La christologie de Hegel: Verbum Crucis* (Hegel's Christology:Verbum Crucis; Paris: Beauchesne, 1983); and *Dieu et l'être d'après Thomas d'Aquin et Hegel* (God and Being According to Thomas Aquinas and Hegel; Paris: Presses Universitaires de France, 1991).

3. See, above all, Bultmann's Gifford lectures. Rudolf Karl Bultmann, *Geschichte und Eschatologie* (Tübingen: Mohr, 1958); *History and Eschatology: The Presence of Eternity* (New York: Harper and Row, 1958).

4. Martin Heidegger, "Hegels Begriff der Erfahrung," in *Holzwege*, 120, 124, 125, 130; *Hegel's Concept of Experience*, trans. J. Glenn Gray (New York: Harper and Row, 1970). Let us be clear: we are *not* taking up the Heideggerian interpretation that is absolutely intent on erasing from Hegel's text every reference to the historical process in which the Absolute makes itself present and manifest.

5. Alexandre Kojève, *Introduction à la lecture de Hegel* (Paris: Gallimard, 1947), 301; *Introduction to the Reading of Hegel*, ed. Allan Bloom, trans. James H. Nicholas Jr. (Ithaca, N.Y.: Cornell University Press, 1980), 225.

6. 1 Corinthians 2:10.

7. Kojève, *Lecture de Hegel*, 324; Reading of Hegel.

8. Kojève, *Lecture de Hegel*, 426; Reading of Hegel.

9. Boethius, *De consolatione philosophiae*; *The Consolation of Philosophy*, trans. P. G. Walsh (Oxford: Clarendon Press, 1999), book 5, prosa 6.

10. See chapter 5, note 8.

11. On this point, see Brito's succinct and rather eloquent commentary on the Hegelian theology of Easter in his quite lengthy study of Hegel's *Christology*. Brito, *Christologie*, 455–64, 519–22, 650–56.

12. See Rudolf Karl Bultmann, *Neues Testament und Mythologie*, Beiträge zur evangelischen Theologie, 96 (reprint, Munich: Kaiser, 1985), 59; *The New Testament and Mythology and Other Writings*, ed. and trans. Schubert M. Ogden (Minneapolis: Fortress Press, 1984).

Chapter Eight

1. See Lacoste, *Note*, § 55.

2. TRANS.: 1 Chronicles, 15:29.

3. TRANS.: Given the particular formalities of address in French absent in English, *tutoyer* cannot be faithfully translated into English. It is a verb that ordinarily means to use the informal *tu* rather than more formal *vous* form of address. It has also come to mean "to be on familiar or intimate terms with someone." Lacoste makes use of it in the sense of "to view or address someone else as an 'other,' as a 'you.'"

4. Gilbert Ryle, *The Concept of Mind* (New York: Barnes and Noble, 1949), esp. 15.

5. This concept is introduced in Schleiermacher, *Glaube; Faith*, § 4.

6. This last celebrated expression comes from Rudolf Otto, *Das Heilige* (Breslau: Trewendt and Garnier, 1917); *The Idea of the Holy*, trans. John W. Harvey (Oxford: Oxford University Press, 1958). But is it really a question here (or in the "numinous object" or in the "Totally Other") of divine names? The *mysterium tremendum et fascinosum*, which is experienced as a feeling, incontestably exists outside of the consciousness that bears witness to it. But is everything that exists outside of consciousness and gives rise to terror within it necessarily proper to God? We should at the least be able to agree that this is perhaps a property of the "earth."

7. See Lacoste, *Note*, § 41.

8. We are not retreating to the position adopted by Schleiermacher. The "primal scene" does not, in fact, give itself to be understood in the first place as the emergence of a feeling of "createdness." Here again, it is a question of knowing [*savoir*] and of implementing this knowledge. There is nothing a priori to prevent created Being from being recognized as such in the sphere of *Gefühl*. To the somewhat anxiety-ridden question that opens metaphysics, "Why is there something (why am I) rather than nothing?" nothing prevents the affective consciousness from responding by appealing to the present experience of its being-created. But this response does not employ a knowledge of which the affects are simply an experiential confirmation. Although the recognition of the gift that creates Being is a source of joy, the pure recourse to feeling could also be a source of joy: but this latter joy could very well be nothing but the happiness of "absolute dependence" on the "earth."

9. TRANS.: Because *initial* and *primal* are used in French and English translations of the Freudian term *"Urszene,"* it has not been possible to translate Lacoste's *initial* as "initial" throughout the text.

10. Boethius, *Contra Eutychen et Nestorium*, III, 4: "'*naturae rationabilis individua substantia'*"; "A Treatise against Eutyches and Nestorius," trans. H. F. Stewart and E. K. Rand, in *Boethius: The Theological Tractates* [and] *The Consolation of Philosophy*, Loeb Classical Library (London: Heinemann, 1918), 85: "'The individual substance of a rational nature.'"

11. See, for example, Martin Heidegger, *Nietzsche* (Pfullingen: Neske, 1961), 1:26; *Nietzsche*, trans. David Farrell Krell (San Francisco: HarperCollins, 1984), 1:25.

12. TRANS.: For a brief introduction to the French term *"ressentiment"* as Nietzsche uses it, see Robert Solomon and Kathleen M. Higgins, eds., *Reading Nietzsche* (Oxford: Oxford University Press, 1988), 222–25. Because this usage only vaguely resembles the notion of resentment in English, translating *ressentiment* as "resentment" would be misleading. I have therefore left it untranslated.

13. Friedrich Nietzsche, *Wille zur Macht, Kritische Gesamtausgabe der Werke und des Briefwechsels Nietzsches (KGW)*, ed. Giorgio Colli and Mazzino Montinari (Berlin: de Gruyter), part 8, 1:123; *The Will to Power*, ed. Walter Kaufmann, trans. Walter Kaufmann and R. J. Hollingdale (New York: Random House, 1968), 7.

14. Nietzsche, *Wille, KGW,* part 8, 2:299; *Will.*

Chapter Nine

1. See Ladislaus Boros, *Mysterium Mortis: Der Mensch in der letzten Entscheidung*, 4th ed. (Olten: Walter, 1964); *The Mystery of Death* (New York: Herder and Herder, 1965); Karl Rahner, *Zur Theologie des Todes*, Quaestiones Disputatae, 2 (Freiburg: Herder, 1958); *On the Theology of Death*, trans. C. H. Henkey (New York: Herder and Herder, 1961). See also Johannes Baptist Lotz, *Tod als Vollendung* (Death as Completion; Frankfurt: Knecht, 1976).

2. See Lacoste, *Note*, § 24.

3. The expression "theoretical splendor" comes from Guy Bedouelle, "La meilleure part: Aphorismes et apophtegmes sur la vie religieuse" (The Good Part: Aphorisms and Apothegms on the Religious Life), *Communio* 6, no. 4 (1981): 54.

4. "The pathways associated with it": the two traditional dispossessions associated with voluntary poverty are the disappropriation of the will [*le vouloir*] (see Lacoste, *Note*, § 90, for its Christological treatment) and the disappropriation of desire [*le désir*], the rejection of conjugality.

5. TRANS.: Lacoste is alluding here to the expression *"la foi du charbonnier,"* the faith of the collier—ascribed to the "simple man" who unquestioningly takes the Church's teachings to be true.

6. On "holy madness," see John Saward, *Perfect Fools* (Oxford: Oxford University Press, 1980) and Irina Goraïnoff, *Les fols en Christ dans la tradition orthodoxe* (The Fools of Christ in the Orthodox Tradition; Paris: Desclée de Brouwer, 1983), although the second of these is at fault for its utterly noncritical usage of hagiographic material.

7. See Lacoste, *Note,* § 79.

8. This is the thesis of Thomas Aquinas, *Summa theologica*; *Summa Theologica,* trans. Fathers of the Dominican English Province (London: Burns, Oates, and Washbourne, 1913–42), IIIa, question 46, article 8.

9. Saint Francis of Assisi, *Ecrits,* SC 285: 118–20; *The Writings of Saint Francis Assisi,* trans. by Benen Fahy (London: Burns and Oates, 1964).

Index

hermeneutics of initial, heuristic of
originary and keeping, 88–93
necessary, surplus and keeping,
80–82
sleep and keeping, 79–80
world, earth, kingdom and keeping,
97–98
Violence, history and, 55, 56–57, 127
Vita contemplativa, 202n4
von Humboldt, Alexander, 3

Wanderer
building, dwelling, prayer and, 37
liturgy prior to world, earth and, 32
Wandering, 32
Weltgeschichte, 51, 56
Will, powerlessness and, 163–67
Wine, 92, 144

Wodehouse, P. G., 3
Wohnen, 12, 15, 34
"Work," liturgy as, 78, 80, 203n1
World, 12n4, 31, 37, 74, 198n20, 200n3
"disclosure" and, 10–11
"earth" and, 13–15, 18–20, 26, 27,
42, 144
foreignness and, 11–13
godless, 17
inherence and, 9, 10
kingdom, earth and, 97–98
liturgy prior to Earth and, 40
place in relation to, 8–10, 26, 35
Worship, 197n17

Xeniteia, 29, 31, 32, 34, 200n4

Zuhause (being-at-home), 19

Perspectives in Continental Philosophy Series
John D. Caputo, series editor